The Freedom...!" Cage
Moy
Luong H. Ung-Lai

Dear Ms. Wong,

THE VOICES OF MY FAMILY AND ALL THE PEOPLE IN THIS BOOK WILL BE HEARD WHEN YOU HAVE THE REVIEW ON YOUR NEWSPAPER. Thank you

Luong ung-lai

The Freedom...Cage II copyright © 1991 by Luong H. Ung-Lai

The Freedom...Cage II, Moy copyright © 2014 by Luong H. Ung-Lai

All rights reserved. No part of this book may be used, copied, or reproduced in any manner whatsoever without written permission from the author, Luong H. Ung-Lai.

ISBN: 1500104574
ISBN 13: 9781500104573
Library of Congress Control Number: 2014910447
CreateSpace Independent Publishing Platform
North Charleston, South Carolina

Keem Lai's Love Echo for Her Child

*Keem's smiles, imprinted in her daughter's memories,
her love gave her child courage to stand up against enemies.
The power of her love echoed in her child's heart and soul,
and it gave Moy strength to carry on. And
Moy determined to fight and see a better day.*

Sue Chae Lai, 1935 to June 18, 1977

Keem is Ma's nickname.
Ma was between twenty-nine and thirty years old.
She was also five months pregnant (with me).

Sue Chae Lai

Keem

Ma told me, "I take this picture when you five month
old and still inside my belly!"
Ma carried me inside her womb, and she adored me
by patting her abdomen.
As a spirit, Ma always stays close to me; she guides me
away from harm to safety and to a better future.

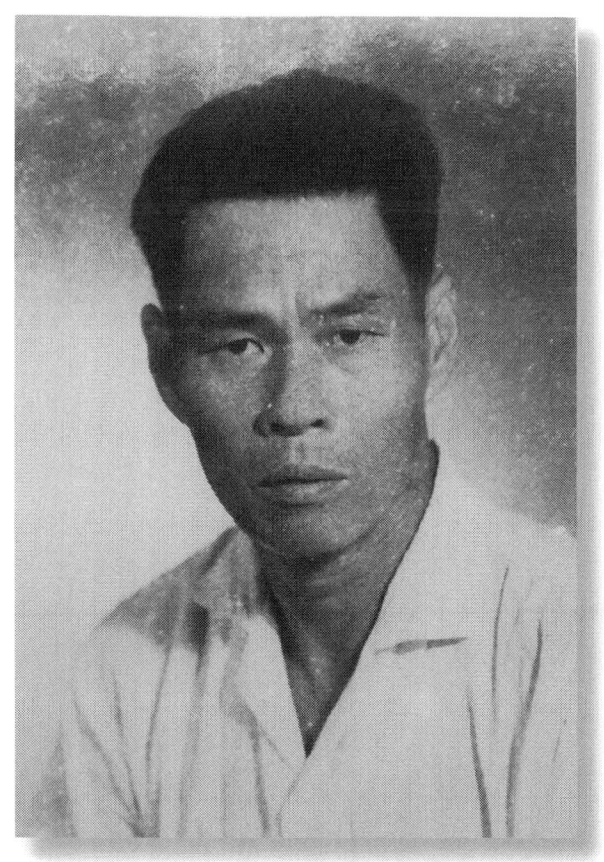

Wong Lai, 1913 or 1925, to June 8, 1977

I don't know how old he is or where Papa/Grandpa took this picture. This is the only picture I have of Grandpa by himself.

A Dragon Child

The lions roared and
Ruled the streets.
The golden dragons
Growled and zigzagged from above
As the red candles burned.
The white dragons
Came to life,
Zigzagging upward, toward
Heaven
At the tips
Of the burning incense
In people's hands,
And were accompanied by
The Eight Angels Music.
The firecrackers exploded
At the front doors,
Welcoming the mighty dragon
Into the New Year
As the sun king rose
From behind the mountains.
A baby arrived.
You held her
In your protective arms and
Welcomed her with
Warm motherly love.
You called me
"My child" or "puppy."
Then
You sacrificed everything,
Including your lives, and
You wished me,

"Child, in future I give you good day."

My ma Keem Lai and my grandpa Wong Lai

Yours forever,
Moy
by
Luong Ung-Lai

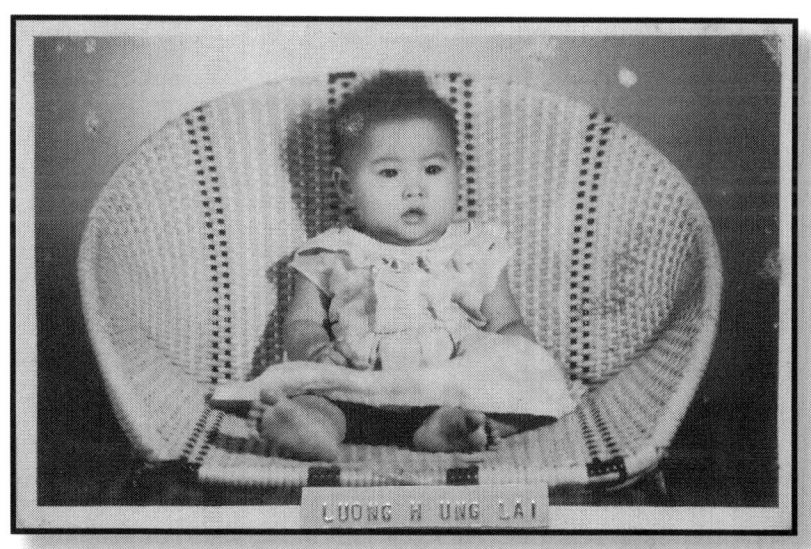

Moy

Ma told me this picture was taken when I was five months old. I couldn't sit up yet. Papa/Grandpa is hiding behind the chair, pulling my dress back, helping me sit up straight.

A Reminder

You may find that the dialogue in this book sounds strange. These conversations were originally in Teochew, a Chinese dialect, and Khmer. To the best of my ability, I have tried to translate the Chinese and Khmer/Cambodian spoken languages directly into English, keeping some of the features of those original languages. For example, in Chinese, there are no verb tenses; instead of "I went," and "I will go," one says, "I go yesterday," and "I go tomorrow," respectively. There are also no articles and no plural markers. So for "two men," the Khmer say "man, man." Further, some words in Chinese and Khmer don't exist in English, and some English words don't have correlates in Chinese or Khmer.

Please keep in mind that this book is based on memories.

Prologue

No matter where you look—left or right, high or low—all you see is line after line of sugarcane for hundreds and thousands of acres. Sharp, long leaves wrap around the canes from three-quarters of the way up, and most look like rabbits' ears. The leaves at the centers of the canes stick up straight like needles. They swing gently left and right, back and forth, following the wind's direction.

A bald-headed girl wears a heavy, white long-sleeved shirt and a long, white cotton sarong. She looks down carefully as she walks almost on tiptoes in the master sugarcane field. She tries not to step on the little pine-needle branches on the ground. Carrying a bent shovel over one shoulder, she holds her free hand out for balance. She stops suddenly, looking around as if someone is nearby. When she is satisfied there isn't anyone around, she takes the shovel from her shoulder and rests the tip on the ground. She holds on to the handle for a second longer and is about to swing it up when she hears something. She freezes and listens carefully. Hearing nothing, she swings the shovel up over her shoulder, but as it comes down, she freezes in midair when she hears a scream. She puts the shovel down, holding onto the handle, and listens. It's as quiet as nighttime, though the sun is straight above her head.

I must be hearing things, she thinks. Then she hears a scream of fear, and she tilts her head in the direction the scream came from. There it is again! It is a man's voice.

The bald-headed girl stands and listens. The voices aren't loud, but they are clear enough for her to hear every word from a couple of rows of sugarcane away.

"Don't kill me, Comrade Brother! Don't kill me!" the man screams in terror. The words are in English, and the other voices also speak English.

"He yells like a baby," the first voice laughs.

"Tie him up!" the second voice tells someone.

"Tie him to the tree," another voice says cheerfully.

"Don't kill me, Comrade Brother. Don't kill me!" the man begs.

The bald-headed girl isn't sure if she heard right. How can anyone kill a person in the middle of the day?

"Nooo!" The man screams in extreme fear.

The girl can't help it and takes a step closer. She puts her ear on the sugarcanes and listens. She wants to make sure that she isn't imagining hearing things in the field.

"Take his heart out and fry it with pig oil. It's good to eat!" one of the three voices remarks. The terrified man screams again as the three voices laugh. They sound like hungry human wolves who can't wait to eat a human's heart.

"No! Mercy, mercy! Don't kill me…nooo!" The man's voice slowly fades.

The girl can't hear the man's voice anymore. Her eyes are big, and her mouth hangs open. She can't move and can't speak. She just stands there, listening helplessly.

"He's bleeding like a pig, a thin human like him!" one of the voices says.

The girl feels hot and weak, and sweat rolls down her face.

She hears one of the voices say, "A thin human like him has such a big heart!"

"Don't worry; the bigger the better. Let's cut it small and cook it with something, then eat it with rice!"

"I'm hungry now. Let's go!"

"Let's go!"

The girl remains where she is; she can't do anything. She feels like she can't breathe, and she is getting warmer. Her throat is dry. *I need a drink of water!* She tastes her own sweat rolling past her mouth. It gets in her eyes and on her lips. She doesn't know how long she has been standing there, but now it is no longer noontime. It seems like the sun is almost going down, or...

She—*I* blink. I see sunlight peeking in from both sides of the white plastic curtain over the window. One of my ears hurts, and my body feels dead. My free hand rubs my face and comes back with a handful of sweat. I turn over and moan. That side of my body is hurt. I lie on my back and kick the thin blue blanket off.

This awful New England weather! When it's hot, it's too hot; and when it's cold, it's too cold.

I sit up on the small bed and look at sweat rolling down my chest. I see my light-pink, short sleeping jumpsuit. I laugh as I get up and look skyward.

Then I see Ma's black-and-white picture, her hair pulled to the right and resting on her shoulder. *She was forty-one when that picture was taken for her last passport.* I had it enlarged to five by seven, framed it, and hung it on the wall next to the small window above the long table I use as a desk. Books, dictionaries, pens, and my book bag are on the table. I hope Ma is not looking. If she does, she might not like seeing me dressed like this. Ma knew me the other side of life. At the thought of Ma, I feel guilty. I miss Ma every day, and my heart aches. I love her with all my heart and soul.

When Ma died, I held on to the gold-and-silver key, because I'd still have someone to hold onto. After she died, I walked into the gold-and-silver cage and locked myself in. Then I threw that key far away and hoped I'd be free in the cage. What I didn't know was I'd locked the nightmares inside the freedom…cage with me. Perhaps there might still be a way. Someone may come this way and free me from the freedom…cage.

Will I ever be free from the nightmares? I ask myself.

Memories from the past were coming back gradually when Ma died, like they always did. Memories of the injustice, pain from the loss of my loved ones, and the betrayal. I was thirteen years old then, when I fell under the shadow of the freedom…cage. And I lived in hell on earth, in a land called Cambodia—a name reminding me of the nightmare.

Now, I present to you the story of *The Freedom…Cage II, Moy.*

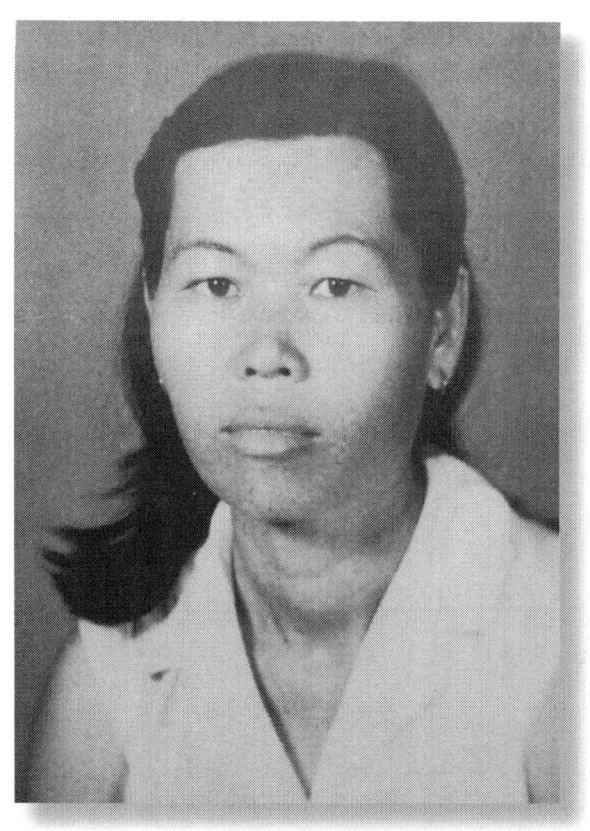

Keem Lai

This was Ma's last picture.
She was forty-one.

This picture was taken in Phnom Penh in 1973.

It was Chinese New Year.
I was nine years old. Moy is my nickname.

The Freedom Cage!! Moy

Book II

Half the sky was colored in light and dark shades of orange, red, yellow, pink, and a bit of white here and there. The other half of the sky was dark gray, almost black. Black...like the living dead. The dead were at peace—beautiful and surrounded by angels. The living will live without the bright sunlight to guide them through each day of hell.

Thirteen-year-old Moy was one of the many who lived in hell on earth, ruled by evil. Would she defeat the evil? Only time would tell.

* * *

June 21, 1977

It was thirteen days after Wong Lai passed away, three days after Keem Lai went to heaven.

"Moy!" someone called to her in Khmer.

Moy looked away from the beautiful sunset. The small bird was gone...to heaven, to its new home, a new kingdom. *Like Ma had gone to heaven, Ma's new home*, Moy thought, blinking tears away.

"Moy! Child, what you do in water?" someone asked in Khmer.

Moy looked at Pon and his wife. They stood on a tiny bridge across the small stream, not far from her.

MOY

"Moy, you hear me? What you do in water?" Pon's wife shouted to her.

"I pull water lily to cook for dinner," Moy shouted back in Khmer.

"Come up now. You cold," Pon's wife told her.

"Child, child, come out from water. It dark now; come up. Let's go home and eat rice," Pon told her.

"Yes," Moy whispered. She turned around and noticed the water was only a bit below her neck. She didn't know she had gone that deep, and she couldn't swim. She moved toward the shore, where Pon now was. He grabbed her small hand and pulled her out. Water dripped from her wet clothes as she walked next to him. Pon's large hand rested on top of her head, directing Moy toward his wife, and they walked home together.

On the way home, Pon and his wife told Moy the townies had been worried when they couldn't find her anywhere. They looked everywhere for two hours and finally gave up. Their last hope was to find Moy at her ma's grave, but no one dared to go there. Everyone was afraid of Keem Lai's spirit.

"We see the corn that you throw away on road. And we know where to find you. Pity her. She stand in water and pull water lily, like in movie. My heart break for her; pity her much!" Pon's wife told Moy. Then she whispered to her husband.

"I don't want pity! I want my ma back! Why everyone pity me? Why no one give me my ma back?" Moy cried aloud.

Pon wrapped his arm around Moy's shoulder.

When they entered their town, some people stopped on the small road or peeked out from their houses, asking, where did Pon and his wife find the Chinese child? Did they go to the grave and find her there? Were they not afraid of the Chinese woman's ghost? Pon told the townies where they had found the Chinese child and what she had been doing. The townspeople looked a little sad, pitying the Chinese

child. Some women almost cried when they heard the Chinese child was in the stream, pulling water lilies.

Moy just cried and felt very scared. Somehow, she knew life must go on. And she must face the world alone, no Ma and no Grandpa to hug. She felt hollow, lonely; an awful coldness settled inside her that she couldn't define in words.

She lived with Pon's family for a week or two after she returned from visiting her ma's grave. They were kind enough to her then. She treated Pon and his wife as father and mother. She ate whatever Pon's family and the Khmer Rouge gave her.

"I want Ma back! I miss Ma!" She cried for her ma every day, and she cried herself to sleep every night. She missed her ma hugging her. She just wanted her ma back!

One afternoon, Moy's adopted big brother, Chi Minh/Ming and his wife, Chan, showed up at Pon's front door. Ming's face was sort of oval, with high cheekbones, thick lips, and a somewhat round chin. He had black hair and eyes, and a small black mole on his left cheekbone. Ming looked sad when he saw Moy crying. She sat on the low bamboo bed in front of the house and cried harder when she saw him. She didn't jump up and run to him. Ming and his wife came to sit on their feet next to her, trying their best to comfort her. Then Ming left his wife with Moy and went to talk to Pon and his wife. They were talking at first, but then they shouted at each other in Khmer.

Moy was still crying. Chan tried her best to comfort Moy, in both Teochew, a Chinese dialect, and Khmer. Moy watched and listened to the shouting between Ming, Pon, and Pon's wife.

"She is my little sister; she must go with me!" Ming shouted.

"Her mother want her live with us," Pon shouted back angrily.

"She like my own child and she call me 'Mother,'" Pon's wife shouted.

"I her big brother," Ming told them.

"Big brother outside from pants," Pon's daughter spoke up, smiling sweetly, like a vulture. Then again, she always smiled. An execution might not chase her vulture smile away.

"What about you? You not father, mother, and big sister outside from pants?" Ming asked. He was right. None of them was Moy's blood family. But Ming and Moy had sworn to heaven and earth to be big brother and little sister for life.

"Why we no ask sister-in-law and listen who she want to live with? We want, you want; what about her? Let her decide. No one pity her?" Chan asked in Khmer. (She was short and a little overweight.)

"I no want people pity me! I want my ma back! Ma! I want my ma back," Moy screamed, heartbroken. Large tears dripped from her eyes. Some landed on her bare feet and some on Mother Earth.

"She can scream like the dead," Pon's daughter complained, with a smile.

"My mother and grandfather just pass away. If my little sister want to cry, then she can cry. If she want to scream, then she can scream," Ming snapped sharply at the young widow. He turned his back on Pon's family. Then he came over to his wife and sister and knelt in front of his grieving sister, his hands on her shoulders. Then he lifted her chin with his large fingers. He looked into her eyes and spoke softly in Khmer, "Little sister, I sad, too. I know your heart broken. We big brother and little sister. I want to take you and go live with me and your sister-in-law." He paused.

Moy looked at him; he did look sad. She continued listening to his speech.

"You go live at the factory with us. Khmer Red feed us better over there. You stay with Chan's stepmother. You live near me, and I come see you every day. I no want to worry about you not have rice to eat." He brushed her tears off with his fingers.

"Grandma must want you go live with us," Chan spoke in Teochew, referring to Keem. It is the Chinese custom and rule that a son or daughter-in-law addresses her in-laws as "Grandpa and grandma," or "dad and mother."

Ming nodded in agreement. Chan barely finished her sentence before Pon's wife marched over like a hungry vulture. She grabbed Moy's hand and dragged her away from her startled brother, taking Moy up and into her house. Pon's wife and daughter told Ming and Chan to wait outside.

Inside Pon's house, his wife and daughter told Moy not to go with her brother and his wife. They said Ming is not her blood brother, that Ming and his wife don't want her with them; they just want her ma's jewelry! Moy told them her brother didn't know anything about the jewelry. The mother and daughter looked as if the Khmer Rouge had just removed guns from their foreheads. Their faces became as bright as the summer sun.

Now the mother and daughter told Moy if she wanted to go and live with her brother, go. But Moy must let "her own mother," meaning Pon's wife, keep the jewelry.

"Child, you very young; you not know how to keep them. Child wait until you older; then you can keep them yourself. Buddha! I love you like my own child!" Pon's wife said as she hugged Moy.

"Right now, let mother and big sister keep them for little sister. When little sister older, come and take them any time you want. Mother and big sister love little sister like our family." Big sister Small smiled like a hungry cat smelling and seeing a fish on a plate for her meal.

Keem's jewelry was all 24-karat gold, and there was more than a kilo. Moy thought there was only just a kilo.

"If you let that brother outside from pants take the gold, he will spend them all! Remember? Your Ma want you come to live with us.

Mother is good person." Pon's wife tapped her own chest. "Buddha, I love child very much! You like my own child. If you take the gold, you might lose them. What you do? Mother not use child's gold. Child very smart, let mother keep them for child. Good child say yes." She dried Moy's tears and hugged her some more.

Moy listed to the mother and daughter. What they had said so far reminded her of something. About a year ago, Ming had come to his Ma with a sad face. He told his adopted Ma, Keem, and Grandpa Wong that he had been turned down by Chan many times. But now that she agreed to marry him, her stepmother wanted one hundred thousand ning—"just a little Chinese custom." Ming finished the tale and looked worried. Keem and Wong laughed.

"Child, if you want her for a wife, no worry. You must have her!" Keem spoke in Teochew.

"No worry. If you want her daughter, you must have her daughter," Wong also told him in Teochew.

Keem turned toward a small red suitcase and pulled out four packs of paper money. Each pack was an inch or two thick, all in five-hundred-ning bills. She handed him the money. Ming's chin almost touched his knees! His eyes were bigger than an owl's. He was an orphan and had lived on a small farm in Vietnam. He had never seen so much money in his life. Shocking him further, Keem pulled two more five-hundred-ning bills out of the fourth pack.

"Tell Chan's stepmother, 'My ma say you know our custom well.' Give her the one hundred thousand first. Then give her this one thousand ning. Don't say another word. Give her all the money; then walk away. Don't forget to smile; then walk out from her house," Keem told him.

After Ming was gone, Keem was mad. "She look down at my son!" She and Wong shook their heads. The paper money was no longer useful under the Khmer Rouge's leadership. Keem and Wong thought Chan's stepmother was testing the family's well.

Keem

Three days later, Ming came to take his Ma and sister to the wedding. Wong didn't go, because he couldn't walk that far. The morning of the wedding, Keem and Moy met a Chinese man who knew Chan's family. The Chinese man told Keem her daughter-in-law to be was the type of person who counts every penny first, before she thinks of asking to whom it belongs. In short, she would take and keep everything.

Do I want to go and live with this type of person? Big brother and I did swear to Father Sky and Mother Earth to become brother and sister. And that we will take care of each other for life, Moy thought.

At first, Moy didn't know what to do. She was scared and missed her ma. Then she remembered Keem and Wong sent her off with Ming to live at the factory in the sugarcane fields over a year ago. She spent one night then ran home the next morning. But now Moy told Pon's wife and daughter she wanted to go and live with her big brother, and that she must take some jewelry with her. The women agreed, telling her to take all of Keem's and her clothes but "not the jewelry."

Moy had two large suitcases filled with clothes belonging to her ma and grandpa, as well as her own clothes. Ming and his wife took turns carrying them, as they walked on the small footpath in the middle of the jungle to the sugar factory. Ming didn't let Moy carry the suitcases.

"You very small. No worry; big brother has big, big muscle," he told her in Khmer.

Ming told Moy he hadn't known their Ma was sick, and that if he had known, he would have come to help. He said that today, he and his wife had gone to visit, and saw the old house was empty. They asked the people who lived next door and were told their grandpa and ma had passed away. He promised Moy he would take good care of her, and he would make sure his wife was kind to her.

2

When they entered the gate of the sugar factory, the sun was down. They heard the sound of the dinner bell ringing over the fields and town. Moy waited at the sharing kitchen while Ming and Chan went straight to Chan's stepmother's house and left the suitcases there. After dinner, the three of them stood in front of a small metal door. It was Chan's stepmother's house.

"Little sister, swear to me you no run away again." Ming sat on his feet as he looked at her.

Moy stared at him like she was just seeing him for the first time in her life.

"*That day*, when you come here and sleep one night; then you run home to Ma and Grandpa. But you no tell me one word before you go. The commander of Khmer Red no happy; he know you come back. I beg him let you stay. I tell him you no run away again. Khmer Red say he let you stay here for two day. If you still here, he let you live with me forever. Swear to me you no run away again. Ma and Grandpa gone. We have only each other now. If you run away this time, I can no help you. Khmer Red will say I lie to him. Swear to me." He spoke softly in Khmer. Ming looked and sounded serious.

"I swear," Moy promised.

Keem

That night, as she was about to fall asleep, Moy heard Chan's stepmother and her son get up from the bed they shared. "Eat quietly. I no want her to eat," she told her small son. They sat behind Moy's back.

"Ma, I want you!" Moy wept quietly behind her hands. Hot tears fell from her eyes. She remembered that when her family lived in Pailin, sometimes when Keem or Wong was hungry they would get up in the middle of the night and cook rice to eat.

"Moy wake up. Ma cook rice for you to eat," Keem would say, waking her up gently.

"Puppy, get up. Your Ma cook rice for you to eat," Wong would shout, helping Keem get her up.

Most of the time Moy wouldn't get up; she liked her sleep. A few times, Keem had to carry her to the dinner table.

"Sad! You this old and still let your Ma carry you. You no embarrass?" Wong laughed.

"This child very spoil." Keem spanked her gently.

"Grandpa." Moy smiled and reached for him.

"So little!" they would tease.

Ming and his wife lived in a small tent at the edge of a sugarcane field, a few minutes from Chan's stepmother's house. Moy met them at the common kitchen every day for lunch and dinner. She didn't go to work—she ate, slept, and cried whenever she felt like it.

After Wong Lai and Keem Lai had passed away, the whole world turned upside down on her. One evening about two weeks later, Moy walked to the water well. She hoped a nice, cool bath might chase her sad mood away. When she got there, she met a Chinese-Cambodian man. He had lived behind her house in Pailin. He and Wong knew each other, but they weren't close. Moy and the man walked toward each other and made some small talk. He asked where her ma and Grandpa were. She told him they had passed away. He looked like he wanted to say something but didn't. Moy asked if he had something to tell her.

He looked at her and said, "You know, your grandpa is not your grandpa. He is your...father." Then he looked away. (If you want a quick answer, please read the author's note.)

Silence.

"Yes," Moy replied, and walked away.

It was a polite way to drop the subject. This was how Keem and Wong taught her; never argue with elders, if she could help it. She hadn't gotten over the shock of Ma and Grandpa's deaths yet. As if the poor girl hadn't gone through enough.

About a week after she met the Chinese-Cambodian man at the water well, Moy met another Chinese man, who had gone to Vietnam with her uncles and aunts over a year earlier, at the common kitchen. She was waiting for Ming and his wife. The Chinese man came over and sat next to her, and they ate dinner together, without Ming and Chan.

They didn't talk much. Moy didn't know him well enough to ask him anything. He knew her better because of her grandpa and uncles. After their dinner, the Chinese man asked her to walk with him. She did. They walked up to the bamboo gate. They stood there in silence and stared at the sugarcane fields. All the canes were seven to ten feet tall, or taller. The Chinese man looked sad when he looked at Moy. He asked her, in Teochew, "You remember all your aunt and uncle?"

"Yes," she answered, and stared at her bare feet on the brown soil. Her hands held onto the bamboo gate.

After what seemed like forever, he told her, "Black Shirt...kill all of them. Those people in the boat at the big Mekong River—Chinese, Khmer, and Vietnamese—who want go to Vietnam. Black Shirt kill everyone. They rape all young girl, then kill them."

Moy listened and stared at the sugarcane fields. Nether she nor the man knew what was hidden inside those fields and under those

Keem

sugarcanes bushes. They are so sweet, but so hard to chew. Sweet, but all for nothing. Like her life. *Yes, I remember Grandpa's children and grandchildren went to Vietnam. Only Grandpa, Ma, and I remained. Now, Grandpa and Ma are gone to heaven,* Moy thought in Chinese.

"I think you must know. Black Shirt kill everyone in your family," the Chinese man informed her.

"Yes," she answered, without feeling. Her eyes were on the sugarcane as memories came back about Wong's children. They always wanted her grandpa and Ma's money and gold. Keem and Wong always gave, and what did they get in return? Nothing! It was like a slap to Keem and Wong's faces. Then, when the paper money was useless, none of them knew Wong and Keem existed.

Moy remembered the past like it was only a second ago. Before her aunts and uncles went to Vietnam, all of them lived to the west, close to the river, about two hours from where she was. Moy remembered how she went to the river and brought water home for cooking. She saw them lay hundreds of fish on the mat, drying them in the sun. They knew Wong was sick, but none of them thought of or came to see their sick father. No one brought a small, dry fish for him to eat. Why should any of them bother to come see their sick old father?

Grandpa didn't have money for them anymore. Why waste the time to go see a sick old man? He had no money and no house. When Grandpa had money, he was their father. When he didn't have money, he was just a worthless old man, Moy thought angrily.

If the paper money were still good, those people would be like ants smelling candy. They would come, but not to see Wong or care for his health. They would come and wait until he drew his last breath, then take his money. They always presented their faces full of sorrow to Wong to get his money. When he couldn't see their faces, they would smile. Moy felt nothing for her four uncles and four aunts. She didn't know much about Wong's second daughter.

The only uncle Moy loved was her youngest uncle. He had been missing since she was four years old, and everyone assumed he was killed. Moy and young uncle were like big brother and little sister. He took her everywhere with him. They played together. They stole ice and made ice balls from third uncle's shop. They emptied half a bottle of colorful, liquid sugar onto their ice balls. Then both took off, eating and giggling together. They got caught by third uncle, because their lips and hands were stained with colors. Young uncle got yelled at by third uncle and Keem. Then Keem paid third uncle for the two ice balls and the half bottle of liquid sugar. Young uncle dragged Moy to hide behind Grandpa, where they giggled. Wong protected them from getting beaten by third uncle and Keem. Whenever Moy had thought about her young uncle, her face would light up in a smile. Now the memory of him only brought pain to her heart.

Everyone wanted money, but it couldn't buy *everything*. When Keem died, Moy had more than a billion in paper money and jewelry in the red bag sitting next to her. However, she couldn't buy Keem's *life* back.

* * *

A few days later after lunch, there was a big meeting at the factory. Men, babies in their mothers' arms, and children like Moy all gathered inside the wall-less common kitchen. The commander told them that all the teenagers and married people with no children must go to Head Tiger right away. The town was about an hour by truck from where they were. The elder people were to stay behind.

Moy hadn't seen a truck for almost two years. Now there they were, the roofless army trucks, so many of them. Each truck was half loaded with long sugarcane. People sat on top of the canes with their belongings on their laps or next to them. Some people had small

Keem

bags of clothes with them. Some people had chairs and small boxes with knives and spoons inside. Moy sat almost in the middle of the truck, facing Chan, and Ming sat behind Moy. Moy turned around and looked past her brother's shoulder, and she watched.

People sat on the edge of each truck, reaching down, and helping people from below climb up. Some elderly women, men, and small children were crying as they reached up to their loves ones on the trucks. Moy looked past them and saw the gate was closed.

"Why such sour face? Smile," Ming said, peeking at her. He smiled and rested one large hand on her head.

She didn't feel like smiling. She knew what it was like, to be forced apart from your parents and grandparents. But she did her best to smile for him.

"Your smile very sour," Ming laughed. He always spoke in Khmer. Not that he didn't want to speak Teochew, but he was not good with the language. If he did speak in Chinese, it came out as one word in Teochew and twenty words in Khmer. He eventually gave up trying.

Ming had done his best to speak in Teochew to their ma and grandpa when they were alive. If he couldn't think of the word in Chinese, he would whisper quietly to Moy in Khmer, "How you say this word in Chinese?" Then he and Moy would giggle. Their grandpa and ma just shook their heads at his poor Chinese.

Moy gave her big brother another smile. She wanted him to leave her alone.

She listened to people shout good-bye to each other. Ming held onto her when the trucks moved. She looked over her shoulder again, but he stopped her and had her face his wife in front of her. Then he told Moy that the trucks didn't go through the gateway because they would take a shortcut on a small road at the back of the townhouses. It wasn't long before the trucks came up to the big highway, covered in concrete, in the middle of the jungle. Ming told her that was the main road to Battambang and Pailin. They were on that highway a long time. Then the trucks turned right onto a dirt road lined with grass and big and small trees. After a while Moy saw a few small houses on both sides of the road. A few minutes later, the trucks came to their stop.

The silver moon hung in the dark sky as everyone got out of the trucks. Moy sat alone on the roadside with her suitcases and Ming and Chan's belonging. Everyone was in a meeting not far from her. She heard a word here and there. After the meeting, Ming and his wife returned. All three of them picked up their belongings and walked to their new home.

The brown wooden house was about sixty or seventy feet long, thirty feet wide. It was about nine or ten feet off the ground. Large, round, wooden poles were arranged in three lines, and each line had six or seven large poles. The walls were all beautiful brown wood, and the roof was metal. The staircases were all wood, about twenty-five steps or more to reach a large entrance in the middle of the house. There was no door. Another staircase stood at the side of the large house.

Inside the house, Moy's chin dropped slowly. *I dare not live here! Where are the monks? Black Shirt couldn't chase the monks out from the temple, could they?* she thought, then turned around. Ming's face appeared from below. He was out of breath from carrying the two big suitcases up the stairs. He dropped them on the wooden floor, sweat rolling from his face, and he wiped them off with the backs of his hands.

"What?" he asked, gulping for air.

"I can no live here," she told him.

"Why?"

"I a girl," she whispered.

Keem

"No worry about sin. There no sin nowadays. Come, we pick a spot to sleep," Ming understood her worry and smiled. He left her to stare after him. "Come!" He picked up the suitcases and laughed.

* * *

Moy watched people keep coming up, women and men. No one look worried. They all picked a spot, dropped their belongings, then lay down. When Moy and her family lived in Pailin, one Cambodian New Year she went to play with some Cambodian children at the temple, where she overheard the elders talking about sins. They said that young girls must be careful to watch where they were going around the temple. If the girls walked into the monks' bedroom, the girls would go to hell and be burned by the devil. Buddha wouldn't help girls who had no respect for the monks by walking into the monks' room with their dirty bodies. Moy asked her ma what it meant. She got an angry look from Keem but also an answer: "Woman has period. No ask so much!"

Moy didn't understand why all the Chinese and Cambodians consider a woman dirtier than a man, just because of the little period. She didn't see what it had to do with being dirty. *If the women were dirty, then take a bath to wash and clean like the men did. There, done!* she thought. The Cambodians were even worse than the Chinese. They considered a man to be like Buddha. *Buddha is in heaven, but the men live on earth. Men no Buddha, no!* Moy brushed that idea away. To her understanding, the difference between boys and girls was that the younger boys had cute little things hanging down between their legs. The thirteen, fourteen, or older boys had bigger ones, and uglier, too!

Moy got yelled at many times by her ma and grandpa for staring at naked boys in the store and on the streets at night. She didn't chase after the boys to stare at them. The boys held onto their private things and shook or swung them around, like long water balloons, in front of her. She didn't like to look, but she was just a girl and saw something…different. This would happen while the family packed up their belongings from their business table to go home. One time, Keem yelled at her tomboy daughter, "Lady no stare at boy's penis with her mouth open big, big like that!"

"The boy want me to see their penis. And I want to see how long their penis grow." She could hardly get the last word out.

"You!" Keem had a carry stick in both hands and went after her. Moy ran and laughed.

* * *

Now that she was older, she understood better, and much more. Very soon, hell would not scare her anymore. She lived in hell on earth now, and it was only getting worse as each day went by. Moy and Ming picked a spot on the left side of the temple converted to house, toward the middle. The house was one large room for everyone. No beds. The wooden floor was everyone's bed. They all slept in three long lines. One line on the left, heads to the wall; one line on the right, heads to the wall; and a line in the middle, between people's feet. Husbands and wives had a little space farther away from other couples. If they wanted to make some babies the others could watch. (Mind your manners; it's only a joke!) The single women slept closer to each other, and it was the same for the single men.

Moy was half asleep. She lay a bit farther away from her sister-in-law. She heard Ming tell his wife what Moy had said to him. Moy didn't get every word, but she heard, "She scare…she no want go to hell when she die," Ming whispered.

Keem

"Khmer Red go to hell. They kill monk like they kill Buddha," Chan whispered back.

"Explain to her…tomorrow…tell your captain you stay with Moy for one day. She not know anyone. She scare…very young…only…self."

"Why you no stay home with her?" Chan asked.

"I must go back tomorrow…three o'clock," he told her.

"Where?"

"Back to my group…Think I want to go?" He sound irritated.

"No yell! She hear you!"

"She sleep," he whispered

"Yell like that…wake…" Chan told him.

"…right…sleep!"

Big brother doesn't want to stay here with me, Moy thought. Tears fell from her open eyes. But no one saw her cry. The room was dark, and she had her back to Chan. *Ma, come back!* Moy whispered in silence. "Ma help me!" she said as she covered her mouth with both hands, and the tears kept coming. She didn't want to wake anyone up because of her sadness. She listened carefully, and when she was sure everyone was asleep, she got up slowly, tiptoed to the door, and went down each step as quietly as she could.

She forgot that the silver moon was almost full. Inside, the house was dark. There weren't any windows, so the moonlight couldn't get in. Outside, she had no trouble seeing where she was going. Moy stepped on the ground and looked around. A large house stood across a small footpath in front of her. The footpath was fenced in by the grass and small and big trees on both sides. That house was like the one she had just come from. A narrow, long road was on her left.

To her right, and across from her large house, there was a long line of eight or ten small townhouses. A small footpath wound between her house and the townhouses. In front of the townhouses stood a tiny house, with a small bamboo bed about a foot above the ground in front of it. A little farther down was the sharing kitchen. The common kitchen had a metal roof and no walls. There were about forty or fifty long wooden tables and benches inside. Three large, square-shaped cooking stoves made of concrete sat side by side at one end.

Moy looked up and down at the two small footpaths in front of her. She had no idea where the two dirt roads would take her. She gave up, turned around, and looked under the large house—*darkness*. She walked to the back of the house and sat on the large, gray, square stone where the monks used to sit, the trees and grass in front her. She felt so alone, and she cried.

"Ma no run away from me. Come back!" she whispered and cried in her hands.

Her whole body shook from crying. She missed her ma. Moy's small form was trapped under and inside the temple, like a dark cage that kept her from any light. The powerful silver moonlight helplessly sat aside and stared at a small, lonely girl crying under the enormous shadow a Buddhist temple cast on her.

After her storm of tears was over, she dried her face with the backs of her hands. She continued sitting there, looking up at the black sky. The moon wasn't completely full, but it was bright, and millions of stars twinkled all over the black sky. Moy stared long and hard at one of the smallest stars. *It is so small*. She could hardly see it; it seemed so far away from all the others—just by itself in the whole black sky. However, the power of its light twinkled to earth. Not much, just enough to make out a small star was up there.

Everyone seemed to be happy. They had their families. If their families were not already with them, then they were somewhere where they could go and see them again. But Moy's ma and grandpa were high up, in heaven, bright and beautiful. They were very far away, and Moy couldn't go and see them. Keem Lai and Wong Lai were

Keem

in heaven. Moy couldn't reach up and touch their warm faces or feel their warm, loving arms around her again. She was that lonely little star. That tiny, bright star was all alone in the dark sky.

"You cry enough yet?" Ming asked.

Moy looked up. She had no idea how long he had watched her cry. He was sitting on his heels in front of her. He got up and went to sit on a tree trunk, closer to the stone where she was sitting.

"You cry like that, you die soon. They no have good medicine for you. You cry all you want; Ma no come back. She good person." He seemed lost somewhere as he continued. "She like help people. Ma has good heart." He paused.

Moy looked away from him and kept crying.

"Good people die young. They no suffer like us. Moy," he called for her attention.

She wouldn't look at him.

"Look at me!" he yelled in anger.

She shook her head and cried harder. A long pause. Then Ming sounded like he was talking to himself. "When I twenty-one, I die, too." He sounded lost.

Moy stopped crying. She stared at him like he had three heads on his shoulders. *Big brother is crazy. He just said it to scare me and stop me from crying,* she thought. Ming looked sad, and he reached for her with both hands. She cringed away and shouted to his face, "I want my ma back! Ma no run away from me! Take me with you, Ma!" She screamed louder.

"Stop cry like baby! You old enough to be someone's wife; stop it now!" He dropped his hands, looking hurt. This was the second time he had shouted at her since she knew him.

Moy stared at him through tears.

"Get up, go upstair, and sleep." He jumped to his feet and pointed upward.

"No yell at her," Chan spoke up behind Moy.

"No talk back! You my wife, and she my little sister!" he shouted.

"No yell at me!" she shouted back.

"Want a slap?" he snapped.

Moy just stared at him. Chan's face was hard. The girls looked at each other; then they looked at him. Chan gave her husband a murderous stare as she reached for Moy's hand. "Come, sister-in-law."

Moy rooted to the large stone. Chan grabbed Moy's hand and pulled her up to her feet. Moy looked at her big brother like he was a stranger. Ming turned away from her stare and spoke over his shoulder, "Big brother sorry. I no want to yell at you, but you very stubborn." He turned around, again looking sad.

The girls said nothing as they walked to the front of the building, up the stairs, then into the dark house.

3

In the morning, Moy woke up when everyone was ready to go to work. Chan told her to go back to sleep, and Moy did. The house was dark, so she didn't know what time it was. Later, some sunlight woke her up. She heard voices here and there, and then Chan told her to get up, or she'd have nothing to eat. She got up and washed her face with the water Chan gave her in a small can. Then both girls went to the sharing kitchen. Moy sat on a long wooden bench with about thirty women. The women were seated on one side of the common kitchen, and the men were seated on the other side. Everyone wore long, black, cotton pants and black long-sleeved shirts. Moy wore her yellow pants with small red flowers and a red short-sleeved shirt with small pink flowers.

Chan gave Moy a plate of white rice and a small bowl of banana tree soup with small pieces of meat. Moy looked at the women at her table, all eating the same food as she had. A group of ten people shared a large, metal bowl of soup on the table; five people seated on each side of the long bench. Moy got the soup in a small bowl by herself because she didn't belong to any group.

After lunch, Chan showed Moy around. There was nothing to see, just grass, trees, and sugarcane. Chan told her the commander of the Khmer Rouge and his family lived in the small townhouses. A Khmer Rouge doctor and his wife lived in the tiny house with the small bamboo bed in front. All the tall common houses, like the one they shared with the others, were Buddhist temples. The Cambodians used to come to worship on Sundays, holidays, and New Years. The monks used to pray and worship Buddha every day and night. Now the monks had all been killed.

"And Black Shirt make us live in Buddha's temple," Chan whispered in Teochew, then explained in Khmer. Chan's Chinese was a little better than Ming's.

At the sugarcane fields, the Khmer Rouge called the sixteen- to thirty-year-old males and females "Bike One." (I'm not sure if "Bike" is the correct word in English, but in Khmer it was bike.) They were the strongest group and the fastest working people. They were the Khmer Rouge's favorite. "Bike One" had white rice to eat for lunch and dinner. The boys and girls from age thirteen to fifteen were "Bike Two." From ten to twelve years old were "Bike Three." And "Bike Old, Old" was the name for the elder people.

"They walk slow, slow; work slow, slow; talk, talk, talk; and eat fast, fast! Keep them, no gain; hit them away/kill them, no lose!" The Khmer Rouge always made fun of the elders. Everyone from "Bike Two" to "Bike Old, Old" got thin rice soup and banana tree soup from the Khmer Rouge.

After half an hour for lunch, people went back to work. Chan took Moy to the fields where people planted sugarcane. Moy looked as far as her eyes could see, and all she saw was sugarcane. Women worked on one side of the field, and men worked on the other.

* * *

Three people worked on each row. Two people worked facing each other, the first person with a bent shovel, standing with his or her foot on each side of a row. That person dug a hole by swinging the bent shovel up and down over his or her shoulders a few times. Then he or she would take two steps backward and repeat the same action, digging another hole. The holes were over a foot long, nine inches wide, and about six inches deep. The second person had an armful of the foot-long sugarcane, and bent over to put a cane in the hole, then moved forward and placed another cane in the next hole. The third person of the group pulled the dirt in and over the sugarcane with a shovel, then tapped his or her foot gently on the soil before moving on to the next one. If the hole digger was slow, the other two people would get to rest a little. When the three people finished their row, they would go with their group to the next area.

* * *

Moy looked at the people at the far end of the row. They seemed to be only a couple of inches tall. No one dared stop working. They finished one row and went on to next. Black Shirts were everywhere. They carried long guns on their shoulders or in their hands as they walked up and down the fields, chatting and laughing. Some of them chewed sugarcane, swallowing the sweet liquid. The whole work field had only three colors: the black of the people's clothes, silver shovels, and the light pink soil.

Each group had two people carrying together a metal bucket of water on a stick. The Khmer Rouge called them "Car Water." The Car Water walked around shouting, "Water! Who want water?"

"Car Water over here!" the workers shouted left and right, from all over the fields, since the temperature was well over ninety degrees. The Car Water would dip a small metal soup can into the water and give it to the worker. Some unlucky Car Waters tripped and fell, and Mother Earth got to drink a whole bucket of water. Then the thirsty workers had to wait for their Car Water to find more water for them.

Moy asked Chan why those people were called Car Water.

"They carry water and go around like car water," Chan explained.

Moy looked longingly at the large piles of foot-long sugarcane. A pile here and a pile there; they were everywhere for the workers to plant. Moy watched as a group of boys or girls around seven to nine years old sat with elders next to a big pile of long sugarcane, chopping them into foot-long canes with curled hunting knives. Then they threw the foot-long canes onto a large pile in front of them.

Moy looked away from the workers and stared at a pile of sugarcane not far from her. She asked Chan if she could have a cane. The older girl said yes and walked Moy over to a large pile of canes, where Moy picked one up. She bit and pulled the thick, outer skins away, then chewed on the softer white part, swallowing the sweet liquid.

Moy sat on her knees and chewed the sugarcane. As soon as she finished one cane, she started another. She chewed until her jaws got sore and her lips ached. Then she licked her lips, looked up, and shouted in Teochew, "Big brother!" Her face lit up when she saw Ming walking toward them from the small dirt road.

He smiled at her welcome, then stood behind his wife, hands on Chan's shoulders. He frowned at the small mountain of sugarcane skins in front of Moy's feet. He shook his head, bent down, picked up a cane, and gave it to her. "Eat another one," he teased.

"My mouth hurt," Moy replied.

"Straight Bird has a lot of water," he told her.

Moy just stared at him.

"You eat Straight Bird." He picked up a black and off-white colored cane and waved it in front of her. "Straight Bird has a lot of water. Very sweet, very soft. We like to grow many Straight Bird, understand?" he laughed.

Moy nodded.

"Let go home. Let go eat rice. Those people get out soon," he said, reaching over and rubbing Moy's head.

Moy picked up three short canes, but they weren't the ones he liked, so she put them back and picked up the ones Ming preferred.

"I take Straight Bird home with us," she told him.

"She no understand," Chan told her husband, and she laughed with him.

"Why take so many?" Ming asked as they walked home together.

"I take one for big brother, one for sister-in-law, and one for me." *Big brother came home! He didn't run away from me!* Moy thought, feeling happy. But evil was lurking just under the surface, waiting to take away whatever happiness she had.

Ming had gone to his group that morning, where they came from yesterday. After dinner that evening, Moy asked her big brother if he was going to stay there. He told her, no, that he would live in the same town with them. The tractors and drivers were sent there to Head Tiger that morning. He would work and sleep with his group in a tent in the work fields. The men had to take turns plowing the fields day and night, to grow more sugarcane. If they didn't plow the land first, it would be too hard for the workers to dig with their shovels. Ming told her she could come and visit him anytime she wanted. Just follow the small dirt road toward the main highway and turn right at the small road on the work field. She would never miss the big tent there.

The next day, Moy went to see her big brother. She walked past the sharing kitchen on the left of the road, and a couple of small wooden houses on the right. After she passed the houses, there were trees, grass, and brush on both sides of the old, small, muddy road. She walked twenty or thirty minutes. Then she saw a small road on her right, just like Ming told her. She stood on the corner of the two roads and looked at the large fields.

A tractor here and there plowed the fields. The drivers turned the tractors around from one line to another. The masters/drivers did nothing, just guided their slaves around wherever they wanted work to be done, like the Khmer Rouge treated the workers in the fields. None of the drivers looked unfit, and each tractor looked as if it could swallow the whole earth. When the tractors were overused, the engines simply died. The Khmer Rouge treated their people like pieces of machinery. Chinese, Vietnamese, and Khmer, rich or poor, all were treated alike; everyone must work like a tractor. Black Shirt told people every day, "Have one, no gain. Take one out, no lose."

Moy looked toward a big army tent under a large tree, away from the tractors, and not far from her. She walked down the small road, then stepped onto the cool, pink soil, and continued toward the front of the large tent. A couple of men were resting on a grass mat under a big tree. She walked toward them. One of the older men saw her and shouted toward the tent, "Chi Minh, your little sister come play with you!"

The men were eating. Moy was embarrassed she had come at their lunchtime. She looked away from the men and waited for Ming. When Ming came out, his hair was a mess, sticking up and pointing in all different directions. He could hardly open his eyes. He pushed his hair back and rubbed his face, his bare chest tossed out to welcome the hot sun. She looked away from the sleepwalking young man.

Big brother needs more sleep, she thought, ready to go home.

Then she heard him ask, "Moy, what you do here?"

Before she could answer, one of the men criticized Ming for questioning what Moy was doing there. He also said that Ming was lucky to have a little sister who missed and loved him and came to visit. The man said he wanted a little sister visit him, too, but he didn't have one.

"Little sister, come. Eat rice with big brother." The man invited Moy in a friendly and respectful tone of voice.

Keem

"Thank you. I no hungry," she told him in Khmer. Then she walked back toward the road where she came from.

"Moy, come here!" Ming shouted to her back. Then he was next to her, apologizing and explaining he didn't mean to be unfriendly, but he hadn't gotten much sleep the night before. He had to stay up all night plowing the field. He asked her to return with him, and she did. He told her to sit with the men and wait for him. She did. When he came back, his hair was combed back to one side, and he looked like her big brother Ming again.

"Wait here!" he pointed at her.

She watched him disappear inside a small, white tent. Then he came out with two big bowls of rice and a few small fish on top of each rice bowl. Ming gave her a bowl, and they sat side by side, eating their lunch in silence. After a few mouthfuls, Moy dropped two fish into Ming's rice bowl. She said that a big man like him can eat more than her. That brought laughter from all the men nearby. The men told her if she kept that up, her big brother would be fat like a pig!

Ming looked embarrassed and pleased at the same time as he returned the fish to Moy's rice bowl. "Eat; no worry about me," he told her.

After lunch, Moy went home. And she continued to visit Ming every day. He always had rice, fish, pork, or beef for her to eat. Moy loved to eat! Sometimes she ate more than him. Ming and his co-workers knew Moy was growing and always hungry. The men didn't mind. She visited them almost every day at lunchtime. She just ate with her brother, then went home. She didn't talk much, but whenever she said something, the men always laughed. It didn't matter what she said; they laughed and teased her.

"Why you always call Chi Minh *Big Brother* in Chinese; then you say everything else in Khmer?" one of Ming's friends asked.

"My big brother is Chinese. He no speak Chinese, but he a good Chinese."

"Good Chinese not know how speak Chinese?" Ming's co-worker asked.

"He no speak Chinese, but no worry. My big brother has good Chinese heart, but his ear and lip all Khmer," she told the men, and they had a good laugh.

"I understand more than I can speak. I understand everything you say in Chinese," Ming said, shaking a finger at her. He teased that if she didn't defend him, he wouldn't give her any more rice to eat, and that brought more laughter from his co-workers.

About two weeks later, Moy went to work in the field with five boys and four girls close to her age. Sometimes the children went to work in the cornfield. Other times, the cooks sent the children to the banana groves to cut down banana trees and bring them to the kitchen. The children peeled off the outer layers of the banana tree skin, all the way to the center. The hearts were either white or pink, and soft. They would cut the hearts like onion rings, to make fish soup. People ate fish soup with dry rice or rice soup every day.

About a week later, the children started to pick on Moy. It was a long walk from the kitchen to the banana groves. Moy didn't have shoes, and she walked slower than the others. Everyone would leave her alone in the enormous banana field and wait for her at the corner of the road. When she got close to them, they all jumped out from both sides, screaming as loud as they could, and frightening her to death. She would scream and cry from the fright. The children would laugh and point to shame her. This went on every day, when they waited for her in different places. Poor Moy cried every day from fright.

One day, the children made Moy carry the biggest banana tree they could find. It was almost two armfuls, more than ten feet tall, with additional five- or six-foot-long banana leaves. Each leaf was about two feet wide or bigger. That tree weighed over a hundred pounds, maybe

Keem

even close to two hundred. She couldn't move it. She didn't know what to do when everyone left her in the middle of the field. The children told her if she didn't carry the tree out, they'd make her go back to get it.

Moy cried, sitting next to the banana tree. She felt so alone and missed her ma. She was also afraid of the ghosts in the jungle. "Ma, help me! No run away from me, Ma. Take me with you, Ma!" she sobbed aloud. Moy just wanted her ma back!

A cool, soft breeze brushed her right cheek and ear gently—then it was gone. It had felt more like a hand than a breeze touching her. Moy felt such comfort from that touch! It was like someone trying to tell her something. At the time, Moy didn't think about it. Years later, and to this day, she believes it must have been Keem's spirit coming to comfort her. Moy had no doubt that her ma and grandpa's spirits were with her at all times. They helped and protected her from danger, any way they could, especially Keem's spirit, who was always by her daughter's side, protecting Moy.

Almost immediately after Moy felt that cool breeze touch her, she stopped crying. She got up on her knees and went to work. She picked up the two-foot-long hunting knife near her foot and chopped off the head and tail from the banana tree. She kept only the center, about three or four feet long. Sitting on her knees, she peeled off all the thick, old, green bark. She stopped peeling when she had it to the size of her ankle. The heart of the tree was all white and pink. She looked at it for second longer; then she picked the heart up, threw it over her shoulder, and walked away from all the old, green bark. She was close to the road where, sure enough, the children were waiting for her. But this time, when they came out from both sides with loud screams, Moy held her head high and walked past them. *No more!* She walked in front of the Cambodian children, with the heart of that banana tree bouncing up and down on her shoulder.

MOY

Don't ever mess around with Keem Lai's daughter! They could pick on her and make her cry, but in the end, it will be Keem Lai's daughter walking in front of them!

Moy heard the children mumbling behind her that they didn't have fun scaring her today. She didn't care. When she got to the kitchen, the headwoman there gave her small pieces of sweet, sticky rice to eat. The elderly headwoman pointed at each kid and yelled, "Look at Chinese child. Very smart. Look at you; just eat the rice away!"

Three or four children had carried a whole banana tree, with the leaves, to the sharing kitchen. Then the cooks had to peel all the bark away and cut off the leaves. The headwoman told the children to learn from Moy. Peel off the bark, cut off the head and tail from the banana trees. "Then you bring them to me."

All the children sat at the long table, heads hung low, listening to the headwoman's lecture. Moy sat near the cooking stove, enjoying the sweet, sticky rice cakes, licking her fingers when she had finished. The other children didn't get any. She heard the headwoman mumble something to her co-workers about Ming's little sister. The other women stared and smiled at Moy. Moy smiled back. She didn't know what they talked about. The headwoman gave Moy another piece of sweet, sticky rice cake to eat, and she thanked the elderly woman. Then the headwoman gave her something wrapped in a banana leaf and told Moy to go home. Moy walked across the small dirt road home, but she didn't go up into the house.

She stopped under the house and opened the bag. There were five or six small pieces of sweet, sticky rice cakes. Moy took them upstairs, where she kept two pieces under her clothes bag for her sister-in-law. Then she went downstairs with the rest of the sweet cakes in both hands. As she walked past the sharing kitchen, the cooks laughed and pointed at her. She smiled at them.

Keem

Ming was sitting under a big tree having his lunch. Moy didn't wait for him to ask; she just sat next to him and handed him the little bag. He took the bag but couldn't speak because his mouth was full. He put his rice bowl down and unwrapped the bag.

"That grandma in the kitchen give it to me. It sweet rice cake. Big brother like them," she told him.

"Which grandma?" he asked

"That buddy grandma who work in the kitchen."

"'That buddy grandma,' now you talk like Khmer Red. Just call her grandma." He laughed aloud.

"Enough! I learn from Big Brother. Big Brother call Ma 'Buddy Mother.'" But at the word Ma, they stopped smiling. Moy lowered her eyes. Ming looked away. She rose to her feet and spoke to him like a mother, "Eat; they good. They no make sweet rice cake often. I go home now. Big Brother look after yourself."

Ming's chin dropped lower as he stared at her. Moy was forced to grow up overnight because of their grandpa and ma's deaths. She looked at him for a second longer; then she turned around and went home. This might be the last time Ming and Moy saw each other as big brother and little sister, and not as strangers.

4

Under the Khmer Rouge's control, all the girls and women had their hair cut short, just a bit below their ears. Moy's hair was longer than everyone else, but no one seemed to care. Every child, woman, and man went by his or her first name only. If two people had the same first name, they would be identified as Tall Le or Short Le, or Thin Le or Old Le.

Moy continued to work with the children, and they went on picking on her. Nowadays, she didn't cry as much as she used to. She didn't cry as much from missing her ma or being frightened by the children's games. She changed gradually from the day the cool breeze touched her like a hand. Day by day, she changed from a carefree kid to a woman-child. Physically and emotionally Moy changed, but she didn't know it. Ming, his co-workers, the women, and the men living in that big house with her all knew. Everyone witnessed the scared little kitten turn herself into a tiger, slowly. However, Moy was not a free tiger. She was a captive tiger. Would that tiger remain captive forever? Would that tiger transform back into that frightened kitten again, or would she remain a tiger forever after?

Lately, Moy didn't visit Ming as often as she had before. And later, a new Cambodian girl came to the group. Her name was Lee, and she and Girl, the leader of the group, were good friends. Girl had high cheekbones and a small, pointy chin. Lee had a round face. Girl was

Keem

the evil one in the group. She always thought up some way to pick on Moy.

One day, the children were working in the cornfield; eleven children working in five rows. One person used a stick about the size of an arm, with a sharp and pointy end, to punch the holes on the row. The second person used three fingers to throw three or four corn seeds in each hole, then pulled the dirt back into the hole with his or her feet, tapped gently once or twice, and moved on to the next.

Moy knew she was a slow worker. That day she was partnered with Lee. They worked a couple of feet apart from each other. The hole punchers went faster than the planters with the corn seeds. Moy was concerned she was too far behind and worked hard to catch up to Lee. She threw the corn seeds in the holes, pulled dirt in from left and right with her feet, and moved on. As she worked, she didn't look up and bumped into Lee's back. Lee whipped around and yelled, "Chinese rag! You blink; why you no look?"

"I beg forgiveness," Moy whispered, staring at her bare feet with her head hung low.

"I no forgive Chinese rag," Lee shouted.

Moy looked up sharply.

Lee smiled sweetly.

Moy looked around.

Everyone else stood still, watching and smiling.

"Buddy Lee, be careful!" Girl warned her friend.

"Look at her, like she want eat Buddy Lee's flesh!" some children shouted with laughter.

"I no afraid of Chinese rag," Lee laughed.

"No call me Chinese rag again. Khmer rag!" Moy took a step toward her.

"Beat the Chinese rag, buddy Lee. She dare call us Khmer, Khmer rag," everyone encouraged Lee.

33

Lee and Moy reached for each other. They pulled and yanked each other's hair out and dug their fingernails into each other's face. All the children surrounded the two girls as they fell and rolled around in the dirt, yelling at each other. The two girls were the same size and height. Moy was on top of Lee most of the time and yanked a few hairs out of Lee's head. But when Lee was on top of Moy, Moy felt someone kick at her sides.

Nothing was going to stop Moy winning this fight! *No one!* She meant it. She didn't want to be called a "Chinese rag." Just a couple of hairs yanked out from Lee's head didn't satisfy her hunger.

"I will beat Khmer rag to death!" Moy shouted angrily. She was a tomboy most of her life and mean like a hungry tiger when she was mad.

"Don't make you angry; you mean like an old mother tiger," Keem told her countless times.

Lee was more like a rose in a vase, and she got beaten up by Moy.

* * *

This was not the first time Moy fought with the Cambodian children when they insulted her. When she was nine or ten years old and living in Pailin, she had a fistfight with a boy. He was twice her size and about five or six years older. He almost beat her to death. She had blood on her face and swollen eyes and cried her eyeballs out. But she felt good and proud of herself! She knew she was no match for him but fought him anyway. She didn't like him calling her, her ma, and her grandpa, "Chinese rag, Chinese dog."

If he had only insulted her, she might have let it go. But she wouldn't let him get away with insulting her beloved Ma or Grandpa. And Moy wouldn't let the Cambodians say, "The Chinese give up before a fight"—maybe another Chinese, but *not this Chinese girl*. After

Keem

the fight with that big boy, people looked at her strangely. The businessmen and women called her a stupid little girl, fighting someone twice her size and age. And they nicknamed her baby tiger.

Moy not only got into fistfights, she also climbed trees. One day, Keem caught her climbing up a lop cop tree in front of their house in Pailin. The tree was about twenty feet tall and about an armful around. Moy adored sweets, and the lop cop tree had green, pink, yellow, and red round fruit the size of a pencil that were sweet, and she loved them. She sat on the tree, picking and eating, picking and eating, just for fun. Keem wanted to murder her. She yelled at her daughter to come down. Then she shook a finger under Moy's nose.

"You climb up that tree like baby monkey! I break your arm and leg myself if you climb up that tree again. I no wait until you fall and break them. Boy climb tree, not girl! Lady no climb tree or fistfight like you! Lady no kick their leg up high, high like you, either," Keem lectured her daughter.

Well—Moy was not a lady. She was a tomboy, "baby monkey," or "baby tiger." *She believed in fighting for her rights!*

* * *

This fight between her and Lee was no different than the one before. Moy was afraid the other kids might help Lee beat her up. But she didn't let that fear get in the way. She was fired up and ready to burn Lee alive with her dragon fire of anger. She sat on top of Lee and beat the life out of her with both hands. Moy pulled and yanked Lee's hair out. Suddenly, someone peeled her hands away from Lee's white face, then lifted her up and away from Lee. Moy kicked and screamed at the person to put her down. She was going to beat Lee to death.

"Stop now! Why you so mean?" said the voice of whoever held Moy. He had difficulty keeping her in his arms.

"She call me Chinese rag! I no Chinese rag. I want to kill that Khmer rag!" Moy went wild, kicking and screaming.

"Stop now! Quiet!" a man yelled.

"You quiet!" she shouted back. Two large arms held her closer and refused to let her go until she calmed down.

"She heavy like elephant," Lee told the others and laughed weakly, her face white as a ghost.

When Moy had calmed down some, a dark-skinned man yanked her around to face him. He lived in the same house with her but farther toward the corner. "I go tell Chi Minh you fistfight today," he told her.

"Chi Minh not my father. I fight Chi Minh, too, if he dare hit me," she shouted to his face.

"You yell at me again, I slap you," he threatened.

"You dare slap me, I slap you back," she shouted right back.

The man looked shocked. He just stood staring at her. He was three times larger and stronger than she. She barely reached up to his stomach. He wanted to say something but changed his mind, instead pulling her along with him toward their house. Each time she tried to pull her wrist from his hand, he tightened his grip. She looked behind and saw Lee was surrounded by the others.

"Go up, now!" The man shoved her toward the staircase and pointed.

"Short life!" she cursed loudly, and stormed angrily up the staircase.

That evening after dinner, she sat in someone's dark-navy hammock, under the tall common house. It was tied to the poles of the second lines. The moonlight shone on her small face, and she closed her eyes. She was off somewhere in her own world, remembering another time when she had been angry like today. Back then, it was Wong who had made her mad. She remembered it like it was yesterday.

At the time, Moy's family had just moved from Phnom Penh to Pailin. For the first eight or nine months, they sold Lucky Tickets

Keem

(lottery tickets) and cigarettes for a living. It was a Sunday, the day of the drawing for the winning number. Moy got to sleep late that morning because she had sold all the tickets the day before. Later, she went to the busy bus station where her family sold different cigarette packages and Lucky Tickets from a homemade business table.

Wong smiled when he saw her. "Your customer come look for you," he told her.

"Really? What my customer want?" She smiled back.

"Your Lucky Ticket. Your big aunt bring two hundred ticket over this morning. Your customer say, 'I only want Moy's Lucky Ticket.' I tell your customer, 'This is Moy's Lucky Ticket,' and he buy them all!" Wong smiled, happy that he had helped sell the tickets for his eldest daughter-in-law.

"My ticket? I sell all my ticket yesterday!" Moy shouted angrily for all to hear.

She yelled at her grandpa. He had a good heart and always helped his children, no matter what they did to him. Moy was different. She reminded her grandpa and Ma that big aunt didn't give them any tickets to sell because Keem and Wong didn't have the money to pay her. However, a stranger, a young husband and wife, gave Keem and Wong two or three hundred pairs of Lucky Tickets to sell, to start the business. Then they paid the young couple later. Each week, that young couple gave more and more tickets for Keem and Wong to sell. At the end, Keem bought three to five thousand pairs of tickets from that couple, and they became good business partners. Moy called the young couple "Lucky Ticket big brother and big sister." Moy walked from noodle soup shops to jewelry shops, and house to house, to sell the tickets six days a week, starting in the morning and going until evening.

Keem shouted at her not to yell at Grandpa for helping her aunt.

"I dare yell!" she cried and screamed angrily.

All the bus drivers sat in their buses, listening quietly. If that aunt was nice, Moy wouldn't be so angry. Her aunt slept late, and her seven children stayed at home doing nothing. Her aunt never walked around to sell anything.

"Ma must run around and help me sell Lucky Ticket when business is slow. Not big aunt or her children. Big aunt sit on her chair! My ma run back and forth, making money to feed me. Grandpa happy to see Ma run around? You happy to see me run around like a beggar every day? You no care for my ma or me. You want help them? Help them; I no care!" Moy ran off crying.

After that, Wong tried to avoid Moy's anger and stay out of her line of dragon's fire. Whenever he felt Moy get a little angry, he walked the other way. Wong and Keem looked at her strangely after that day.

Moy remembered she didn't go out to sell tickets the first three days of that next week. She didn't speak to Grandpa for weeks. Both Keem and Wong were nervous. They relied on her to sell the tickets, but Keem and Wong didn't dare yell at her. Keem took the tickets and went to sell from house to house and shop to shop like Moy did. Moy felt guilty when she saw her poor Ma working so hard, so Moy took the tickets and went out to sell. Wong tried to talk to Moy, but she only answered yes or no. After a few weeks of Moy not talking to Grandpa, Keem took her daughter home and had a talk with her.

"Your grandpa is older, but he is willing to step back. You must do the same. It not right, not speak to your elder. You embarrass Grandpa by not respect him. He always call you first. He ask you go eat pork noodle soup with him. You say no. He ask you go see movie with him; you say no. Don't make him sad. He old and no live that much longer. When he gone you can no have him back. Grandpa love you. Be a good child to your grandpa."

Moy didn't say anything. She listened and helped her ma cook their lunch.

Keem

"You hear me?" Keem demanded.

"Yes."

"When you see Grandpa again, you must call him first. Show people we teach you how to respect your elder. Show them you love and respect your grandpa. Don't let people laugh at our family."

That did it! *Laugh at my family? Never!* She didn't talk to Grandpa that same day. She felt awkward. But the next morning, at their business table, Grandpa asked awkwardly, "Moy, you want go eat pork noodle soup with me?"

She was about to say *no,* but she saw her ma looked very unhappy. Keem didn't say anything or look at her.

"Yes," Moy answered.

His face lit up like the sun just coming out from behind dark clouds. Grandfather and granddaughter walked side by side, headed toward the pork noodle shop.

"She talk to her grandpa again," Moy heard some of bus drivers whisper to each other as she and Grandpa walked past them.

Wong took her to his favorite, and expensive, pork noodle shop. They went there every morning, ten minutes away from their business table. They had just sat down at a round table when three of Wong's other grandchildren came running from across the street.

"Grandpa," they shouted, and sat around the table immediately, *uninvited.*

"Good," Wong returned his grandchildren's greeting. He didn't dare look at Moy sitting next to him.

"Big Brother, Big Sister, Moy/Little Sister." Moy greeted her big aunt's children. Wong looked uncomfortable as he smiled at his grandchildren.

"Moy," her cousins returned her greeting.

Moy looked across the street at her big aunt's large business table. Big aunt smiled.

"Grandpa come to eat noodle soup?" her cousin Pig asked.

No. Grandpa came to eat your head. I want to eat your head! Moy thought, her blood boiling hot. When the waiter came to ask for their order, Moy told him, "Big Brother, today I buy a bowl of noodle soup and a glass of iced coffee for my grandpa to eat. And I want a bowl of noodle soup."

"You good child!" the teenaged waiter was surprised, and he looked at Wong with great respect. Wong tossed his chest out like a proud peacock.

"I buy a bowl of noodle soup and a glass of iced coffee for Grandpa to eat. You want help me pay?" Moy asked, looking at her cousins.

They didn't answer. They just sat there and talked to each other or to Grandpa. Grandpa answered them now and then. Then the shop owner came out and told Wong, "Uncle, my little boy tell me Moy buy noodle soup and iced coffee for you to eat! This one equal to more than one hundred children!" She rubbed Moy's head.

"No have!" Wong smiled and replied proudly. It is the Chinese custom and a polite way to accept a good compliment. Or remain silent for criticisms.

"Have, have!" She shook a finger skyward, which meant only heaven has one this special.

And Wong went around smiling for weeks.

"Why you keep smile like that; what is it?" Keem asked.

"I happy!" He looked at Moy with such pride. Later he told Keem what Moy did.

"She very smart. It her money; don't try it. That child very tight with her money when she angry," Keem laughed.

* * *

Keem

Gradually, someone pulled Moy out from her happy world.

"You sit in my hammock. Get up!" A teasing male voice came from above her head.

Moy smiled dreamily, opened her eyes, and saw it was not Grandpa's smiling face. It was her brother and sister-in-law's faces hanging over her. *Big brother is all I have,* Moy thought and pushed her sadness down to the bottom of the ocean. "Big Brother," she greeted him. She saw that bad man stood next to Ming. *Did he tell big brother I fistfight today? It doesn't matter; I'm not afraid of big brother.* Moy got out of the hammock and asked, "Is this big brother's hammock?"

"My hammock, not Chi Minh's hammock," the large, dark-skinned man answered.

Moy didn't look at him. She brushed her backside with both hands as if telling him, "You can go and hang your neck there!" She didn't like him, because he'd stopped her from pulling a few more hairs out of Lee's head.

"I not know it Uncle's hammock. If I know, I no touch it," she told him.

"Be careful. Soeun not that old. Call him Big Brother is enough," Ming smiled and warned her.

"Big Brother, call him 'Big Brother' yourself," she told him.

(In Teochew and Khmer, the words "big brother" or "little sister" are used like sweetheart or honey in English. It depends how the word is used.)

"Mean, mean like baby tiger!" Soeun laughed, and walked away from the hammock.

"Come; let make sugar," Ming told Moy.

Ming, Chan, Soeun, and Moy followed each other to the other side of the house. Soeun and Ming made a cooking stove with three big rocks. Chan made the fire. Moy used Ming's army knife to peel off the hard skin of the sugarcane. Later, people came down from the house. They worked together like Ming's family and Soeun were doing. Ming and Soeun found a long chair from somewhere and put a clean piece of board on top, sideways. They took the sugarcanes from Moy and put them on the board. Then they placed a second board on top of the sugarcanes. Then Ming and Soeun sat at each end of the board and squeezed liquid out of the sugarcanes into a large pot below. When no more liquid came out, they got up and folded the canes in half, then sat on each end of the board again, causing more liquid to come out. They repeated this until no more liquid came from the canes. Then they threw the dry canes away and put new canes in, repeating the entire procedure. When the large pot was half full, they put the pot on the cooking stove.

After the liquid boiled for about ten or fifteen minutes, Chan used a stick to stir it around in the pot until the liquid turned black and became thick and sticky. Ming and Soeun lifted the pot off the stove and let it cool. Then they went to sit on the monks' stones, farther away from Moy and Chan. The girls sat near their stove and homemade sugar. Like all the other men and women in their house, they waited for their sugar.

Moy and Chan chewed on the sugarcane for fun. Moy heard Soeun tell Ming, "She mean like baby tiger. If I her age, I no want to fight her. She will win." Soeun laughed.

"She very small. I not know she know how to fistfight!" Ming chuckled.

"Small? Yes, but strong like baby tiger!" Both men laughed aloud.

Chan stared at Moy, and Moy smiled.

"How old is she?" Soeun asked.

"Moy, how old you?" Ming shouted over his shoulder.

"What kind of big brother, not know your little sister's age?" he said to Ming.

"You know your mother's age?" Ming shouted back.

"No, but…"

"What kind of son? You not know your mother's age? Moy, what your age?" Ming shouted to his sister again.

"Ninety!" she shouted loud enough for everyone to hear. Chan narrowed her eyes.

"Buddha! Buddha! We have one old, old grandma living with us young, young people!" Soeun shouted, making everyone under the large house laugh.

That night in bed, Chan lay between her husband and sister-in-law. Ming told Moy to try not to be too stubborn or too reckless when she got mad, and to learn to control her temper. Or else people wouldn't help her like Soeun. He was a good person. He helped her end the fist-fight. Ming told her to apologize to Soeun for threatening to slap him.

That no good man. He told on me, Moy thought in Chinese. She wondered if Soeun told her big brother that she said she would beat Ming back if he dared hit her. *I'm not going to worry about it.* She closed her eyes and went to sleep. That would be the last night Moy slept without fear. And her relationship with Ming would crumble slowly.

5

A couple of months after Keem Lai and Wong Lai had passed way, and Moy came to live with Ming and Chan, Moy told Chan she wanted to go to Chan's stepmother's house to see her ma's clothes. She missed her ma. Ming had taken the suitcases back the morning after they came to Head Tiger, because they didn't have a safe place for them. He said the suitcases would be safer at his mother-in-law's house. His mother-in-law had the whole house with her small son.

Moy walked with a large group of people toward the main highway, where the army trucks loaded with the long sugarcanes waited to take people to the fields. She was about to get on the truck when a Khmer Rouge stopped her. (To spell out that evil creature's name in my book is like a slap to my face. Therefore, I'm going to call that Khmer Rouge's son Vulture.) Vulture was in his midtwenties, about five-foot-seven, and very dark-skinned, almost black. He wore long black sleeves, a cotton shirt, long cotton pants, and black sandals made from car tires, like all the Khmer Rouge wore. He told Moy to go back to work at the field but wait for him while he gave the truck drivers orders. After all the trucks left and no one were there, he ordered, "Walk!" On the way to town he asked, "Little sister angry at big brother?" His tone was friendly and overly sweet.

"No," Moy whispered, looking at the earth as she walked.

"Why little sister girl want to run away from big brother?" In this sentence, he meant the term in a romantic sense.

"I want go see my friend," she told him innocently.

They walked side by side. She didn't like his tone of voice or his meaning. But she couldn't do anything about it. He was a Khmer Rouge and the commander's son. Moy kept her mouth shut. She just wanted to get home, about forty-five minutes away.

About half the way home, without a house or a soul in sight, Vulture stopped and ordered her to stand still. He looked around, up and down the road, carefully. "Turn right," he told her.

Moy did as she was told. She turned onto a tiny footpath leading into the jungle. He told her he had something for her to carry to the sharing kitchen. She walked in front of him for a long time but saw nothing as they went deeper into the jungle. She felt something was not right. Without turning around, she asked, "Where is it, buddy Big Brother?"

"Not far. No call me buddy Big Brother, just call me *Big Brother*," he told her.

She said nothing, but kept walking. Later, she saw a small shelter on her right. It was no more than six feet square. The roof and one wall were covered in dry, brown grass and had a platform of brown wooden boards about two feet off the ground. Moy was in the center of a bowl in the jungle. Trees and tall and short grass folded in around her and Vulture. She walked past the shelter.

"Stop! Come back!" he shouted, his voice heavy. He breathed in and out rapidly, like he was having trouble breathing.

She turned around to ask if he was all right. Not that she cared, but she didn't want him to drop dead right in front of her.

"Go up and sleep there!" the Khmer Rouge's son pointed toward the bed. His face and eyes had changed, and his breathing, too.

Moy was afraid. He just might drop dead in front of her, and there was no one to help. Without warning, Vulture grabbed her upper arm and threw her toward the bed.

"Go up there now!" he ordered through his heavy breathing.

Without thinking or understanding why, Moy screamed as loud as she could. He ran like a wild animal into the deep jungle. She continued to scream and cry as she ran toward the road. She was shaking. She didn't like how that Khmer Rouge yanked her arm and tossed her toward that bed.

She ran out of the jungle and onto the road, and he was there waiting for her. His face was hard, and he looked at her with extreme hatred. "Why buddy scream?" Vulture asked, looking up and down the road. "Stop your scream now!" he commanded when he saw a group of people coming from home toward them.

Moy wanted to yell and ask the people for help. But she was too scared and couldn't find her voice. She rooted to the spot and cried, shaking like a baby bird with broken wings.

"If you dare tell them, I kill you!" the Khmer Rouge threatened her.

She nodded helplessly, still crying from fright.

He continued his threatening, "I will kill Chi Minh; then I'll kill Chan. Then I'll kill you! If you dare tell anyone, I'll cut Chi Minh in half. I tell this to your face! I will take Chan's clothes off. Then I fuck her in front of you. Then I'll sleep on top of you. Then I fuck you until you can't sit down. If you dare tell anyone, I'll fuck you until you die. I will cut Chi Minh in half, take his heart out, fry it with pig's oil, and eat it with rice. You hear me?" he hissed like a mad dog.

Moy cried without tears. The Khmer Rouge's words kept ringing over and over in her head—her brain memorized every word. She screamed in silence; her voice was strangled by fear. *She had no voice.* In the real world, she didn't understand what rape was. But she remembered the Chinese and Cambodian movies she saw about how

Keem

men forcing themselves on women. The women screamed, cried, and begged for mercy when strange men yanked and pulled them to bed. The men tore the women's clothes off, especially the women's pants or sarong, and then the men jumped on top of the women. The women screamed and cried in shame. The men laughed, and some men slapped the women around when they were on top of them. Afterward, the women hung their heads in shame, crying. The men laughed and spat at the weeping women. The married women were different. They seemed shy and happy when their husbands held their hands and led them to bed. There were no screams, no crying, and no shame afterward. Instead, the women smiled. Their husbands didn't laugh at them. The husbands brushed their wives' cheeks and smiled in a teasing manner.

Moy had a sick feeling and a stomach full of ice. She was about to become like one of those women in the movies who hung their heads down in shame.

"Walk slow, slow; no talk to them," the Khmer Rouge ordered.

Moy's legs couldn't move.

"Walk!" he hissed angrily.

She couldn't move.

"Buddy Big Brother Vulture," one of the women greeted the dark-hearted dog with a smile.

Moy wanted to shout at the woman not to smile at this Khmer Rouge dog, but her voice squeezed tight in her throat.

"Buddy Sister where you go?" Vulture returned her smile.

"We go to work. Who is she?" one of the women wanted to know.

"Sick person; I take her home. Work hard!" he smiled genially as they walked past him.

When Moy was able to move again, she walked slowly. He walked very close to her. When they came to the road to Ming's tent, the Khmer Rouge ordered her to stop. "Now, I go see Chi Minh. I know where he live. You dare say anything, I tell his captain to kill him." He stepped in front of her.

They engaged in a staring war, their eyes only inches apart. His black eyes were hard and filled with hatred. Her light brown eyes were like steel.

"I go tell Chi Minh's captain, take Chi Minh to the jungle and cut his heart out. Then I cut Chi Minh's heart small, small, fry it with pig's oil, and eat it with rice. It good to eat! I share Chi Minh's heart with other people. Wait here. No go anywhere." The Khmer Rouge turned away and walked slowly toward Ming's tent.

Vulture's words rang inside Moy's head and wouldn't go away. Moy's brain recorded every word, imprinting an image of Ming being mutilated alive. Moy couldn't scream. Her voice would not come out. She wanted to run, but her legs wouldn't move. Her tears got frozen somewhere inside, so she couldn't even cry. She just stood there, watching helplessly.

Vulture walked to the front of the large tent to talk to some men. They laughed at something, and then Vulture walked into the tent and came out with Ming.

A funny sound escaped from Moy's throat. She hoped Ming would turn around and see her, but Vulture blocked Ming from turning around. Then he led Ming to the other side of the tent. Ming kept shaking his head. Moy kept watching. Vulture pointed to one of the men, who came over and stood next to Vulture. Standing between Ming and the other man, Vulture pointed to the jungle.

Moy fell to her knees and screamed without sound, crying without tears. She wrapped her arms around herself. She knelt there shaking like a little bird, half bending over, rocking back and forth. She watched helplessly from afar.

Ming walked between the two men, heading for the jungle. The two men had long, curled hunting knives in their hands. Ming was empty-handed.

Moy covered her mouth with both hands. She screamed and cried like a baby eagle trapped in a cage, being taken away from its mother's protective wings. She fell on her face and pulled her knees up to her chest. Then she got up slowly on one arm, her free hand reaching toward her big brother. Her mouth hung open, screaming silently, as she stared after Ming. Her eyes were dry. Moy tried to get up on her feet and run to save her big brother, but each time she rose to her knees, she fell flat on her face again and again. Strange sounds escaped from her throat as she screamed noiselessly. Then Ming and the men were gone from her sight. Vulture turned around and came back.

"Buddy pray for Chi Minh's ghost already?" He laughed aloud and smiled with satisfaction.

With difficulty, Moy managed to get to her feet. She stared at him with all the hate she felt in her heart. She felt cold from the inside out because she was incapable of doing anything. She had no one to help her. Her hands were empty, and she was only thirteen years old.

She wept silent tears that drowned her carefree heart and soul, killing her there and then. She looked away from evil Vulture and walked toward town. Vulture ordered her to stop walking. She didn't. He followed her and threatened her some more. He threatened to kill her if she didn't stop walking right then. When that didn't work, he threatened to kill Chan that night. Moy walked on. He stopped at the side of the dirt road, picked up a pin stick the size of an arm and came running at her like a mad dog. Swinging the pin stick over his shoulder, he brought it down toward Moy's head.

She felt the hot air coming down forcefully to her head, like a pot of boiling oil. The pin stick froze only an inch from her head. She didn't scream or cry. She just stood there and stared him in the eyes.

"Let see it. Hit me; go ahead," she challenged him in a calm voice.

Vulture's face was hard. He again swung the pin stick over his shoulder, then brought it down very hard. The powerful air pressure was like fire hitting her head, but she just stood there, arms and hands hanging straight down. And she stared harder into his eyes. Moy didn't even blink. She drew up to her full height, stood there, and waited. He was smart. He stopped before the pin stick touched her. His face and eyes slowly softened. Then he smiled and threw the pin stick away.

Moy might have been a young Chinese girl, but she was not stupid. She knew all there was to know about the rules set by the Khmer Rouge government. The rules were that if a woman and a man went to bed together without first being married by Onka, the Khmer Rouge government, Onka, called it "wrong rule." If Onka found out about the couple's love affair, Onka would "hit them away," execute them.

Perhaps Vulture understood what she might do if he hit her but didn't kill her. He was also afraid of getting killed by his own father's men. Vulture was such a coward. He picked on a helpless thirteen-year-old girl. He was like an actual vulture, picking on the dead, and cowering away from the living. Because of his quick thinking, he thought he had won and smiled for his victory. Moy lost the battle, and the game hadn't begun. After he threw the pin stick away, Vulture threatened that he would tell the kitchen not to give her any food. But she was very stubborn, and he couldn't control her.

"You meet your punishment tonight," he told her.

His threat meant nothing to her. Moy was numb, sleepwalking. She couldn't blink, couldn't cry. She made no sound, had no tears. She just walked.

Then they met a young Khmer Rouge on the road. Vulture ordered the boy to tie Moy up. The boy was maybe fifteen years old. The boy and Moy stood still and just stared at each other. The young Khmer Rouge didn't move until Vulture was out of sight.

"Why Buddy Big Brother Vulture want me tie you up?" he asked, keeping his eyes on her face.

"He order me to sleep with him. I no listen to him. I no want to sleep with him. Now he angry with me." For the first time, tears dripped from her eyes, and she wiped them away.

The young Khmer Rouge looked thoughtful; then he smiled. "Go home, go. Don't be afraid. Buddy Big Brother Vulture play with you," he told her. His chin pointed toward town.

She was going to tell him about Vulture's threats, but the young Khmer Rouge had already walked away, shaking his head. Moy walked past her captain, Girl. For once, Girl looked away from her, like she was afraid of Moy. Moy walked up the staircase and into the dark house. She walked to the spot where Ming had slept the night before and lay down on her side. She inhaled his sweet scent, breathing deeply, and closed her eyes...

6

Moy felt a gentle shake on her shoulder and opened her eyes. She stared at her sister-in-law. Chan told her to get up; it was time for dinner. Moy had slept through lunch and couldn't miss another meal. Moy got up and went downstairs. She took a small cup of water from a large gasoline tank to wash her face. She walked next to Chan to the sharing kitchen. Chan looked at her strangely and asked if Moy was all right. If not, she could stay home and Chan would bring food for her. Moy shook her head.

Vulture sat at a long table, his feet on the bench, at the entrance of the sharing kitchen. Moy walked past him, but then she stopped. She turned around and walked back. She stood in front of him and stared him in the eyes. He looked startled and smiled strangely. Chan didn't know what was happening. Pulling Moy away from Vulture, Chan asked his forgiveness. She told him that Moy was very young, that she didn't know any better, and she was sick.

"I not sick! I not too young, and I know everything and what happen!" Moy shouted loudly over her shoulder.

Everyone heard her and turned around in their seats to stare at her and Vulture. His face was pale, and he looked at her with big eyes.

"That child very disrespectful. She look at elders like that!" people whispered to each to each other.

"Buddy Big Brother, forgive us," Chan shouted over her shoulder, as she pushed Moy onto a bench. "You crazy, talk to Big Brother Vulture like that?" Chan hissed in Khmer.

Moy said nothing.

"Vulture is Black Shirt; you not know?" Chan whispered in Teochew, and she went on and on.

Moy heard nothing. After dinner, she went straight to bed. Sometime later, she felt something heavy and warm on her forehead. She opened her eyes and stared into the candlelight and at the face behind it.

"Little sister sick?" a male's voice asked.

She knew that voice.

"Get up. I have some food for you. Go downstair and wash your face. I have sweet banana soup for you to eat. Chan already eat some," Ming's ghost told her.

She got up and looked at him sitting in front of her.

"Big Brother?" Moy asked in Chinese.

"What?" He frowned.

"Big Brother Ming?" she repeated.

"What wrong with her?" he asked his wife, pointing at Moy.

"Crazy pig," Chan told her husband.

"Big Brother," Moy touched his face. She felt the heat under her hands. Then she touched his chest where the heart was and felt it beating. She wept and mumbled, "Big Brother, Big Brother," in Chinese, over and over.

"Why you cry like that? You cry like Khmer Red take me away and kill me," Ming said.

Moy cried harder and louder. She couldn't stop mumbling, "Big Brother, Big Brother."

Poor Ming! He didn't know what had happened. By the pictures that Vulture drew for her, Ming had been executed that morning, in such a horrible way. And that image would live in Moy's mind for the rest of her life. Ming looked helpless, sitting next to her.

"Stop cry like baby! I not know what to do," he told his wife. He got up and shifted from foot to foot. "Go wash your face. Big Brother must go back to work," he told Moy. Then he touched her shoulder gently.

It took Moy a while to control her tears. Then she got up and walked toward the staircase. She stopped and looked at her handsome big brother. She still couldn't stop mumbling, "Big Brother, Big Brother."

He looked confused. Moy heard people in the house whispering to each other and to Ming that Moy must be very frightened of something to cry like that. She must love her big brother very much and scared something bad might happen to him. People told Ming he was very lucky to have an adopted little sister who loved him that much. They told him to ask Moy nicely what had frightened her.

Later, she sat between Ming and Chan. Moy ate the sweet banana soup he had saved for her.

"Why you cry when you see me?" Ming asked between bites of the soup with a spoon.

Moy didn't answer and lowered her head. She thought if she waited long enough, he'd forget.

"Moy, you hear me?" he asked.

"This sweet banana soup is good to eat," she told him.

"Answer your big brother," Chan told her.

"I want more soup," she told them.

"Answer first," Ming looked thoughtful.

"I…dream bad thing about Big Brother," she lowered her eyes toward the empty bowl in her hands. She couldn't tell anyone what had happened. If she did, people might tell her, "Big Brother Vulture only play with you," like the young Khmer Rouge did that morning.

Keem

If I tell Big Brother, he wouldn't believe me anyway, she thought. And then that would be the last time Moy heard and saw Ming. Then, mentally and emotionally, she went deaf and blind for a period. Ming had to wait a long time before Moy could see and hear him again.

Moy kept changing after that night. She was not the same carefree and talkative little girl everyone in that large house knew. She isolated herself more each day. She didn't smile or laugh like she used to. She cried more and more each day. She cried for her ma's comfort. Most of all, she cried in fear of losing her one and only big brother, and from the pain of the loss of her ma and grandpa. She cried for someone to hug her or hold her hand. But there wasn't anyone who understood her longing, and she didn't know how to ask. What little comfort Ming could give, she no longer wanted. She was afraid to lose him, so she withdrew from him. It was the only way young Moy knew of to protect him from harm. However, Ming didn't understand.

Those days, Moy only talked to women, if she talked at all. And she avoided all men and boys. She was afraid of people who live in this evil world. Many people had given her pain, tears, and fears since her beloved Ma Keem Lai had gone to heaven. Currently, she lived in a world where she had no one to love or care for her. She cared little whether she lived or died. Yet, she still cared for her big brother, from afar. Not that he would harm her or hurt her in any way. *Big Brother is a man. A man could change from a friend to a deadly enemy in the blink of an eye. Like Vulture.*

Since that awful day, wherever Moy worked, in the cornfield, or at the mung bean (small, hard, green beans) field, Vulture was there. He worked with the children, talking, laughing, and joking around with them. He didn't talk to Moy. Then he became Girl's best friend. Together, they always thought of something to have the children do to insult Moy, like taunting, "Chinese rag. Lazy Chinese, Chinese dog." They tried to get her angry so she would fistfight with them.

Moy didn't fistfight with anyone; she just cried from the insults.

"Chinese rag! Chinese only wash rag and eat rag!" all the children shouted and laughed at her. Vulture and Girl would laugh and chatter loudly after the children.

The more Moy cried, the meaner they became. But Moy was a fast learner. She knew their games. Vulture was a coward, hiding behind the children. He fought against thirteen-year-old Moy from behind them. However, he and the children couldn't get Moy to fistfight.

Vulture would tell one of the children to shove Moy on the back. Sometimes, the kids pushed her so hard that Moy fell on her face. She just wiped tears away with the backs of her hands, picked herself up on her feet, and went to work. One time, one or two kids walked up and slapped Moy's cheeks. Then they ran off laughing. Other times, they threw dirt and grass at her face, head, and body. She didn't fight back. She didn't care anymore. If one of the Cambodian children had a knife to shatter her heart, she might even welcome it.

Moy simply let her captive tears free, free to wet Mother Earth's dry throat, for more corn to grow. Then the children and Vulture would have more corn to eat.

She stopped talking to people in the large house. If someone asked her a question, her answer was only yes or no. She was very tired for her age. She couldn't get out from under evil Vulture's claws! He was such a coward, like a scary little lizard, hiding behind the children and getting them to fight his battle for him. Evil always hides behind smiling and friendly faces. It is the only way evil can get people to fall for his tricks. And Ming and the children fell for it.

One day in the cornfield, Vulture worked next to Moy, and he shouted in a friendly voice, "Moy, two!" The number one in Khmer sounds like Moy. All the kids laughed with him. He threw corn seeds into the holes and pulled the dirt in with his foot. To the children and onlookers, he was helping her.

Keem

"Why buddy eat so fast and work so slow?" he shouted loudly, then looked around at the children in the field. Everyone laughed with him. Then he turned around, face to face with Moy. His smile was gone, and he whispered just loud enough for her to hear, "I no kill Chi Minh the other day. It no fun. I already tell you. You wait and see. I still want to eat Chi Minh's heart. Moy two not just stand there like a scarecrow! Work!" he shouted, laughed, and smiled for all to see. Then he whispered to her again, "One of these days I'll eat Chi Minh's heart. Work, Moy two, work!" he shouted with laughter.

Moy rooted to the spot. She didn't blink. She stared into his eyes, stone-faced. She wanted to see his evil soul behind his eyes. Time stood still. Finally, he turned around and walked away. She felt like a large sheet of ice covered her, and icy water flowed up and down in her throat. Feeling dizzy, she shut her eyes, holding her stick tightly, with her head dropped forward. When the dizziness passed, she went back to work as if he hadn't said anything to her.

She ate whatever the sharing kitchen gave her. She never asked for more. She didn't bathe or change her clothes. Moy lived in an unknown world of darkness. She never knew when Vulture might come and take Ming away. She didn't know when Vulture's men would come and take Chan and herself away, when the Khmer Rouge would rape them in front of her big brother, before killing them all. *Would he cut me in half, too? Then take my heart out, chop it in small pieces, fry it with pig's oil, and eat it with rice?* she thought, seeing that picture inside her head every day. During the day, she walked, worked, and lived like all the other living dead. Better dead than alive. But Moy was neither dead nor alive. Still, she must go on.

She stopped visiting Ming. When he came home, she went off somewhere. When Ming was inside the house, she went outside. If he was downstairs, she went upstairs. She stopped sleeping next to her sister-in-law and big brother. She went to sleep with the single women, on the other side of the large house. That hurt Ming and his wife's feelings.

About a week later, Chan sent Moy to wash the family's clothes at the small stream next to Girl's house. While washing the clothes, Moy broke down in tears, feeling sorry for herself. She remembered when they lived in Pailin. Keem had told her daughter that some brothers' wives will abuse their sisters-in-law if their parents weren't there and the husbands were too busy to notice their sisters' condition.

It is the Chinese custom. The husband's sister has authority over his wife. The wife must be the one to take care of the husband's sister and respect her. Sometimes a bad wife would look down on the husband's family if his parents had passed away. She would abuse his little sisters or brothers. Sometimes a bad wife would abuse her parents-in-law, too. The Chinese custom and rule is that the daughter-in-law must service her husband's family, by cooking, washing the clothes, cleaning the house, and so on.

On other the hand, sometimes a husband's family members might abuse his wife. If they were lucky, everyone would help each other, and they would live happily. However, the daughter-in-law must always respect her in-laws if she is a good wife.

I don't want to wash her clothes! Moy cried and threw Chan's shirt into the water. *She should wash my clothes! I never dare ask her to wash my clothes. She has no respect for Big Brother, and she no respect Ma and Grandpa!* Moy thought. She picked up the wet, unwashed clothes and went home. She did spread them out on the bushes to dry. Then she went to sit on the monk's stone and cried her fill. The shadow of the large house was like a cage over her. She couldn't get up and walk out of the cool, dark shadow into the bright, warm sunlight. She simply didn't have the will to get up from the monk's stone.

"Why you cry so much? Now you no talk to anyone and you no play with the children. You go off somewhere and cry. You embarrass

Keem

me. Want talk?" Ming asked. He sat on another monk's stone, next to her.

Moy didn't know when he had gotten there. *Yes! I want to talk! But no one is here to see or hear me! I want to tell you about Vulture. He wants to kill you! But you're not going to believe me! Big Brother can't see or hear me!* she thought. But she shouted something else, "I no want to wash sister-in-law's clothes!" She wept behind her hands, rocking back and forth.

"If something happen to you, tell Big Brother. I find way to help you. I can no help you if you no talk to me." Ming sound frustrated.

"I no want to wash sister-in-law's clothes," she told him.

"What?" One minute he was sitting on the monk's stone next to her; then he was gone.

Good! He gone, now I can cry all I want. No one is here to bother me! Moy thought. Then she heard people whispering to each other, "She no respects her husband or his sister!" People didn't approve of Chan. They were resting under the other side of the house.

Moy might be younger than Chan, but she knew the Cambodian custom and rule was like the Chinese. Then Ming was back quickly with his angry wife. "Sister-in-law, I beg forgiveness. I dare not ask you to wash my clothes again. I no have time today to wash our clothes," Chan tried to explain. Moy cried harder.

"If you no have time to wash your own clothes, then no ask someone else to wash your clothes!" Ming snapped at his poor wife.

"I ask for forgiveness. What else Mr. Husband want me to do?" Chan gave him a hard stare.

"You wash Moy's clothes. You hear me?" he pointed at Chan.

Moy cried harder as she watched and listened to Ming yell at his poor wife.

"Yes, Mr. Husband," Chan said and then stormed off.

MOY

Ming went to sit on the monk's stone again. He didn't know what to do. He just sat there and watched Moy cry. Then he told her, "My co-worker and I will make sweet banana soup tomorrow. Come at noon, and I give you some."

"I no want sweet banana soup," she told him. She got up, ready to turn away from him. But she couldn't move when she saw his disappointment. "Big Brother bring some home tomorrow?" she asked.

"Moy?" He reached for her.

She backed away from his hand. And she rubbed her upper right arm where Vulture had grabbed her.

"Why you afraid of Big Brother?" he frowned and dropped his hands into his lap. Ming watched her carefully.

"I no afraid of Big Brother." *I just want you to go away from me. Go somewhere Vulture can't hurt you!* she wanted to tell him.

He looked very disappointed.

"Big Brother, bring some sweet banana soup home?" she asked.

"If you want some, you go where there is some!" Ming was angry. He jumped to his feet and tossed his hand into his hair, as if to hold back his anger. "I can no bring it home," he snapped sharply. Then he turned around and walked away. Friendship ended quicker than the blink of an eye. He didn't know what had happened, and he tossed their friendship away.

"Big Brother, come back! Come back," Moy whispered, holding both her hands out toward his back. He didn't hear her. *Big Brother hates me now. I have to save my big brother. I want him to live,* she cried in silence.

One night, Moy awoke and lay still, listening to an elderly woman and some other people who were older than Chan and Ming. They told Ming and Chan they had never seen anyone so sad and heartbroken as Moy. They pitied the Chinese child whose ma and grandpa had died, leaving her alone. The elderly woman told Chan and Ming that something very bad had happened to the Chinese child, or she had to be very afraid of something, to cry like that every day. Some single women who slept close to Moy told Chan and Ming that Moy cried herself to sleep every night. Some nights, they listened to Moy cry for her ma, grandpa, and big brother in her sleep.

The elderly woman and some single women advised Chan and Ming to ask Moy nicely and gently about the bad thing that had happened to her. They said especially Ming had to make Moy trust him and get her to talk to him. They said that if Moy didn't worry about or love him, she wouldn't cry for him in her sleep. Ming and Chan said they had tried to talk to Moy, but she wouldn't talk. Chan asked her co-workers for help. The elderly woman told everyone in the large house to help the Chinese child, like she was their own little sister. But right then, the only person who could help the Chinese child was Ming.

A few days later, Ming came to tell her he was leaving town. The tractors and the drivers were being sent to Kompong Kol, the headquarters of the sugar factory. A lot of land needed to be plowed there. But Chan's group would remain in Head Tiger, and Moy would stay with her. He sounded like a grown up stranger talking to a child without feeling, not the big brother that Moy adored. But he did say, "Look after yourself."

"I beg Big Brother forgiveness if I make Big Brother unhappy," Moy said. She hoped he would say something.

He looked like he wanted to but changed his mind. He turned around and walked away from her. She wanted to run after her big brother and beg him not to leave her in this evil town. But if she did that, he would ask why. She couldn't tell him. And she remembered what Ming had done a few weeks earlier. One day, coming back from somewhere, she was walking past the sharing kitchen and saw them. They were sitting next to each other at the table, talking, laughing, pushing, and shoving at each other like two children.

"Moy two, you go where? Come here, my little sister!" Ming shouted through his laughter.

At first, she was too shocked to move. She just stared at Ming and Vulture. She almost threw up. Her own big brother had actually called her "one, two," like Vulture did.

"Moy two, come here and sit with Big Brother, Little Sister!" Vulture shouted through his laughter, and Ming laughed with him.

She ran home, hearing their laughter after her. After that day, Ming, Chan, and Vulture became good friends! Vulture talked and laughed with Chan every day, and she fell for his charm. He gave Ming and Chan clothes and shoes. Ming and Chan told each other and other people in the house how nice and friendly Vulture was. Moy said nothing. She simply walked away. Then one day, Ming told Moy, "Big Brother Vulture ask me to give this new sarong to you. He pity you, an orphan." He handed her a black sarong.

Ice water flowed up and down Moy's throat and through her whole body. She just sat there and stared at Ming. When Moy yanked that sarong from Ming's hands and tore it in half, Ming and Chan were shocked. Moy jumped to her feet, ran to the entrance, and threw it down from the house. Chan ran downstairs and got the sarong. Everyone in the house called Moy crazy.

"That Chinese child so mean. She throw the gift away!" people said to each other.

Perhaps that night Ming thought Moy was mad at him for calling her "one, two" earlier that day. He didn't know that Vulture never let a day go by without reminding Moy, "I act nice to Chi Minh and Chan. They not know which night I come to take them away and kill them. When I done with them, I come to take you and fuck you; then I shoot you away."

Every day, Moy came home heavyhearted. She was afraid Chan wouldn't be there. She was terrified that her big brother might disappear! Now, she stood and watched Ming leaving her. Tears dripped from her eyes as he walked away. Not once did he look back.

Big Brother hates me. Everyone hates me. Big Brother is angry—but he is alive, she thought.

7

A couple of days after Ming left town, the commander of Head Tiger, Vulture's father, called the eleven children to the common kitchen for a meeting with a strange man in his late thirties, and a young girl about fifteen years old, both light-skinned. The strange man was in charge of the eight- to sixteen-year-old children who worked in the sugarcane fields. He came to ask for the children in town to join the Bike One Children, the strongest workers. The young girl who came with him looked friendly. She was the girls' general, overseeing all the girls. The meeting went on for a while.

Afterward, the children went home to get their clothes and say goodbye to their parents. The children put their belongings in old cloth book bags, if their parents had them for them. Some children wrapped their clothes and mosquito net in a piece of cloth or a plaid towel. Moy had only a change of clothes and her grandpa's old mosquito net, wrapped in an old, thin, plaid towel. Some of the children hugged their clothes bags to their chests or carried them over their shoulders. Most of the children cried, scared to leave their families. When any of them looked at Moy strangely, she stared back. She held her head high and marched after the children's commander. Before she left, she asked some of the sick people at home to tell Chan where she was going.

Moy's new home was about thirty minutes from the common house where she lived with the others. She looked around her new home. It

Keem

was about forty feet wide and fifty feet long. The building had only one wall and a white, standard metal roof. She looked at the little beds inside the house. A piece of wood here, a piece of white metal there, a small pile of dry brown grass on the left, a piece of green or red plastic on the right, and so on. Some of those little beds had old mosquito nets tied over, held up by small sticks on the four corners. There were so many lines of those tiny beds that Moy couldn't count them all. The girls' and boys' sleeping places were separated by a two-foot-wide dirt footpath, but the girls slept on one side and the boys slept on the other, *under the same roof.*

Some sick girls and boys had stayed home and were sleeping. Some sat crying for their mother, father, grandma, grandpa, big brother, or big sister, missing them very much.

Other children sobbed aloud, "Mother, come take me home!" or "Father, come take me home! I miss Mother and Father very much!"

Some children sat on homemade beds, looking tired and sad. Some just sat staring at their bare feet. Some of the children were all skin and bones!

Moy walked past the children. They looked up and stared at her with dull eyes that spoke of their hunger. A hunger for their mother and father's warm arms wrapped around them. They were very young and helpless. Moy knew and understood. If she could have seen her own face when the Khmer Rouge took her from her ma and grandpa, she'd know this is what she looked like—dull eyes, frightened, sad, and hungry, but not for food.

When Keem was alive, she went through it, and said many times that a person could die from missing someone she loves.

Most of these children were starving to death, slowly and painfully, from missing their parents. Some of these sick children were like the rotten, empty eggshells Moy had seen on the sidewalks many times. Large, green-headed flies and mosquitos were everywhere, on the sick children's heads, faces, hands, backs, chests, fingers, legs, and toes. They were being eaten alive by flies and mosquitos, but these children didn't have the energy to lift their hands or move their fingers to chase the flies and mosquitos away. Some flies and mosquitos were even on the children's lips! A few children swept the bugs away from their faces with their little bony hands. Their black hair looked like they had been through a firestorm. Some of the children's faces were caked with dried mud, and they had black, broken fingernails. And most of these children were *four or five years old*, not eight.

In Cambodia's middle or lower class families, parents started to train their four- or five-year-old children to care for their younger siblings, or help make a living, such as by selling iced coffee in plastic bags, fish noodle soup, sweet banana soup, and other goods in the open market.

Keem had had Moy cook rice for the family when Moy was four years old. After dinner, Moy did the dishes, every night.

Moy looked away from the sad, wounded children. She was about to walk past a five, or maybe seven, year old little girl.

"Buddy!" the little girl called out to her.

She looked at the girl's big, dull eyes. A happy, but tired smile spread over the girl's little, pale, wood-and paper-covered face. The girl was like a skeleton. Moy could see every bone in the girl's body under her pale, dry skin. That poor child's knees were drawn up under her wooden chin. Her skeleton cheek rested upon her wooden knees, her toothpick arms wrapped around chopstick legs. She didn't have the energy to lift her hand, but her fingers wriggled in greeting. Moy read the girl's lips as they moved slowly, "Buddy."

"Buddy sick?" Moy said, kneeling in front of the girl.

"Yes," she whispered, and her smile became wider. She spoke in a weak, but very sweet, little voice. This girl gave Moy the impression she might have come from an upper class family.

"They give buddy medicine to eat?" Moy wanted to know.

"Yes, but I no get better." She put all her energy into each word. "And they take me to hospital next week. There, I see my mother again!" She looked and sounded very happy.

"Where is the hospital?" Moy asked.

The girl stared at her strangely, then asked if Moy didn't know where the hospital was.

"No," Moy told her.

"The hospital is at the factory in Kompong Kol. We have only one hospital," she told Moy.

"Buddy sleep. You no have strength," Moy told her. Then Moy got up.

"Buddy! Buddy come and play with me again?" The little girl grabbed Moy's hand with a strong grip. She sounded and looked hopeful.

Moy looked at the skeleton hand on her arm. The girl's touch was hot like fire, and her skin was dry. She looked at the child's thin, pale skeleton face and into her dull eyes. She wanted to hug and comfort her and take away her sickness. *I'm not her mother. I want my ma, too!* Moy thought.

"Yes. Sleep now. I come back to play with you when you wake up," Moy told her.

The girl turned around and walked on her skeleton hands and knees to her dry, brown grass bed to lay down. She smiled and whispered weakly, "No forget and come back to play with me." Then she closed her eyes and went to sleep with a smile on her skeleton face.

Moy turned around and walked away. *After dinner, I'll come and play with her,* Moy thought. Then she quickly thought, *I want to go back and live with Sister-in-Law.* She knew Chan was a good actress, always smiling when someone was nearby. She never smiled when no one was watching. Not that she did anything mean to Moy, but Moy felt a coldness from Chan whenever Ming wasn't home. Still, Chan was the closest person to her, now that Ming wasn't there. Keem and Wong weren't there anymore, and Moy had to take care of herself. She couldn't wait for Ming to come back to take care of her.

Moy went around and looked for a spot for her belongings. She looked toward the right and saw a long room with two large entrances, one on each side of the room. She walked up the four steps and onto the platform, then into the large, clean room. In the room, there were about five to ten small mosquito nets tied to both walls. The girls' general was there with another, shorter, girl. Both girls smiled and asked if they could help her. It was nice to see someone smile at her for a change.

Moy told them she was looking for a spot to sleep. They told her she had to look outside, that this room belonged to the generals only. The two girls giggled and offered to help Moy find a spot, and she thanked them. They found a spot for Moy across from their room. They even found two boards to make a bed for her. Then they found four small sticks and tied the mosquito net over her tiny bed. The two girls went to their room, and Moy waited for the children to come back from the fields to go have their dinner.

It was about six in the evening when the children returned from the work field. Moy was sitting on her new bed when she heard the children singing one of the Khmer Rouge's songs, "…get rid of the American!" *Who is the American? Oh, Red Hair!* Moy thought. In Cambodia, the Chinese called the French Red Hair.

She remembered once, when she was about two or three years old, she'd seen a cute red-headed baby in its mother's arms. Moy went crazy; she wanted the baby. She cried and begged her ma for that baby. Keem laughed and told her daughter she'd tell Grandpa to buy a Western doll for her to play with. That didn't stop her from crying.

Keem

"Crazy child, you want Ma sell you to Red Hair? Red Hair want to buy you." Keem told her daughter. That shut Moy up nicely. Nevertheless, she looked longingly at that cute little baby in its mother's protective arms.

Moy looked out from the one-walled house. The girls walked in one long line, and the boys walked in another. All the girls wore long black sarongs or pants and black long-sleeved shirts. The boys wore long black pants and black long-sleeved shirts. Some children carried bent shovels; others carried long, bent hunting knives on their shoulders or held them in their hands. When the children got in the house, everyone went to their bed areas, but five minutes later, all the girls and boys were outside standing in line— girls on one side, boys on the other, about ten to twelve children in a group.

Each group had a number: Bike One, Bike Two, and so on. The youngest group was Bike Seven, four to six years old. The oldest group was Bike One, fifteen to seventeen years old. All of them looked clean, but sweaty, and none of them were thin. Some were outright fat. Everyone had a small, deep plate and a spoon in hand, waving them back and forth impatiently. They couldn't wait to get to the common kitchen for their dinner.

Some children had very little energy; a few looked about to fall asleep on their feet. When everyone was at attention, the commander came out and said a few words. He reminded the children to work harder, have good manners, eat slowly, not steal food from each other, and not get into fistfights. He ended by shouting, "Success, success. Communist Cambodia!" and thrust his fist upward. The children imitated him, repeating after him three times.

Moy held her hand up, like knocking on someone's head in front of her.

The children walked in two straight, long lines. If the person in front was a slow walker, the others would yell, "I hungry. Walk faster!"

It took the children about fifteen minutes to walk to the common kitchen. Four groups sat on two long wooden benches, facing each other. Each table had eight large, round, deep metal bowls. The bowls were about a foot wide on top and five inches wide at the bottom. Each group had a big captain and a small captain. The pairs of captains took the bowls to the headman or headwoman of the kitchen to get rice and banana tree soup for their groups. Then the two captains divided the rice and soup among the group members at their table. Each girl and boy got only two small dippers of rice mixed with corn or mung beans. Some groups shared the soup out of the big bowl. Whoever ate fastest got full, while the slow eaters went hungry. There was yelling at every table, "You eat up everything!"

"Why buddy eat so slow?"

"It not my fault; I hungry!"

Moy held her spoon and stared at the empty soup bowl. Girl smiled at her. Moy had eaten only one spoonful of soup. Then she ate the rice mixed with corn, with salt. She ate slowly, like her ma and grandpa had taught her.

"Eat like a lady. Lady no eat fast, fast like boy." Keem and Wong also told her, "Look around; see what people do. If it is good, then learn from them."

When Moy came home from dinner, she heard a boy crying and shouting. "All the short life, no one care for her, now she died. My little sister died like a dog." He was about ten or twelve years old. The commander tried to hug the angry and grieving boy, but the brother stepped away and shouted every bad word he could think of that no mother wanted her children to hear.

"Watch your word! Get him!" the commander shouted.

A tall boy blocked Moy's view, so she stepped aside to watch. The brother shouted a very colorful bad word at the two older boys, who caught him and held him tight in their arms. He cried, brokenhearted.

Keem

"Watch your word! We want to help you. No curse people like that," the commander and two older boys told him.

Some children, like Moy, stood farther away from the corpse. Other children stood closer, to watch and listen. Some children hung their heads. Some thrust their heads up higher, or turned left and right, trying to get a better view. A strange sound escaped from Moy's throat when she saw where the corpse lay. She stared at the dirty, little brown blanket covering the small body.

It was the sick girl Moy had spoken to that afternoon. The one who had urged Moy to not forget to come play with her again. She had been very happy! She'd be going to the hospital next week so she'd see her mother again. Now...she had died. She died like a hungry dog. She was abused by her own people. They took all her pride and dignity away, like they had with Wong and Keem.

Wong had sobbed aloud, brokenhearted. Someone had stolen the family's chicken and he didn't get to eat it. Much later, he ate a cooked baby mouse the size of Moy's pinky. He died the next morning, wearing only a towel around his waist. Keem was buried without a small towel to cover her beautiful face!

This little girl carefree childhood and life were stolen from her, like Moy and the others. The Khmer Rouge abused her, forcing her to live and work inside the jungle, like everyone in the country. When she got sick, they kicked her aside like a dog. And they starved her of her mother's warmth, care, and loving arms so much that she had asked a stranger, Moy, to be her friend.

"I come back and play you again," Moy had promised her.

The girl's dull eyes had lit up with hope, and she'd gone to sleep with a smile. But no one else cared enough to check on her. And she died like a street dog inside a one-walled house. She was only a child. She was Moy's friend.

Keem Lai

In this small picture of Ma inside a frame, she was forty-one.
It was the picture I took to work with me every day
when I was in the freedom...cage in Cambodia.

8

The next morning, Moy was awakened by a strange sound. She opened her eyes and listened carefully. It was the sound of a whistle.

"Get up!" Girl peeked inside Moy's mosquito net to shout in Moy's face.

Moy got up, looked around, and saw almost everyone else was up. Outside, the sky was still black. She looked around but couldn't find any water to wash her face. Some boys and girls were half asleep as they walked to the front of the house in lines. She didn't know who her captain was, and she went to Girl's line, where there were only four girls. The girls' general pulled some ten- and twelve-year-old girls from other groups and sent them to Girl's group, so now there were ten girls, in Bike Three group.

Moy didn't know why they had to get up in the dark. She looked around; some girls were nodding off on their feet. Moy watched and listened. The two generals, about fifteen years old, stood in front of the all the girls, who had formed about thirty lines. The big and small captains stood in front of their groups. The generals called for the captains' attention and asked how many sick people each captain had in her group. The captains called the names of the sick girls to come out and sit on their feet in front of the not sick.

Sometimes, the two generals told sick girls, "Go back in line and go to work. You sick too much!"

Other times, the two generals debated each other about which girls could stay home sick and who should get back to work. So some girls ended up going to work, whether sick or not. Later, Moy found out that when there were too many sick people, the generals sent everyone back to work. Sick or not, the generals didn't care. Then the generals ordered the captains to bring out the bent shovels and the long, curled hunting knives for everyone and gave a final order, "Go!" After everyone left, the two generals went back to sleep.

Moy walked with the girls and boys for a long time. Most of the children flew by her, like there was food somewhere waiting for them. Some children walked in groups, others walked alone, like Moy. About an hour's walk from their house, Moy looked around at the girls and boys who were sound asleep on the side of the road, near the sugarcane fields. A few older girls and boys sat in groups talking quietly to each other. Sugarcane twice her height stretched as far as Moy could see. She stood between a large mountain and the master sugarcane fields. In the sky, the stars twinkled down upon the sleeping children and on Mother Earth.

Moy sat by herself, knees under her chin, the bent shovel lying next to her. She looked at the dark sky and the bright stars twinkling down at her. *So high and bright…*

Girl kicked Moy's back and yelled at her to get up. Moy sat up quickly, not sure where she was, and looked around. The captains went around shaking the girls and boys awake. Most of the children sat up, rubbing their sleepy eyes, and looked around like Moy. Moy glanced at the sky. The sun was not up yet! It was only bright enough for the children to see the tips of their noses. Each captain ordered his or her group into the sugarcane fields.

The members of each group worked together. Two people worked between rows of sugarcane. The person with a long hunting knife went ahead, cutting down bushes and tall grasses. The second person

Keem

used a shovel to dig out the roots of the bushes and grasses away from each sugarcane bunch, cleaning up the space between the rows. Each bunch of sugarcane had between five and fifteen canes, with two feet between each bunch. Some rows had sharp pin bushes and needle vines on the ground that were very hard to dig out from below and pile up at the center.

It was a nightmare for Moy. She didn't have shoes. She had no choice but to work in the row that Girl assigned to her. She cried whenever she stepped on the sharp vine needles, sitting down to pull them out of her feet. Later, and many times afterward, when she didn't know she had thorns in her feet, the punctures got infected. When that would happen, she would borrow a safety pin from someone to poke a hole in the area and squeeze out the infection. Then she would tear a little bit of skin off and wash the area with salt water. Keem had taught her that.

Everyone else in Moy's group had shoes, and they worked much faster than she did, so they would rest at the end of her row before starting a new one. By the time Moy finished her first rows, the others were halfway through in their second rows. At the end of the day, the generals ordered everyone to help Moy finish all her rows. It was like that every day. Moy was the slowest worker in the fields, and everyone hated her for having to do most of her work. She tried her best to work as fast as she could, and her rows were the cleanest. But she was also the fastest eater! Girl had to divide the fish with banana tree and juice equally to everyone.

The children's lunch was carried by four wooden wagons to the field for them. Each wagon was pulled by two cows and accompanied by four Khmer Rouges. They had long guns hanging down from gun belts over their shoulders. The girls and boys formed four lines—two wagons for the girls and two wagons for the boys. Each girl or boy got two small dippers of rice, mixed with bananas, mung beans, or corn, and a small dipper of banana tree soup on top. The children took their food and went to eat under the sugarcane. Most days, the temperature was ninety to one hundred degrees or over. The leaves on the trees hung down nice and straight, not a breeze anywhere. The heavy, long black clothing made everything worse for the children. They had an hour for lunch, and most children ate their meal quickly then went around looking for grasshoppers, mushrooms, or some leaves that they would take home and boil with a little salt to eat.

Every day during lunch, Moy sat alone and cried under the sugarcane. She had a small picture of Keem, a two-by-three, that she would hold in both hands. She stared at Keem's beautiful face and longed for Keem's love. Moy wanted her ma back!

"You cold?" or "If I can pull the moon down for you, I pull it down for you"—Moy longed to hear her ma whisper those words in her ear again. Sometimes she would sob aloud and whisper to Keem's picture, "Ma, come back! I miss you, Ma. Come back. Take me with you!" She wished her ma were there, holding Moy in her arms again.

Moy didn't know that the generals found out about her crying, missing her ma. They threatened to take Keem's picture away if Moy didn't stop crying over it. Though Moy was afraid they might take her beloved Ma's picture away, she continued to take it to work with her. But during lunch hour she was more careful, and she sat farther away from the others. She whispered softly in Teochew, "Ma, I miss you. Come back! Help me, Ma!" She would hold her ma's picture to her chest, or up close to her face, and hold the rice bowl with her free hand.

She worked with the children for a few months. Then she got sick. Everyone yelled at her that she was too dirty, and that was why she got sick. She didn't wash her dark brown hair, which reached the middle of her back. Her mind had shut off from the world. It was as if she had been locked up in a cage and couldn't get out—or she refused to get

Keem

out and face an empty world without Keem Lai and Wong Lai's love. She didn't take care of herself. She let the children abuse her, and then she abused herself some more by not bathing. Her excuse was there wasn't enough water to bathe, only enough to drink. Her head was full of lice that dropped from her head like black pepper when she combed her fingers through her hair. Lice crawled around her neck and shoulders, and her head itched like crazy! No one wanted to sit or sleep next to her.

"You smell worse than a dead body!" they yelled at her.

Her head hurt, and she stayed home sick a lot. Then one day, Moy stayed home sick and remembered that Girl had led some of the children to pull away the small piece of white cloth attached to Moy's shirt. Having the cloth attached to her shirt was a Chinese custom, the way she paid her respects to Keem and Wong after they passed away. Moy cried, brokenhearted over the assault on her beloved Ma and Grandpa.

Then Moy remembered the assault on Keem Lai's remains, a pain that would stay in Moy's heart for the rest of her life. Keem had worn a light jade bracelet/wrist-ring before she passed away. Moy wanted her ma to have it. However, a large Cambodian man who helped Pon carry Keem's remains to be buried broke Keem's wrist and hand to take it! And Moy wasn't there to stop him.

Ming and Chan had asked Moy countless times before the assault to take the white cloth off her shirt. People and the Khmer Rouge didn't like it. They wanted her to take it off. She didn't listen. However, there was another way to pay her respect to her beloved Ma and Grandpa, and it would kill two birds with one stone! Without thinking, she rose to her feet and walked out of the one-walled house. If the baby tiger, Moy, wanted to be free, there wasn't a lock or a cage that could keep her in. And she was about to become a teacher for everyone at the sugarcane fields.

She walked toward the common house where she used to live with Chan. Moy went to a small shelter covered in dry, brown grass. She climbed up on a large chair and told the man to shave off her hair.

"I never see a head so dirty like yours! Who want you for a wife?" the man yelled at her.

She didn't care and felt no shame. Afterward, she went home and got a metal bucket half filled with water. She took it outside to wash her head for the first time in weeks. Then she went to see the children's nurse, in the generals' room. The nurse cleaned out the infection on Moy's head with salt water. Finally, Moy wrapped her old plaid scarf around her baldhead.

The children didn't know about it until the next morning. She went to sleep with the scarf around her head, but it fell off when she got up, and her head got stuck on the mosquito net when she tried to get out. The girl who slept next to her shouted for everyone to hear that Moy was bald-headed. Moy grabbed the scarf and wrapped it around her head again. Everyone laughed at her as she walked toward her group. Even the generals laughed. Moy wanted to cry but fought back the tears. The children all called her Grandma Nun.

For the first couple of months, she wrapped the scarf around her head. It kept the flies away from her infection, and she was also embarrassed at being called Grandma Nun. Girl always yanked the scarf from poor Moy's head; then everyone would shout, "Grandma Nun!" making her cry.

It took Moy a while to put a stop to the abuse. But one day, Girl tiptoed up behind Moy and yanked the scarf off her head. "Grandma Nun!" she shouted with laughter.

This time, Moy wiped the stupid smile off Girl's face, making Girl choke on her own laughter. Moy turned around, stared her in the eyes, and asked, "Yes, grandchild? You abuse people and hurt their feelings. You have sin. You want Grandma Nun help you pray?"

Keem

Yanking the scarf from evil Girl's hands, she tied it around her hips instead of wrapping it around her head like she used to. She turned around and walked away, leaving Girl to stare after her.

Everyone stared in shock as Moy walked past them. Moy was no longer a toy for the children to play with or laugh at. *No more!* The mean baby tiger was out of her cage. Now she was ready to take on the evil world. From that day on, she never wrapped that scarf around her head again. She was happy to go around bald-headed. She felt good and proud of herself for doing it. She shaved her head every few months. The barber always complained when she showed up on that large chair, "You have no hair for me to cut."

"Shave." She pointed at her head and asked the barber if he wanted her to wait until she had a head full of lice again.

After that, no one dared call her Grandma Nun. But, since Girl was so evil, she always thought of some way to pick on Moy. She started calling Moy scarecrow, but Moy never cried again. She would answer if the kids addressed her by her name. Otherwise, she walked past them like they didn't exist. They didn't like it. *They can all go and hang their necks. I don't care!* she thought. *Don't make me mad. I'll get even!*

"No argue with people. If they want to push you to the edge, stand up tall, tall. Not let them push you over. If you want to push back, push harder!" Keem had taught her daughter.

One day in the work field, Moy did something and Girl shouted, "Buddy scarecrow!"

"Buddy, you a scarecrow?" Moy walked up to Girl, staring her in the eyes, and told her that only a scarecrow would call another person a scarecrow. A person wouldn't call another person a scarecrow.

All the girls and boys who worked nearby stopped whatever they were doing to watch and listen.

"Buddha, that hurt and embarrass!" a boy said, and then he laughed with other children. Girl was pale faced, staring at Moy with big eyes.

In those days, Moy was happier. She went around bald-headed and didn't care what people thought or said. She wouldn't let anyone get in her way again, ever! She lived and worked with the children in Head Tiger for a while; then the children were sent to Kompong Kol, where the factory and headquarters were, and where Ming also worked. The children carried their clothes bags on their shoulders or backs, walking in two long lines for a few minutes. Then everyone began walking faster, and some children ran. They couldn't wait to see their parents in Kompong Kol. The dirt road to the main town, about ten feet wide, ran through the middle of the jungle.

Moy alternately ran and walked, like all the others, to Kompong Kol. She heard wolves calling for each other during the middle of the day. Perhaps the wolves were mourning the loss of a meal that ran past their sharp teeth and hungry jaws. No one wanted to be left behind and get eaten alive by them. The wolves hid behind the tall trees, thick bushes, and grass on both sides of the dirt road. Moy looked behind often to make sure that she was not the last person on the road.

She felt bad for the four- to six-year-old boys and girls. They walked and ran like the older children but couldn't keep up and got left behind. Some little children fell and picked themselves up, crying and running again. There were four wagons pulled by eight cows that were filled with large pots and bags of rice, and a few of the youngest children got to sit on the back of the wagons. The children's commander walked behind the wagons, along with some of the youngest children. Three or four Khmer Rouge also walked behind the wagons, their long guns slung over their shoulders. They yelled at the youngest children to walk and run faster, or they'd be left behind and get eaten alive by wolves. The little children cried harder and tried their best to go faster. Finally, halfway to the main town, all the youngest children

Keem

jumped onto the cow-pulled wagons. The sun was getting lower in the sky, and the Khmer Rouge didn't want to hang around in the middle of the jungle where the hungry wolves waited for a meal.

The trip was about two hours' walk and run for Moy. Her jaw dropped when she entered Kompong Kol, where the human wolves were. The first thing she saw was the large glass house. She had seen a house like that one when she lived in Phnom Penh, the capital of Cambodia. She was told that the house belonged to a member of the king's family.

To the right of this glass house stood lines of townhouses made of brown wooden boards, with white, standard metal roofs. And to the left of the glass house stood three identical white concrete houses with docks. They were about ten feet off the ground, and their staircases were also white concrete, about twenty feet wide and thirty feet long. It was said the owner of the factory had had three wives, and each wife had lived in one of those houses. Much later, Moy's group lived in one of those houses for a couple of weeks, but then the Khmer Rouge moved in. Inside the house there was a single large room, an entrance to and from the dock, and a smaller room at the back, like a bedroom, near the staircase. But there were no doors.

The Khmer Rouge had torn down every house and turned the cities and towns into banana groves. A few years earlier, when Moy and Keem went to work near a town between Pailin and Battambang, they saw it had been turned into a banana grove.

This glass house, in Kompong Kol, had a wall-less stadium next to it. At the right corner of the stadium and up high, a large and angry black dragon zigzagged furiously upward from the top of a white building's chimney. It circled around lazily in midair, looking down at the people of Kompong Kol.

Moy stood still and watched the Khmer Rouge pacing back and forth inside the glass house. Some of them carried guns; some were empty-handed. Then she looked around and made her way slowly toward the common kitchen, to meet the children and the Khmer Rouge. She had no idea where she was going or where the common kitchen was. She walked past a couple of men and women talking and laughing. They carried bent shovels or hunting knives on their shoulders. Moy walked backward, staring after the happy people. She felt carefree and smiled. The main road into town was covered in concrete. No dirt, no mud. *I like it here! So clean!* she thought. But she didn't know the evil living in this clean town.

Moy turned around and walked right into a big man. She apologized to him, then screamed in delight, "Big Brother!"

"Moy?" Ming was about to walk past her but stopped and stared.

"Yes." She was very happy. She almost hugged her big brother, but she was too old.

"You bald-headed." He looked her up and down strangely.

"Is Big Brother well?" She couldn't tell if Ming's stares were from anger or something else, but it was not friendly. She felt uncomfortable.

Ming didn't answer at first. Then he said, in a harsh tone of voice, "People tell me you shave off your hair." He looked angry.

She told him she had a lot of lice and her head itched and hurt badly, so she kept her head shaved. Then she told him she was on her way to the common kitchen and walked away from him.

"I on my way to look for you," Ming spoke to her back.

"Big Brother go look for me?" She stopped in her tracks and turned around.

"Come home first. The children not at the meeting for many more hours." He nodded, his face softening a little.

"I no have a home." She stared at her bare feet.

"My house, Chan's house, is your home! Moy, where you go?" he shouted after her.

"I no like Big Brother yell at me." She headed in the wrong direction. *I will sleep in the common kitchen. I will not go to his house. No one is going to yell at me again!*

"Where you go sleep tonight?" he walked next to her now.

"I sleep with my group."

"The children will go sleep with their parent tonight," he told her.

"Then I sleep in the house by myself. I no afraid of ghost," she told him.

"Turn right, here," he laughed, but it sounded very bitter.

"I go to the kitchen."

"You go the wrong way," he told her.

Forward or backward, if she headed the wrong way forward, then she'd turn around and go the right way. She whirled around and almost sent him to the ground.

He grabbed onto her shoulders for support as he stumbled backward. "Soeun right; you mean like baby tiger." He reminded her of his friend who had cheated her of pulling more hair from Lee's head. Ming looked like he wanted to say something but changed his mind and said instead, "Follow Big Brother." He grabbed her small clothes bag from her shoulder, then took off with it.

She didn't want to fight with him after they had just met again. She remembered how he had come to see her almost half a year earlier, after they had parted. She was sick at the time. He brought something for her. He looked horrified at the conditions where Moy lived. She couldn't remember if they talked to each other that much. But she remembered he sat next to her general, a couple of feet away from her. The two of them talked quietly. Every now and then Moy looked up and saw Ming looking around the one-walled house, then staring at her. That day, he asked the general's permission to take Moy home for a day.

"Why you so dirty and not take care of yourself? You smell very bad, you no embarrass?" he yelled at her on their way home.

Moy lowered her head and kept quiet. When they got home, he told his wife to bathe and wash Moy's hair. Later, Moy found out her general had told him that Moy was abused by her group and the group captain, Girl.

* * *

"What?" Moy asked. She'd heard him murmur something as she walked behind him.

"What?" Ming looked at her sideways.

"I hear Big Brother say something,"

"I say nothing; quiet!" he replied.

Moy wondered if Ming had heard the rumor from that Chinese man's daughter who lived behind Moy's house in Pailin, that Keem and Moy were Wong's daughters. But Moy couldn't see any possibility it was true. The age gap between them didn't make him old enough to be Keem's father. He was fifty-two, almost fifty-three. Keem was forty-two, almost forty-three, when they both passed away. Moy knew Wong always lied, saying he was ten years older than he really was, because that way Black Shirt couldn't make him work, since he was too old. She also remembered he once told her he was sixty-two, which would make him really fifty-two. Could a ten-year-old boy father a child? Maybe he could, and maybe he couldn't. Or maybe Moy was wrong, and he was really seventy-two.

The only thing that made any sense to Moy was that Keem Lai was the rich casino owner's daughter. It would explain many things! Where did Keem and Wong get the money to buy that large house and big motorcycle in Siem Reap? And they gave hundreds or thousands of ning to this son or that daughter, and there were nine of them. Moy remembered her grandpa carrying steamed fish to sell in the countryside, while Ma stayed home with the baby—Moy. Then, suddenly, they had the five-and-dime shop. Business might be good, but they couldn't have made all that money in such a short period of time. And there wasn't a bank in Cambodia they could borrow the money from. If a house cost a billion, they must pay for it in cash and gold. Keem and Wong couldn't have borrowed a billion from their friends, as not many people had money. And Moy had a nanny to look after her. The family was rich!

When Moy tried to connect everything to get the answer, she decided Keem Lai was the rich casino owner's daughter. When she and Wong first met, they couldn't marry, because he already had a family. So she married Luck. Keem told Moy Luck died when she was three years old. Much later, Moy met a woman who knew her family, and she told Moy that Moy had an older brother who had died when he was a baby, before Moy was born. The woman didn't say anything about Keem and Wong or disrespect them. Moy thought Luck died from a broken heart after his son's death. Then Keem and Wong met again, and this time they got married. So Keem became Wong's second wife.

Moy was proud of her ma and loved her ma with all her heart and soul. Keem Lai was the best, most loving ma on the Mother Earth and under Father Sky! And Moy would always remember her grandpa/papa loved her more than his own life.

In Cambodia, it was common for some men to have more than one or two wives. And some Chinese and Cambodian wives and husbands addressed each other as "Mother" or "Father." It was also common for the youngest child to address her parents as "Grandpa and Grandma," imitating their older siblings' children.

However, the second wife and her children weren't respected by the public. Her children were most likely to get picked on and made fun of, especially for the lower class family. People didn't want to "lose face" or respect by having the second wife's children as sons or daughters-in-law in the family.

Wong and Keem did whatever they had to do to protect Moy.

Now, the story they told her about Keem was one of abuse by *her* mother, in Cambodia. That mother was not Wong's wife, like Moy had first thought. There was also the story that Keem ran after Wong on the train, in China. But Moy thought that wasn't Keem, that it was Wong's daughter, the second aunt. But those were just Moy's thoughts.

In Cambodia, it was also common that the first wives often abused and enslaved most of the second wives and their children, especially if the second wives were from lower class families.

Keem could have been abused by Wong's first wife if he had them live together.

* * *

Perhaps Ming was angry at Moy for some other reason. But he did go looking for her. Moy respected him, though, and slowly withdrew and stayed away from him. She didn't want him to feel uncomfortable being seen with her.

I'm not going to worry about it. I'll take care of myself! Moy thought. Keem and Wong would want her to do that.

Moy looked around in front of the townhouses. There were tomatoes, green beans, and flowers growing in front of each house. Every house had a door and a lock. As she kept walking, she walked past Ming, and he asked where she was going. She turned around and looked at him. Ming was no longer the eighteen-year-old boy he had been when they first met. He was taller and had broader shoulders. The boyish face had been replaced with a grown-up face and grown-up voice. The handsome, boyish smile was not there anymore. She

Keem

returned to where Ming stood. He unlocked the door, and they went into the house.

Inside, a full-sized bed stood against a wall, a large mosquito net hanging over it. There was a small, old table next to the foot of the bed, two or three plates and spoons on the table, and no chair. A tiny, folding army bed was pushed against the opposite wall. Some small wooden boxes sat at the head of the larger bed.

"You sleep here." He dropped her clothes bag on the dark-gray and green army stretcher. Then he froze her in the spot. "Luong, is it true? People tell me…" tears swam in his eyes. He couldn't get the words out. He just stood there, looking sad.

Moy was shocked. No one ever called her Luong, not even her aunts and uncles. Keem and Wong called her Hong Luong during Chinese New Year days, because they were special days. Wong's wife had always called her Hong Luong. In Teochew it means Peacock Palace. Keem and Wong named their little chatterbox after the Gold Palace. Keem told her daughter a story about a Chinese king who loved his queen so much he had a gold palace built for her.

It was such a beautiful name but came with a tragic life. Moy had no beauty to show off, like the Peacock Palace. She lived a minute at a time, not an hour. And Ming shortened it to Luong. What else had their ma and grandpa tell him, besides her name? What did they ask of him? Moy was willing to bet her life that what Keem and Wong had said to Ming was, "If something happen to us, you must love Moy. Look after Moy and take good care of her."

There was no doubt Keem had told him, "Moy's tongue has no brake. It jump up and down from sunrise to sunset. No make her mad. She blows fire like baby dragon when she mad."

Sometimes, Keem said to Moy, "Talk, talk, talk; never stop! I go buy a brake, put it on your tongue, and stop it from jump up and down so much!" Keem would shake her head as Moy giggled.

MOY

After the shock, Moy waited for him to finish his question, but he didn't. Ming turned away like he couldn't bear to look at her and walked out of the house. Now she wondered if she might be wrong.

Ming had found out his friend Vulture had tried to rape Moy. But Moy refused to be Vulture's victim. Ming was a smart boy. He asked around. She saw him talk to Girl. Then he found out later from the girls' general that Girl picked on Moy and made her cry every day. Girl was Vulture's good friend. And the young Khmer Rouge might have told Ming what Moy told him, that Vulture tried to get Moy to sleep with him, but Moy refused. Ming put all the pieces together and got his answer. He had fallen for Vulture's charm. Ming didn't know and couldn't protect Moy, and he had insulted her some more by taking that sarong from Vulture. Ming delivered it to Moy himself. He was embarrassed and ashamed of himself.

Moy didn't see him until late in the evening. While she waited for him to come home, she looked around the one-room house carefully. Brown wooden walls, concrete floor, a curtain that hung around the large bed, pushed aside. Ming's pants and shirts were on the bed. She folded them up for him.

9

A freedom...Cage

I have mouth but I couldn't talk
I have legs but I couldn't walk
I have eyes but I couldn't see
I have ears but I couldn't hear
I have wings! But I couldn't fly
I lived in a cage,
The freedom...cage.
May 2012
By
Luong Ung-Lai

* * *

Ming came home around six o'clock, before dinner at seven. Moy sat in front of the house and played with his army knife. She ran her fingers up and down the blade, then chopped off a handful of grass.

"Black Shirt give us this house to live. Most people have no house. They stay with their group," he whispered in broken Chinese in her ear. He only said Black Shirt in Teochew. Then he gave up and spoke in Khmer.

"Big Brother is Chinese, but Big Brother no speak Chinese?" she teased, in a beautiful moment of brother and a sister talking with each other.

"I know how to speak Teochew," he said, trying to defend himself.

"Big brother say one word in Teochew, everything else in Khmer," she told him in Chinese.

"You…" he spoke in Chinese, shaking a finger under her nose.

Big Brother is going to speak in Khmer now, Moy thought with a smile.

"No criticize your big brother; it's sinful!" he warned.

"I tell Big Brother you not know how to speak Teochew, right or wrong?"

"Grandma bald," he whispered.

She watched him walk into the house.

"Luong, come here." He had something on the floor. "Stand here," he motioned for her to stand in front of him. Then he walked around, looking from box to box for something. He came back with something in his hands. "Put your foot here." He knelt in front of her.

"What is it?" she tried to look over his large shoulders and head bent over her foot.

"Stand still!" he yelled.

Whatever it was, it felt thick and soft under her foot. She looked left and right, trying to see what he was doing, but his head got in the way. He was on his hands and knees, one hand holding onto her foot. She could feel him drawing something around her foot.

"Stand still! Or I draw it wrong!" he yelled again.

"I to want see," she whined.

"Be still!" Ming held her foot tightly, yelling louder.

She couldn't help it and stuck her tongue out over his head. She pulled her lips back and, with her hands, formed claws over his head, like she wanted to bite his head off for ordering her around. "Luong,

Keem

come here. Luong, stand still. Luong, don't move!" *What happened to Moy? Big Brother's little sister?* she thought.

"Dead!" said a deep voice.

She looked up sharply when that deep voice reached her ears. She relaxed her lips and dropped her hands on Ming's head. He looked up.

"She want to eat your head," the deep voice told Ming through his laughter.

I don't like him! Moy thought.

"Soeun, you come to visit my family," Ming greeted him. He still held tightly to Moy's foot.

"I come to help. Why your little sister want to eat your head?" he asked.

"Little Sister want to eat my head?" Ming asked, and smiled handsomely, his beautiful, black eyes soft.

"She stick her tongue out and pull her mouth like this," Soeun showed Ming what Moy had been doing over his head.

She told Soeun she didn't like him. He asked Ming what he was doing on his hands and knees in front of his sister.

"I make shoe for my little sister."

"Big Brother make shoe for me?" Moy felt very happy. Ming was making sandals for her.

Ming told her that the week before, one of the Black Shirts asked him to cut a pair of sandals for him. Ming asked for some tire from the cars or trucks to make a pair of sandals for Luong, because she didn't have any.

"Buddha, Buddha, what a pretty name. Want marry me?" Soeun wrapped an arm around her shoulders.

"Uncle crazy," Moy shouted and pushed his hand off. She ran out of the house, hearing Ming and Soeun's laughter behind her.

That evening, she wore her new sandals to the meeting at the common kitchen. She couldn't stop looking at them. It felt good to walk on sandals again. The children asked where she got them.

"My big brother cut them for me," she told them proudly.

At the meeting, the Khmer Rouge told the children they weren't allowed to go home and sleep with their parents every night. If the children worked hard, they could spend a night with their family every other week, with permission from their generals. The children were to live near a group of Bike One adults and eat with them at the second common kitchen, next to the river. The common house was about twenty minutes from the main common kitchen, where the meeting was. That night, Onka allowed all the children to go home and sleep with their mothers and fathers. But they must go to their new home by the next morning.

After the meeting, Moy sat between her big brother and sister-in-law and ate dinner at the common kitchen. The street was crowded as they walked home. Moy looked at people as they walked past her. Women and men all wore black, long-sleeved shirts and pants, or some women wore sarongs. Everyone had different-colored checkered scarves wrapped around their necks, and black sandals, like hers. Moy held her new black sarong and black, long-sleeved shirt to her chest. For the first time in almost a year, the Khmer Rouge had given her a new outfit.

Because Kompong Kol was the main town, everyone had to dress and talk formally. The first word out of anyone's lips was buddy or comrade. All the women, men, and children carried bent shovels or long, curled hunting knives on their shoulders. Most people walked in groups, talking and laughing. Moy noticed that some people who walked alone, deep in thought, looked scared to death. She didn't have to wait long to understand why.

That evening, Ming's family sat outside their house, enjoying each other's company under the silver moon. They talked softy, smiling now and then. Sometimes they argued, and sometimes they laughed. Moy asked Ming why Soeun had gone crazy over her name.

"You have good and respectful name," he explained. The title of some females in the Cambodian royal family sounded very close to Luong.

Moy didn't know anything about the Cambodian royal family or their titles.

Ming told her he knew that peacocks and dragons are symbols of power, and for Chinese queens and kings. He went on to tell her that their ma and grandpa had told him a Chinese story about naming Moy after the Gold Palace.

Moy didn't know Keem and Wong had shared a lot of things with him, and he understood more than she. She watched Ming with sidelong glances. He looked thoughtful as he stared at the black sky and bright silver moon.

"Smart people always name their children with good name," he mumbled to himself. He looked lost, staring at the sky above their heads. Was there a star, a moon, in Ming's sky? Only he knew.

At ten o'clock, everyone went inside and locked their doors to keep the evil out.

Moy smiled as she lay in Ming's tiny bed. She was very happy! Her big brother didn't hate her, and he had made that pair of sandals for her. Poor Moy—she had no idea the hungry human wolves would soon come out in force. Kompong Kol was like a pretty mask hiding evil behind it. And that mask was about to be lifted.

Sometime late into the night, Moy wasn't sure if she was dreaming or awake.

"Big Brother not go!" Moy heard a woman shout in Khmer, a couple of doors down from Ming's house. She kept her eyes closed and listened.

"Big Brother/sweetheart, not go…Buddy, pity me!" the woman cried.

"Take your hand away from him," a man commanded through his laughter. Then silence.

Moy turned onto her side. Then she rolled onto her back, opened her eyes, and stared into the darkness. She wasn't sure if she had actually heard the yelling. Her fingers walked on the cool wall. *Yes. I'm awake…*

"Why buddy sister cry like that? Onka only want to meet your husband, no worry," a man spoke slowly. It sounded like he was smiling.

Moy couldn't tell if this was a different man's voice. *Meeting in the dead of the night? Black Shirt crazy!* she thought. Everything was calm, and she didn't hear anything else, so she closed her eyes. Then she heard, "At this hour? Big Brother, pity me! No…them…" the woman shouted louder.

"Little Sister/sweetheart, no. Big Brother all right…do…wrong. Little Sister no cry," a man spoke in a weak voice.

"Go, go! Onka no like waiting," a man shouted in anger.

Each long row of the townhouses was a single long room, and each of the ten to twenty houses were separated by two walls and a door.

The shouting sounded like it was coming from next door.

"No. No. No!" The woman screamed louder.

Moy kept her eyes closed. She moved her head a little higher to one side and listened harder. Her eyes popped open wide at the sound of kicking and pulling. Something or someone had fallen down with a loud thud against the wall, and then to the floor.

"No! No! Mercy, Buddy Big Brother. Mercy!" the same woman screamed.

"No kick my wife! You black heart, dog heart!" the husband shouted.

"Go, go! Or I will shoot Buddy away here, now!" a man shouted.

Moy felt icy water run up and down her throat, but she forced it down.

Keem

"Take me! I go with my husband!" There was the sound of someone hitting the wall, then falling to the floor. The banging sound seemed to go on forever.

Moy lay as still as a log and welcomed the darkness inside the house, blocking her from seeing the scene. Unfortunately, the darkness couldn't block her from hearing it.

"Khmer Red dog, dog heart! You like kill your own Khmer people like yourself?" a man shouted loudly.

Bang!

Moy jumped at the loud sound. She continued listening helplessly as the sounds went on.

"Buddy, no hit him! No…mercy, mercy! Buddha! Help my husband! Buddha pity me!" The only living thing in this dark night was the woman's tearful voice pleading for mercy. Everything and everyone else was dead silent.

Moy started to cry quietly. Her eyes got bigger as a large hand covered her mouth.

"No cry! No yell! Hear me?" Ming whispered in her ear. She nodded in his hand. "Take your hands, cover your ears. Close your eyes, and go to sleep!" His hand remained over her mouth. He waited until she nodded again. Then he removed his hand and whispered in her ear, "Whatever you hear, no talk about it. No yell. Understand?"

She couldn't see his face in the darkness, only a shadow. Funny sounds escaped from their throats as they listened helplessly.

"No hurt…wife!" Silence, and more silence.

"Dog heart!" The husband's shout was cut short.

Bang! Bang!

Moy jumped at each bang. *Was it gunfire?* Ming dropped his head onto his arm.

"Mercy!" a woman shouted.

Bang! Bang! Bang!

MOY

The sound was so loud, and then Moy heard nothing. Ming turned around and ran to his bed to comfort his wife. Moy was alone in the dark night. She lay there staring at the darkness. Slowly, she closed her eyes.

The silence of the night had come to life with the singsong of gunfire. The gun sang in its powerful voice for the living to sleep while it claimed two lives. And that no one should dare talk about it when the sun rose in the morning. Perhaps nothing happened, and no one heard anything. Everyone simply lived one second at a time. What else could one do when powerless to stop an execution of innocents?

In the morning, Moy walked like any other day, like everyone else on the main street. She went to meet her group at the common kitchen. A lot of the adults were there, but not Ming. In the meeting, the Khmer Rouge told everyone about the execution, "Last night, Onka hit away [killed] a traitor of our country."

Moy didn't hear anything after that. The sound of gunfire still rang in her ears. She stared at the Black Shirt standing in front of everyone and watched his lips move, but she heard nothing. She understood now. The Khmer Rouge would kill anyone they believed to be a traitor, even a three-month-old baby. She remembered one day when she lived in Head Tiger, a group of Khmer Rouge came from another town to observe the children working in the field. At the time, she was eating her lunch, and she overheard them talking and laughing. One of the Khmer Rouge told his friends he had torn a baby in half by the legs, "Same like a frog."

10

After the meeting, Moy's group moved to the big, wooden house next to the river. That same afternoon, her group and some adult groups went to the work area about half an hour away. She walked and watched. Other groups of men and women were already working in the fields. They swept their hunting knives up once and cut the tails off the cane. Then they swept the knives down, left and right, to get the leaves off. Grabbing a handful of cane with their free hands, they swept the knives as close as they could to the ground, cutting off the canes and throwing them down.

Some men and women were empty-handed. They walked around picking up armfuls of canes, tying them up with the long sugarcane leaves and leaving them piled there.

The third group of men or women worked in pairs. They picked up the stack of canes and carried them on their shoulders to the roofless army trucks. When they were loaded up with sugarcane, the trucks drove away.

Moy and her group worked in another field, like the men and women were doing. Her hands got cut often by the sharp sugarcane leaves, and sometimes blood dripped from the cuts. Some days, her group walked around behind the adults, picking up the sugarcane and tying them up. Other days, Moy and her partner carried the canes to the trucks. The canes were very heavy. At the end of the day, her body was sticky and ached all over. The river was next to her house. She never missed a bath anymore, and most days she bathed twice. Every day she did the same work, like everyone else. The work was hard, but she liked it. She got to chew the sugarcane and drink the sweet liquid. Then one day after lunch, she found out why some canes were larger than all the others in the fields.

She walked deeper into the sugarcane field. She hoped no one nearby was watching. Holding onto her sarong, she walked toward the thickest area of canes. She pulled her sarong up with both hands and was about to sit down on her feet when she saw something through the space between the canes. She stared at the objects. They were white, lying half on and half off the sugarcane row. The cane in that section was the tallest and biggest of all. It was just one row in front of her. She got up, forgetting all about the bathroom. She opened the canes with both hands and looked down in between.

She felt no fear. She just stood there and stared. She could picture the horror and tears from the suffering. Their screams for mercy, and from pain, must have shaken the earth and echoed to heaven. No human being should die like this. The broken skeleton told Moy how she died. Her legs were forced apart, brown rope still fastened her ankles to the sugarcane. Now the knots were too big for just the bones left. Both arms were forced high over her head, with the knot of brown rope on each wrist tied to the cane on both sides. One side of her forehead was missing. There were pieces of torn black shirt and sarong lying on the row of sugarcane near her head and legs.

Moy looked away and saw another skeleton about two feet away from the woman's. The wrists were tied to both sides of the canes. This skeleton was sitting up, leaning against the canes and facing the woman's skeleton. The entire jaw was missing, and there was no nose, no teeth or mouth, just a great big hole. One cheekbone was gone. A big piece of bone was missing from the middle of the head, and a

Keem

couple of chest bones were missing. One leg was also missing. The remains of that skeleton were like pieces of a puzzle. These sugarcane groves drank countless drops of tears and human blood spilled by Khmer Rouge hands.

Moy let go of the bushes, and they closed like a door shutting in her face. All she saw now was the sugarcane. Dragging her hunting knife behind her, she walked through one row of sugarcane after another. Then she stopped and cut off a long cane. She held it up and cut off everything, keeping only a foot near the root, the sweetest part of the cane. She left the rest of the cane behind and didn't look back. As she walked, she ran her knife around the cane, peeling off all the hard, outside skin. Then she bit, chewed, and swallowed the sweet liquid. If the Khmer Rouge wanted to punish her for eating a cane, she didn't care. The Black Shirt didn't want people to eat Straight Bird cane. But she ate the white- and black-spotted cane. The Black Shirt also prohibited people from talking back to their group captains. But Moy talked back to her captain.

Every day after lunch, the children had their meeting. They reformed each other from whatever the other did wrong. The captains loved having the authority to abuse their workers. One day at the meeting, Moy sat on her feet like everyone else. The general asked if anyone needed to be reformed. If someone shouted an individual's name, that individual must stand up, walk out from the line, stand in front of the others, and get whipped. A girl in Moy's group shouted, "Buddy Moy!" and about a hundred girls repeated after her. The general told Moy to come out to the front and someone would give her ten whips.

"I do nothing wrong. I not get up," Moy told the general.

"She dare talk back to the general!" everyone whispered.

"Buddy Moy get up and come out. Or I give buddy twelve whip," the general told her.

"I do nothing wrong," Moy repeated stubbornly. *If I get up, it means I did something wrong. If they want to whip me, let them!*

"Fifteen whip. Buddy Moy, if I tell buddy again, it will be twenty whip!" The general demanded she get up.

"No." Moy remained seated on her feet.

"Everyone get out," the general ordered.

All the girls got up, stood back, and watched. The general had a captain whip Moy's back with a small stick. Moy kept her eyes on the general and the girl who had shouted her name.

"Hit harder!" the general told the captain.

Moy jumped at the first five or ten whips on her back. But she didn't scream or cry, just stared harder at the general. Moy didn't even whisper. The general smiled and waited for Moy's tears. Moy didn't have any tears left for the general's pleasure. The whipping seemed to go on forever. Some of the youngest girls in Bike Seven started to cry. One little girl jumped up and down, sobbing aloud and shouting, "Buddy, scream! Buddy Scarecrow, scream, and they stop hit buddy! Scream!"

Moy kept her lips tight. She looked at the little girl hopping up and down on her feet, crying. Then more girls cried. Some older girls shifted from foot to foot and cried in silence. But other girls told the general to give Moy five more whips.

"Scream one sound, Buddy Scarecrow! Say one word! Why Buddy so stubborn? Scream!" a girl from Moy's group yelled at her, crying.

Moy looked at the girls from Bike Two to Bike Seven. Tears dampened their little faces. They looked horrified as they wiped the tears away with the backs of their hands.

You want to whip me? Go ahead and whip me, Moy thought. Some of these little girls got whipped for nothing, every day!

"Thirty!" the general shouted, and she looked away from Moy.

"Buddy want to kill her?" a couple of the older girls looked very scared.

"Quiet. Whoever dare say one word, that buddy will get five whip."

"Buddy Big Sister, enough. She no cry. Buddy Big Sister want to kill her?" more girls cried, terrified. The girl who got Moy the whipping looked away and began crying, too.

"Thirty!" the general's voice cracked as she shouted the order. Then she looked away again.

I won! Moy thought, as she stared harder at the general's back.

The general wiped her face. Then she turned around and ordered everyone back to work. Moy picked up the shovel next to her and rose to her feet. She held her head high and felt proud. She walked past all the girls, toward the work field, leaving them to stare after her. Her back was numb.

"Buddy very stubborn!" the general yelled at Moy.

Moy stopped, turned around, and stared at the general's watery eyes. But Moy said nothing. She just walked away and went to work. That evening, there was another general with Moy's general, and all the captains laughed at something as Moy walked into the house. She didn't know what they were talking or laughing about. She didn't care. She went to bed. She pulled the mosquito net down and lay on her back.

The laughter died down, and then she heard, "That scarecrow very stubborn!"

"Her back not hurt?" a girl asked.

My back is too numb to feel any pain. Ma put something on my back to make it not hurt. Ma's spirit won't let them hurt me. Ma won't let anything happen to me, she thought, then closed her eyes and went to sleep.

Soon after Moy was whipped, some of the youngest girls learned to sit for their rights, refusing to get up and get whipped.

"I do nothing wrong; I not get up," the girls told the general. Those little girls got ten to fifteen whips on their backs while they sobbed into their hands.

"Buddy, you very stubborn, like Buddy Moy," the general and captains told them.

* * *

Later, the children and some adult groups were sent to a village, Kompong Klang. They went to join the other Bike One men and women who were already there. It was too far to walk, so the army trucks took them there. The sun was almost down when they got to Kompong Klang, which had no dirt, only sand. There were two long rows of new townhouses on left and right, a couple feet apart, and a common kitchen across from them. The Khmer Rouge's doctor lived in a small house close to the edge of the river and next to the townhouses.

I know this place! I came here many, many times, Moy realized but couldn't remember when. The memories were bitter.

All the children and some of the adults went every day to clear more land from the foot to the middle of the mountain. They got bitten by the big, red ants living there. It was a nightmare for women and girls wearing sarongs. It was better for people who wore pants. Moy learned from watching some men and women to tie her pants legs around the ankles with thin, long vines. But no one could keep the red ants out of their shirts. As the days went by, people learned to deal with the big red ants, and eat them, too!

They learned to look carefully before cutting down any trees. If they saw a nest of red ants, they used a stick with a hook to take the nest down, dropped it in a large bucket of water, and covered it. At the end of the day, they took out the bucket full of dead ants and mixed a few red ants with "frog leaves" or other leaves, and large white eggs, then ate them happily! If the mixture was 90 percent white eggs and just a few red ants, it tasted like sweet-and-sour soup. If the mixture was fewer white eggs and more red ants, the soup tasted bitter, like vinegar. Still, everyone was happy to have the red ants and eggs for dinner!

The red ant nests were usually on the smaller trees and bushes, but if there was a nest on a larger tree, it would be enormous. When the tree came down, the red ants had everyone running, screaming, and brushing them off left and right. Sometimes people had to set fires to burn the red ants away. Later, some people cut down the trees and piled them up, then let them dry in the sun for a few weeks before burning them away to get more land to grow sugarcane and mung beans.

One night, Moy lounged next to her new Chinese friend, Lee Moy, who also spoke Teochew. They shared a room with twenty-five others girls. Moy and Lee Moy were the same size and height. Moy was about a year older than her friend. The two Chinese girls were like day and night. Lee Moy was like a chick that had just come out from under her mother's protective wings, or a countryside kitten. Moy was a city tiger and mean like a baby tiger, blowing fire like a baby dragon when she was mad.

The girls whispered stories in Chinese. Sometimes they ended up giggling. If someone came in the house or sat near them, they spoke in Khmer. Suddenly, Moy remembered she had been here when her ma and grandpa were alive. At that time, they lived about two hours from here. Moy came to the river almost every day. She carried water home for cooking, and for Keem and Wong's baths. Her uncles and aunts lived not too far from here. The thought of them hurt her heart, and she dismissed the memories. But a new nightmare was about to enter the children's lives, especially for Moy.

* * *

All the children were sent back to Head Tiger. When Moy arrived in town, she felt an unknown fear charge into her. She looked around. Everything had changed! The large house, Buddhist's temple, where Moy used to live, and all the others houses had been replaced with long common houses. Each common house had four entrances, eight wooden platform beds against both walls, and a two-foot-wide hallway in between. Groups of ten to twelve adults or children slept on a bed. The roof and walls were covered with dry brown grass. A new, larger, common kitchen was in the spot where a temple had been. Moy's group stayed in a long wooden house, where two groups of twenty to twenty-five girls shared a room. Each girl had a small space to sleep.

Moy knew something bad had happened there, and that made her look over her shoulder. With each second that crept by, more fear built inside her, her hands and feet turning to ice. But there was nothing she could do about it. She lived and worked with her group in the sugarcane fields every day. A couple of days later, the Khmer Rouge moved Moy's group out of the long wooden house, and the Khmer Rouge moved in there. The girls went to live in the common house on the other side.

While Moy lived in Head Tiger, a new group of Khmer Rouge came and took control over the former group, like they always did. And they had everyone sit on his or her feet, or on the ground, for a meeting. The Khmer Rouge would identify themselves as the West, North, East, or South side, like they always did.

"We the East side is better than the North side," they would say, taking pride in their group.

Keem

In every meeting, the Khmer Rouge always asked if anyone needed to be reformed. At one meeting, Girl tried to be the hero. She stood up and told them she had caught Moy eating a sugarcane, and Moy must be reformed. Moy was furious, and what she did made everyone laugh. She jumped to her feet, stood up straight, and told the fifteen or twenty Khmer Rouge, "I want reform my captain, Buddy Girl, back. She lie. Onka not like liar! I catch Buddy Girl cut a cane and eat it this morning. Yes, I eat a cane today, but I no cut it. I find it lay on the ground, after wild pig eat half of it off. And I have a witness. That buddy big brother see me find it." She pointed at a Khmer Rouge.

"Me?" All the Khmer Rouge said, smiled, some laughed aloud and pointed at their chests.

"No. That buddy big brother *over there*." She pointed at a Khmer Rouge who stood next to a large tree, by himself.

"Me?" He was startled. He pointed at his chest and came over. Everyone stared at him.

"Yes. I show the cane to buddy big brother, and I ask if I can eat it. Buddy big brother say yes." Moy nodded to confirm it.

"I'm dead!" he laughed aloud, standing next to the other Khmer Rouge. He told everyone, "I a trust Khmer Red. I kill enemy. Now that child make me her witness because she eat a cane after the wild pig. I hope buddy big brother at Kompong Kol no hit me away when he hear about this. Help!" He shook his head and laughed with everyone.

"Who child is she?" the Khmer Rouge asked around.

"Chi Minh adopted little sister," someone answered.

"Very good. Onka like it very much! Come, come, anyone else want to reform buddy Moy?" the commander asked, and everyone laughed some more. He told everyone he'd be careful with what he says and does, or he might end up being called and reformed by "Little Sister Buddy Moy." He encouraged people not to be afraid of their captains and reform them if they saw their captains doing something wrong.

After that meeting, people looked at Moy differently. Sometimes, when people saw her walk by, they would whisper to each other, "That child reform her captain. And she has a Khmer Red as her witness. No fool around her!"

"I no want to be that child witness, no!" some of the Khmer Rouge told each other, laughing, when they saw Moy.

After that, most of the children didn't dare make fun of her. Some kids smiled when they came face to face with her. After that meeting, Girl didn't dare pick on Moy again. But Moy was all wrapped up inside, with a dark fear. Every step she took, she looked over her shoulder. The name of Head Tiger gave her such unknown fear, and she was about to face it.

Would the person who created that fear in her defeat her in the end? Or would she stand up and fight head on again? This time would be the final battle between the two. One of them would stand up and look on. The other would hang his or her head, and lower his or her eyes, in shame.

11

One evening, Moy came back from working with the others. She rooted to the spot and stared at the evil man sitting outside her house, talking and laughing with other Khmer Rouge. His face was sideways to her.

I'll run away. I don't want to see Vulture again, she thought.

Then, it was as if someone told her to straighten up to her full height. She held her head up and walked past the Khmer Rouge and Vulture, going into the house at the entrance next to him. She could have entered the common house through the Bike Four entrance but didn't. Still, she was scared.

After dinner that evening, the children had a meeting, and the Khmer Rouge told them their commander was ordered back to Kompong Kol by Onka's order.

"Now, Buddy Big Brother Vulture is your leader."

Every morning, Vulture had the children up at three or three-thirty, half an hour before a one-hour walk to the field, where they started working right away. He allowed no one to rest until lunchtime, an hour. Dinner was at six or seven o'clock, in the field. After dinner, the children went back to work under electric lights until 10:00 p.m. Vulture told the children he worked very hard, and that he pleaded with Onka to put up the electric lights for them to work.

"You very lucky have me as your commander, I love you very much!" he told the children.

When the children got home, it was almost midnight. Vulture ordered a meeting every night and every morning for the children to reform each other. The children sat on their feet in long lines. Some sat on the ground, nodding off to sleep. But evil Vulture wouldn't let that happen. From the first day he took over, and for the next few weeks, the children had fun reforming their co-workers and watching them get whipped by Vulture.

These whippings were nothing like the thirty whips Moy had gotten from one of her co-workers. Vulture had a handful of sticks the size of pens on the table next to him. When he whipped, Moy could almost hear those sticks hit through to the bone. Those little girls' and boys' eyes almost turned white, and their mouths opened wide, screaming without sound. Their faces were white as ghosts. They stood there, shaking in front of everyone as Vulture whipped them. He gave twenty to thirty whips on the children's backs, backsides, and legs. Most of the children couldn't even stand up. But that Khmer Rouge continued whipping them! Some children had to crawl back in line, crying without sound. Their little hands rubbed their bodies, in shock. Some nights, Vulture whipped ten to twenty children. And he smiled while he whipped them.

After those couple of weeks, everyone shook after dinner. There wouldn't be a sound at the meeting when Vulture asked who needed to be reformed. Every girl and boy sat there, shaking on his or her feet and praying. No one called out a name to get whipped by Vulture.

One night, Girl called out Lee Moy's name, saying Lee Moy must learn to respect her captain and not talk back like she had that morning.

"Lee Moy! One two, come up here. We meet again. Come, come stand in front of me." Vulture said in a singsong voice, laughing. Lee Moy sobbed in silence, looking scared to death.

Moy lowered her head like most of the children. She kept her head low and stared at Vulture without his noticing. She watched him pick up two sticks, *not one*. He got up slowly, circling around Lee Moy like a hungry shark with the smell of new blood in the water. He swung the sticks over his shoulder and brought them crashing down on Lee Moy's back.

Moy and the other girls all jumped at the sound. One little girl fell, landing sideways on the girl next to her. No one said anything, just helped her sit up on her feet again, next to Moy. The girls and boys cried in silence, watching helplessly as Lee Moy screamed in pain. The louder she screamed, the harder Vulture whipped her.

"Lee Moy, you very stubborn before. Now buddy stubborn with me again, yes?" he shouted like a mad man, and kept whipping her.

Me! He was talking to me! Moy thought.

Vulture had mistaken Lee Moy for *Moy,* thinking Lee Moy and *Moy* was the same person. Or he wanted Moy to know how much he hated her. This was how hard he would whip her, if Moy were standing in front of him. Moy could feel Lee Moy's pain; she was a sweet girl. Moy didn't look away from the evil man as he whipped the wrong girl. She felt hatred for this creature.

The large groups of girls and boys were gradually getting smaller and smaller. Every day, one or two boys and girls were sent to the hospital, sick from a whipping. The daylight went by so quickly, and nights fell upon the terrified children faster. Moy was smart. She kept her mouth shut. She never talked back to anyone. She kept her head down and lowered her eyes, waiting for a better day to arrive.

Then one night, the commander of Head Tiger came to save the children.

"It midnight and you have meeting, and you whip the children. You crazy like pig? Go to sleep, everyone!" he yelled angrily at Vulture.

Every now and then, there was a meeting in Head Tiger. Moy listened to the commander tell everyone who got executed the night or day before.

"We no keep traitor. If you not want to work, you not eat. If we can finish two acre today, we finish three acre tomorrow. Success, success, Communist Cambodia!"

The Khmer Rouge shouted, raising their fists, guns in their hands.

They weren't really very successful. They had to ask the Chinese, from China, to come show them how to make sugar! The Khmer Rouge kept their lips sealed about that, but Moy and many other people saw the Chinese men and women wearing gray outfits at the factory. They didn't come out in public.

* * *

This one meeting with Vulture was no different than any other meeting. All the children were terrified, and some of them would get whipped by him. But this was one whipping Moy would watch and smile about inside. It was not hard to be bad, but it was very difficult to be good. The old saying is, "Evil goes in full circle. Whatever you do to others, it will come right back at you, and harder." Girl called on a Vietnamese girl. The Vietnamese girl got up and called Girl's name right back. They'd had a fight that morning. The punishment was twenty whips for each girl.

"Fifty for me, and I go first," Girl told her good friend, Vulture.

Stupid girl! Why can't she say two hundred! Moy had been waiting a long time for this day. All Girl wanted was fifty. A hundred whips would have satisfied Moy, but she was not greedy. She would settle for watching the fifty whips. What made Moy mad was that crazy Vietnamese girl. She also wanted fifty whips.

Her skin, not mine! Moy thought. She tried hard not to stare at Girl's ghost-white face. She was so brave, wanting fifty whips instead of twenty. And she had gotten poor Lee Moy thirty whips for talking back to her. Lee Moy went to the hospital a few days after that whipping and never came back.

Moy watched as Girl screamed in silence and her mouth opened very wide. Vulture's face was grim as he whipped her. Girl's hands held on tight to her upper arms, shaking in pain, bending lower and lower. Large tears dripped from her eyes. She howled aloud a few times.

It sounded very sweet! Moy tried not to smile while she watched and listened. *Stupid girl only asked for fifty. Sixty whips would have been better. Better fifty than none, though!* Moy thought.

Girl tried to kill herself after the meeting. She jumped out of a window and onto the white metal underneath. But she didn't die! The metal did cut through her evil bone at her back of her foot. And she howled for the world to hear. Tears and blood! Blood, tears, screaming, pain from the whipping, and pain from the metal almost cutting the back of her foot off. How that's for justice?

Then one evening, the Khmer Rouge called for a meeting. Moy was tired and sleepy like everyone, sitting on the ground. But she came fully awake when she heard the commander say that Buddy Vulture worked the hardest. Under his ruling, there were no sick people staying home. Everyone was at work. Then there was hardly anyone at work, but all sick in the hospital.

"Now no more room at the hospital. All sick, sick children, and children die and die. Because he so successful, we want him go to adult Bike One." Everyone laughed at the commander's joke.

Thank you, Buddha! Thank you! Moy smiled and looked around openly. The children all smiled, and some giggled aloud.

"Thank you, Buddha!" a couple of girls sitting next to Moy whispered aloud.

Vulture's face was pale, and he looked scared. He was to leave immediately to meet with "Buddy Big Brother, in Kompong Kol."

Vulture had the children working in the field until 10:00 p.m. at night, while he was sound asleep on a pile of sugarcane. Then he took them home and he whipped them. Now he's leaving!

"I very happy that Dog Heart go away!" a girl behind Moy whispered.

"I happy, too." Moy turned to the Cambodian girl. The two girls smiled at each other.

Everything changed in that meeting. Moy's general became a captain of ten girls, ages fifteen to sixteen. The girls' new general was a Khmer Rouge. She had just come from another town or city. Each new group that came in either sent the former group of Khmer Rouge off somewhere or killed them.

Moy's new friend, Le, was a ten- or eleven-year-old Cambodian girl in Bike Four. Le had a round face and round black eyes, and she shaved off her hair, like Moy, because of lice. Moy was three or four years older and in Bike Two. One day Le came looking for Moy in the house; Moy was surprised to see her that day. She told Moy she was going to Kompong Kol to see her family. Moy asked if she was sick. Le's dark-skinned face was white as a sheet.

"Let go play at Aunt Wipe House." She grabbed onto Moy's hand and pulled.

"I no want to play at Aunt Wipe House." Moy didn't want to go to the outhouses.

The Khmer Rouge had cut large gasoline tanks in half to place a foot underneath four outhouses, two for women and two for men. The outhouses were about thirty feet from the girls' houses. People had

Keem

nicknamed them Aunt Wipe House. They used small sticks to wipe their backsides.

"I say go!" Le pulled Moy up from the bed.

"I no want to go!" Moy yanked her hand free. The smell! The black- and green-headed flies were about the size of her fingers, and the little flies were all over everywhere!

"I have something to tell buddy."

"I no want to go to Aunt Wipe House." Moy got mad.

If there was food, no one had to ask her twice. But Aunt Wipe House, no! Moy looked at her friend's pale face. Tears swam in Le's frighten eyes. Moy felt bad then, and told Le, "Go, go! Walk faster or I go back home. I no want to smell your shit." She hoped they wouldn't die from the smell in Aunt Wipe House.

"I tell you I no want to shit. Go over there," Le shouted over her shoulder, pointing.

They walked across the small footpath to the other side of the outhouses, closer to the large wooden house where the Khmer Rouge lived. Le fell behind because she walked slowly. Moy sat on a block of wood waiting for Le to catch up.

When she sat down next to Moy, Le stared at her bare feet. "I see them," she whispered. Her voice trembled.

"See who?" Moy wanted to know.

"I see them kill him." Le's toes swept left and right on the dirt, and she picked on her fingernails.

"Who kill who?" Moy looked at her.

"Khmer Red tie Uncle Soun's hands to his back. Then..." she paused for a long time, her face getting whiter. Her black eyes became almost white, so large against her dark skin. "They take his heart out." Le spoke about the former Head Tiger Commander of the Khmer Rouge.

He was friendly and always smiled at the children—a little, bald-headed, pale-skinned man.

"Buddy talk like crazy pig!" Moy was about to look away from her.

Le looked up, staring at her with big eyes, and told Moy, "Khmer Red take Uncle Soun's heart out. Then they throw his body away, inside the wood, halfway to Kompong Kol. Buddy want go see?" Le looked almost inhuman, like she wasn't there.

"Buddy sick, yes?" Moy thought Le was not well, and worried about her.

"I not sick! I see them kill him! I see them take his heart out! I hear they say, 'Take this heart and go fry with pig oil. Then eat it with rice!'" Le jumped up to her feet and screamed. Tears started dripping from her eyes.

Moy froze. The two girls stared at each other in horror. Then Moy jumped up and covered Le's mouth. Moy looked left and right carefully, hoping no one was nearby to hear Le.

"Buddy want them to kill us, too? Khmer Red will kill you if they know you see them." Moy whispered in Le's ear. Then she shook a finger under Le's nose and told Le, "Buddy will tell no one what you see. Buddy hear nothing, hear me?" Moy held onto the frightened girl's shoulders and shook her. "If people hear you, they might tell Khmer Red what you see. Khmer Red will kill you. Understand?" Moy and her friend hugged each other.

Later Moy found out how Le saw the Khmer Rouge kill one of their own. That day, Le had permission to go home to see her family. On the way home, she had to go to the bathroom, and that was when she witnessed the killing. From that day on, Le and Moy slept next to each other if their captains let them. The Khmer Rouge had forbidden people from singing old romantic songs, but Moy and Le didn't care. They sang the old romantic songs.

Keem

Moy remembered how she had felt sorry for Uncle Soun a couple of weeks before they killed him. He was at the fields with a hunting knife, sweeping the small bushes off after the children. No commander or Khmer Rouge ever did that. That day, he looked sort of lost. None of his men would go anywhere near him, which was strange. Usually, the commander was surrounded by his men. But that day, Uncle Soun's men stared at him from afar and whispered to each other. At the end of the day, he walked alone by himself, headed home. Moy and her co-workers whispered to each other, "Why Uncle Soun look sad?"

"Uncle Soun? Uncle no feel well?" one of the children asked.

"No worry; Uncle fine." He smiled and nodded.

Sometimes Moy was glad both her ma and grandpa had gone to heaven and didn't have to live in this evil world anymore. Then she would feel guilty at that thought.

She didn't know how bad the Khmer Rouge killings in the sugarcane fields were.

Almost every day, Moy and the children saw, stepped on, or walked over people's skeletons. They were often hidden under a couple of dry leaves and bushes. Nowadays, countless children found out that their mothers, fathers, or whole families were killed by the Khmer Rouge. Every other week, someone would come from Kompong Kol and say so-and-so's parents were taken during the middle of night to "go meet with Onka." It sounded better than "killed by Onka." And some children were told their parents got sick and died.

If Keem hadn't died over a year earlier, she might have now. No children were allowed to live with their parents, and Keem would die just from missing her daughter.

Moy wouldn't find out until it was too late, like a lot of these children. Moy didn't know why she fought so hard to live in this evil world. Perhaps there was something she had to live and fight for.

Maybe Keem had planned a better future and new life for her little girl. Her spirit always stayed by Moy's side, helping Moy through this hell on earth. She would get Moy out into a new sunrise to see a better day.

1 2

One day, Moy walked to work with her group. She was sure she hadn't said anything to a Khmer Rouge's daughter, whose father was the former commander from Kompong Kol. He had two wives, and his heart got eaten by his own people. The girl was seventeen or eighteen years old, the second wife's daughter. She was in children's Bike One, and she got permission from the general to whip Moy. She took Moy to an isolated area and whipped her.

"Buddy very stubborn! I teach buddy not to be stubborn again!" she yelled while whipping Moy.

"Who teach a traitor's child not to be a traitor?" Moy got mad and shouted back. She let herself get whipped because she didn't like the story about this girl's father's heart getting eaten.

"The flesh from his thigh jump up like popcorn in the frying-pan." The Khmer Rouge had told the story to some adults.

"You very stubborn!" the girl yelled in a harsh tone of voice.

"Ten whip, no more!" Moy grabbed onto the stick. She stood eyeball to eyeball with the girl.

"Buddy dare talk back to me?"

"I dare tell the traitor's child if buddy hit me again, I'll hit buddy back."

She slapped Moy hard, which Moy hadn't seen coming. Moy saw stars in front of her. She lifted her hand to strike back. But *then it was like someone told her to drop her hand.* Moy got herself under control, smiled, and told the girl, "Flesh hurt but the heart hurt more." Moy turned around and walked away from her.

Nowadays, Moy went all the way. She wore the white, heavy cotton, long-sleeved shirt and sarong the Khmer Rouge gave her. Everyone else wore black or dark brown. She didn't like the muddy smell in her clothes. People took their white clothes to any mud holes they could find, threw the white clothes in the mud, stepped and jumped on them, then left them there for a couple of hours. Later, they took them out and washed off the mud, and thus got their dark brown clothing. Everyone laughed and called Moy Grandma Nun behind her back. Moy was bald-headed and wore white, like the Cambodian nuns.

The Khmer Rouge would laugh and tell each other, "I look at the entire field and at everyone, and I see only one baldhead and white clothes, like Grandma Nun. That's Chi Minh's little sister!"

No doubt Ming got an earful of what Moy did. She was always hungry, and the only thing she could find to eat was grasshoppers. She caught any grasshopper she could get her hands on. She pulled the heads and wings off, and broke off the lower half of the thorny legs. She had about a handful of grasshoppers every day that she'd wrap up in one end of her scarf, and when she got home she threw the grasshoppers in her little can to roast them until they turned light brown. Then she ate—and they tasted like peanuts! At first, she caught only the large grasshoppers, but when they were gone, any size grasshopper would make her happy. Moy loved her grasshopper-peanuts. She ate so many grasshoppers that they were in great danger of extinction!

"We no have any more grasshoppers for Chi Minh's little sister to eat now," the Khmer Rouge told each other and laughed as they walked past her, eating the grasshopper-peanuts, every day.

Keem

Moy embarrassed her big brother but made him proud at the same time. And she was about to make him very famous! And all the men wanted to be like Chi Minh.

* * *

One day, she was sitting on a rock and chewing on a short sugarcane when a man came up from behind and said, "Buddy's cheek very red." He smiled and brushed her cheek gently.

"I no like Buddy Big Brother touch my cheek. Onka no like boy touch girl. I reform Buddy Big Brother; wrong to touch me," she told him with a smile.

He looked shocked but didn't say anything, just turned around and walked away.

If he didn't want to play me, let him. Moy thought, she didn't know who he was. Most of the girls were shocked at what they had heard and witnessed, and they yelled at Moy for a couple of days for embarrassing the man. Then a couple of days later, she was sitting on her feet in front of a little stove made from three small rocks and a little fire. She was roasting the grasshopper-peanuts in her favorite small old can. Moy had just picked the can up with a stick from the stove when a large group of Khmer Rouge showed up. They stood in front of her. She looked up.

About twenty of them showed her all their white teeth. They had long guns hanging from their shoulders. But three Khmer Rouges in front of the group had no guns. A Khmer Rouge at the center of the group asked, "What Buddy Little Sister do?" He looked friendly and smiled.

"I no take anything from Onka. I roast grasshopper; they no belong to Onka. Onka let me eat grasshopper," she told him, getting up to her feet. Her hand held onto the little stick with the small can hanging on it.

"Good to eat?" the leader asked. All the Khmer Rouge smiled wider, and a few chuckled aloud.

"They taste like peanut!" She didn't mean to be funny, but all the Khmer Rouge laughed aloud again. Moy knew from their dark green polyester clothing and the red-checkered scarves around their necks that this group of Khmer Rouge came from a higher-up office. She held the small can up for the leader to see the golden grasshoppers. She told him she didn't have many grasshoppers, but she would like to share them with him.

"This child know Onka's rule to share," the leader complimented her. He looked about thirty. He examined her carefully, and then he reached for a small grasshopper. His right and left hand men each also took a small grasshopper. The three men stared at the insects between their fingers.

"Eat! It taste like peanut," she told them, nodding to confirm it.

The three leaders' smiles became wider, while their men laughed behind them.

"Pity Buddy Big Brother," their men whispered.

Moy watched. The three leaders held the grasshoppers between their white teeth and looked at each other, smiling.

"Yes. It taste like peanut," the leader told her, and then he laughed aloud with all his men.

Moy tossed her chin toward the house. She was happy! This Black Shirt agreed the roasted grasshoppers tasted like peanuts. All the girls yelled at her every day that she ate the grasshoppers because she had nothing better to do. However, she was not happy when the leader told his men to go out and catch grasshoppers and roast them for him. She told him there were no more grasshoppers left. That she had gotten them all. He said there were many large fields, so there must be more grasshoppers for his men to catch.

"I eat them every day. No more grasshopper left," she told him.

The leader turned around and led his men to the large wooden house. All of them laughed. She heard them whisper that she was afraid they might catch all her grasshoppers, and she'd have no more grasshoppers to eat. She heard the men whisper, "That child know nothing; pity her."

There was a lot of loud laughter from the wooden house where the Khmer Rouge slept. Every now and then she caught a word here and there while she sat in front of her house, eating the grasshoppers. The Khmer Rouge were talking about her and Ming. Moy is orphan and Chinese. Chi Minh is her adopted big brother and a Vietnamese. She heard the same comment many times: "That child know nothing!" or "Pity her!" or "Too bad she Chinese and not Khmer," or "We must take her to meet Buddy Big Brother in Phnom Penh."

The next morning, a strange thing happened. In the meeting, a woman commander from the Khmer Rouge pulled Moy out of her group and made her a captain of the Left Over. She was to supervise the six girls who took care of Aunt Wipe House. Everyone laughed at her, but Moy didn't care. Her little group got to sleep until eight or eight-thirty, while everyone else got up between two-thirty and three some mornings, and after dinner, they had to work until 10:00 p.m. By the time they got home, Moy and her group were sound asleep. The girls were from eight to twelve years old, and Moy was the oldest in her group. Every day, she took her little group to the jungle around the sugarcane fields. They cut the wild mint bushes, brought them home, and chopped them up.

There were four outhouses; under each of them was a two-foot-tall gasoline tank that filled with human waste. Two or three times a week, in the morning, Moy and the girls wrapped their scarves around their noses and mouths. Moy used a long stick to lift the handle up from each of those tanks. Three girls on each side of a large wooden pole slipped it through the handle of each tank under the outhouses, and lifted it out. That was the hardest part of the work. They threw the wild mint in and used a very long wooden pole to mix it up. Then they pushed the tank over and left the human waste with mint to dry in the sun. After that, they put the tanks back under each outhouse.

Moy didn't want to wait until the whole tank filled up, because then it was very heavy to lift out. So she and the girls took the tanks out when they were less than half filled. The minute the girls had the human waste out to dry in the sun, Moy and her group took off. The girls would bathe in the pond. They threw water at each other, laughed, and had fun. Then they went mushroom hunting for themselves or did whatever they wanted. Afterward, Moy made sure every girl had a brush of wild mint to take home. Much later, the Khmer Rouge had people use the dried human waste to help grow larger corn, beans, and everything else.

One day, a little girl asked Moy why people called the outhouse Aunt Wipe House.

"If you a girl, you wipe your aunt after you shit. If you a boy, you wipe your uncle after you shit." Moy laughed and ran while her teammates chased after her, also laughing.

The cook's daughter told her mother what Moy said about Aunt Wipe House. All the cooks laughed at Moy's joke in the common kitchen. Then it got to the woman commander and her men, and laughter exploded from the wooden house.

*　*　*

Later, all the children were sent back to Kompong Kol again. The second Moy got into town, she got stared at. People pointed her out to each other.

"That's Chi Minh's little sister!"

"Which one?"

"That bald-headed one."

"The one look like Grandma Nun."

"There! Chi Minh's little sister!"

"I want a little sister who no afraid of anyone, like Chi Minh's little sister," people told each other.

Everyone on the streets stared, pointed, and talked about her. Even the Khmer Rouge pointed her out to each other. They never went anywhere without their guns hanging from their shoulders, but Moy didn't care. She went to live at the same house near the river again. She and the children ate at the second common kitchen. She didn't go see her brother. She was tired from work all day. Then one day, Moy ran into her sister-in-law. Chan had shaved off her hair, and now it was very short.

"Your name very big in Kompong Kol," Chan told her.

"My name very big?" Moy didn't understand.

Chan told her the man who had touched Moy's cheek was not only a Khmer Rouge but also the commander from the State of Battambang. He and his men came to learn how to grow sugarcane. He told people in the meeting that he had met a Chinese bald-headed girl who said, "Onka no like boy touch girl, and I reform Buddy Big Brother," and that he was wrong to have touched her cheek. He was told the child's name was Moy, Chi Minh's little sister.

"She no afraid of anyone; she brave like baby tiger!" he told people in the meeting. He would take the lesson Moy taught him to Battambang and teach his people. He told his hosts that if he saw that bald-headed child on the same street with him again, he'd keep his hands behind his back. He didn't want to get reformed by Chi Minh's little sister again. Everyone laughed at his joke. And he brought pride to the commander of Kompong Kol, who oversaw the whole sugar factory and fields, with his good teaching.

Moy wondered what else he had said in the meeting. She was afraid the commander from Battambang might come back and order his men to kill her.

Moy thought the commander from Battambang was a good, educated, and understanding man. He could have her killed for what she said to him, but he didn't. And he turned his embarrassment into a joke that he shared with a few thousand people in the meeting. She understood that not all Black Shirt were bad people. No matter who and where they came from, there would always be some bad and some good people—like her previous commander, Uncle Soun, who was a Khmer Rouge but was kind, understanding, and always smiled at everyone under his rule.

But because Uncle Soun gave men, women, and children white rice to eat, he got killed by his own people, and they ate his heart. Moy learned to respect some of the nice Khmer Rouge, like Uncle Soun and the commander from Battambang. She was thankful he hadn't hurt her. But she hated the Khmer Rouge like Vulture. So long as she was alive, she'd face the good and the evil. Hopefully, she would defeat the evil.

* * *

A few days later, she ran into Chan on the street again.

"Go see your big brother. He want to see you," Chan told her.

"Yes!" Moy said but kept walking.

She didn't go see Ming. She could almost feel her ears ringing from her big brother's lecture for letting her tongue run wild. One evening, she and Le sat talking in their group's room. A girl came in and asked, "Who name Luong?" She said Luong's big brother was outside waiting to take her home.

Moy went out, hid in the dark shadows, and watched Ming. He leaned on the wooden steps, six steps up the front porch of the house.

Keem

He was talking quietly with the general about Moy, but she couldn't hear what they were saying. Ming must have sensed her staring, and he looked up in her direction.

"Big Brother," she greeted him from the shadows.

"What wrong with Little Sister?" He didn't look angry under the bright electric light. "Come down," he ordered.

She edged slowly out of the shadows.

"Your leg hurt?" he asked

"No."

"Go get your bag; you go home with me." He pointed toward the room.

"I want to stay here," she whispered

"What?"

"I go get my bag." She went to get her things and told her friend she was going home with her big brother.

Ming and Moy walked side by side on the main street. She looked at him from the corner of her eyes and noticed he had grown a lot.

They walked quietly for a while, and then he asked, "Why you no come to play with me?"

"I busy." She kept her eyes on the road in front of her.

"You here three week and you no come to see Big Brother. Why?"

"I busy; I work," she told him.

He let it go. Then he asked the question that Moy wished to forget, "Luong, when we live in Head Tiger, that *night* when you see me, you cry. Why you cry that night?" he asked softy and gently, then waited patiently.

I can't tell Big Brother! Without thinking, she told him instead, "Big Brother is bigger than before."

"Luong, why you cry that night when you see me?" He sounded all grown up. He was very patient and asked as gently as he could.

"Big Brother know what Ma and Grandpa say? If we meet in Pailin, Ma and Grandpa say they give Big Brother money to buy and sell ruby and sapphire in the park, like other men." She told him the truth about what their Ma and Grandpa had wished.

"Ma and Grandpa talk like that?" He sounded pleased.

She looked up.

He smiled handsomely. His smile made Moy wish their Ma and Grandpa were there to tell him, instead of her. Ming was an orphan and a Vietnamese; his parents had died when he was a little boy. He had an aunt and uncle who didn't care for him. He went to live with a stranger, who worked him like a slave on the farm and gave him nothing to eat all day. He had to go to the streets and beg for food. How did he end up in Cambodia? Moy didn't know. Keem Lai and Wong Lai, Ming's adopted ma and grandpa, wished they had met him sooner, in Pailin, so they could have loved him more, to make up for what he had missed as a little boy. Keem would have been overjoyed to have had Ming as a son when they lived in Pailin.

"Yes, Ma and Grandpa talk like that all the time!" She looked up.

"Ma and Grandpa are good people," he said. He sounded very cheerful. Then he looked at her and asked, "Now, why you cry that night?" He laughed aloud.

Oh, Big Brother! Why can't you forget? she growled inwardly. "I have bad dream."

"What kind of dream?" He almost whispered the question, as if trying not to frighten her.

"I dream..." *I'll tell him the truth, now!* "I dream Khmer Red want to kill big brother." Close, but not quite the truth.

"Khmer Red take me away and kill me?" he asked in a casual tone of voice.

"I not remember." She stared at her feet.

Keem

He let it go and waited. Then he went on with his easygoing tone of voice. "You tell Big Brother the truth? If you lie, it a sin."

"Yes." She didn't look at him.

Ming didn't ask any more questions. Perhaps he wondered how to get the truth out of her. They walked side by side in silence, under the bright electric lights on poles on both sides of the sidewalk. As they got closer to their home, the lights blinked on and off three times.

"Walk faster; Khmer Red will turn off the light soon," he told her.

* * *

Moy lay on Ming's small, folding army bed, the same bed she had slept in the last time she was there. She didn't know why, but she was frightened and startled at the smallest sound. Then she heard Chan criticizing Ming. "Snore and snore! Who can sleep if you snore this loud?"

Moy smiled, listening to her big brother murmur something, then silence.

"Stop snoring!" Chan protested louder.

Moy giggled in her hands. She heard someone turn over in bed and whisper something; it must have been poor Ming.

"Stop snoring!" Chan complained angrily.

"Yes…madam wife," the words slipped out of his lips, and then he began snoring again.

Moy faced the wall and giggled in her hands. *Big Brother snore like a pig*, she thought. Then she heard someone turn over or jump up in bed. Ming's angry voice reached her ears, "You do that again, I will kick you under the bed!"

"Yes, Mr. Husband," Chan hissed back.

"'Mr. Husband' one more time, I will kick you out from the house!"

"No yell; your little sister sleep in that bed, over there."

"I know where my little sister sleep," he snapped. He sounded very angry about whatever Chan had done to wake him up. "What you say to my little sister, make her afraid of me?" he whispered.

"I tell Mr. Husband's little sister nothing. I only tell her about that meeting."

"What meeting?"

"The meeting with the commander from Battambang," Chan reminded him.

"I forget about that meeting. My little sister brave like baby tiger." He chuckled, and then he asked, "Chan, do you dare reform some leader, if you see them do something wrong?"

"I dare not."

"Luong dare." He sounded proud.

"Dare and very stubborn. One day they take her and hit her away," Chan whispered.

Kill me? Why? I didn't do anything wrong. I'll watch my big mouth and keep my tongue from jumping up and down. That is all, Moy thought.

When Keem was alive, she always yelled at Moy, "Your tongue jump up and down. Talk and talk all day; your tongue has no brake! I go buy a brake and press your tongue down!" Moy giggled; she thought her ma was funny.

Moy never felt connected to Chan, since they had first met. She didn't know why. Moy was shy when she first met Ming, but she felt grabbed by him. As she listened to her big brother and his wife, she liked Chan even less. And she adored her big brother even more!

"You no better; you as stubborn as Luong." He sounded bitter. "People look down on her; they beat her many time. Many week ago, Moy's former general tell me she order twenty-five whip on Luong, but she no cry. Then she order five more whip. Still, Luong no cry. She tell me she no want to wait until someone else tell me; she order the

Keem

whip on my little sister. She know I will be angry. I tell it straight to her face that Moy is stubborn and can be mean like baby tiger. But she has no right to whip Moy or anyone else children. Now I know why all the mother and father in Kompong Kol call her a mean witch or 'that short-lived mean witch, meaner than Khmer Red.' No mother or father give their child thirty whip. She lucky I a man and not a woman, or I slap her. I tell her, 'Don't let me see your mean witch's face again. Or I will forget I a man.' Ma and Grandpa must be angry with me if they know I not there to protect Luong."

"What can you do? You not live with her every hour." Then Chan's voice became quiet. "What you tell her?" she asked.

"I tell her nothing. If Khmer Red want to rape her, I'll kill her myself! I not let them hurt my little sister." He sounded furious.

What is Big Brother talking about? Moy thought. She kept silent and continued to listen.

"Every day, I see bodies in the field! Khmer Red rape women, then kill them. They beat the men until they die. Khmer Red break the men's arms and legs like stick. Sometime, they yank people's eyeballs out. Khmer Red like to eat human's heart, fry them with pig oil, and eat them with rice!"

Vulture told me the truth! And all those stories of the Black Shirts killing each other off and eating each other's hearts were true, Moy thought.

"Stop! I want to throw up!" Chan moaned.

"If you dare go outside now, it like you walk into a hungry tiger's mouth," Ming told his wife.

"Then stop your story!" Chan whispered.

But Ming went on anyway, "Before, I just plow the land to grow sugarcane. Now, I plow the land to grow sugarcane and bury many, many body. Khmer Red rape women every night and day. They kill every night. Tonight, you kill someone. Tomorrow night, someone else might kill you. I not know when they want to kill me." Ming sounded like he was in another world, not in the present one where he saw so many dead and mutilated bodies.

"Stop talk like crazy pig!" Chan whispered.

"Luong tell me when we live in Head Tiger, she dream bad thing about me. I know she no tell me the truth. She very scared that night, but I no understand then. I remember she cry and cry when she see me. Then she not the same again. I think someone—" he paused.

Moy heard him say something about Khmer Red. She couldn't hear him, his voice sounded like he had turned toward the wall.

"You know? Luong is afraid of me since that night. She no want me go near her. I not know why. Every time I ask, she talk about this or that, and try to make me forget. She no answer me. She very smart, but I wait. One day she'll tell me."

Tears rolled from Moy's closed eyes. His words echoed in her head, "I wait. One day she'll tell me." That one day might be longer than his life. Maybe that one day would come sooner for all the people who lived in this hell on earth. Maybe the sun would rise and shine upon them; maybe the sun would never set from them again. Wait; they would wait. Hope; they would hope. Maybe their wishes would come true *that one day.*

* * *

Moy lived and worked in Kompong Kol for a few months. Once in a while, she went home to see her big brother. But she didn't sleep in his house again. The work was the same, at the sugarcane fields. The Khmer Rouge made people work harder. The work was from five in the morning until ten at night, with an hour for lunch and an hour for dinner. This south-side Khmer Rouge fed people better. No more thin rice soup to drink. People got rice mixed with corn or mung bean or banana, and banana tree soup with fish, or some kind of meat. Some of the meat was very salty, and no one dared think or ask what kind of meat it was or where it came from. *Human flesh?*

The Khmer Rouge picked a couple of hundred men, women, and children to work in the rice paddies, under the same commander. The Khmer Rouge called it the farm side, next to the sugarcane fields. There was no work on Sunday, but the meeting was from nine to eleven or twelve. After lunch, people were free to do whatever they wanted.

Later, the Khmer Rouge had new people take over Ming and his co-workers' job of plowing the fields. After that, Ming and his co-workers planted or cut sugarcane, like everyone else. Moy didn't like to see her big brother work so hard. Ming lost weight, and he looked older than he was. And she couldn't miss his look of concern. His smile never reached his eyes. Nowadays, there were a handful of Grandma Nuns and monks working in the fields, and Ming was one of them. And lice! But Ming looked very handsome with his short hair standing straight up on top on his head.

One day he said to Moy, "You very smart to shave off your hair and become a model for everyone." He laughed but sounded tired.

These days, there was no time for Moy to laugh or worry. After she got home from work in the evening, she could hardly remember her own name. The second she lay down and closed her eyes, she was out. Sometimes, she was awakened at night by mice chewing on her toes or fingertips. She either brushed or kicked them off and went back to sleep again. The next morning, she would get up to the loud sound of whistles at two-thirty or three and be at work in the fields at four-thirty or five. A few times the whistles would blow at eight or nine o'clock because the Khmer Rouge overslept!

"Thank you, Buddha!" people would whisper and smile on those days.

Moy was tired from work but happier because she got to see her big brother almost every day. They ran into each other as they got off work and headed home.

"Big Brother," she would greet him and walk next to him.

"Luong," or "Moy," he returned her greeting. Sometimes he rubbed her baldhead or rested his large hand on top of her head for a second or two. "Tired?" he would ask.

"Yes. Big Brother tired?"

"Yes, but we must work like everyone else. No talk too much. Work and live a little longer," Ming reminded her.

Sometimes on the streets, Moy heard the Khmer Rouge talk to each other, "That Vietnamese Chi Minh," or, "That Vietnamese rag, Chi Minh."

Other times, she heard the Cambodians and some of Ming's co-workers talking behind his back, like the Khmer Rouge did. Moy would turn around and give them a hard stare. As the days went by, she heard more and more about "Chi Minh this," or "Chi Minh that," and it always ended with, "that Vietnamese rag."

She didn't know if anyone called Ming "Vietnamese rag" to his face. If they did, she didn't think her brother could do anything about it. He might laugh it off. It couldn't be easy for a grown man to be called a "Vietnamese rage." Moy was young and would fistfight to stop the insult. But Ming couldn't, or the Khmer Rouge would kill him.

The insult brought Moy and Ming a little closer. She learned to open her heart more to him because he cared for her. Not once did she think he would carry out his threat from over a year before and betray her.

13

1978

The work in Kompong Kol was done. On the last day of work, there was a big meeting in the evening; even the babies were there. The Khmer Rouge said they would give the people the next day off from work. It was not a day of joy for most people. After lunch, all the husbands, wives, parents, and children would go their separate ways, in groups, to different towns. They would grow more sugarcane, cut down more trees on mountains, or work in the rice paddies. Just a few people would remain to work in Kompong Kol.

In the morning, the families spent whatever time they had left together, then said good-bye. Some families went to the river, where they bathed, played in the water, and had fun together. They would hold onto the memories of their times together.

Moy was the only one who didn't have a chance to say good-bye.

She felt uneasy as she sat on a big rock, feet kicking in the water, keeping an eye on her brother. Ming and Chan were bathing with all their clothes on, Ming swimming around, having fun. Then suddenly he disappeared under the water. Moy straightened up and looked around for him, and then she relaxed and giggled while Chan screamed and dove under the water. But she came back up with Ming behind her, laughing.

"You crazy," Chan said. She turned around and slapped her husband's shoulder.

Moy laughed as Ming and Chan threw water at each other. Then Ming turned around and pointed at her. Moy smiled and watched him swim toward her, his mouth under the water, blowing water out in bubbles. Ming's smile reached his beautiful black eyes that were on Moy.

"No!" Moy laughed, pulling her feet out of the water. She moved away from his reach.

"Luong come down and swim with Big Brother," he shouted up to her.

"I can no swim." She stood on the rock and peered down at him.

"Big Brother teach you; come down." He waved her down.

"No, thank you very much."

"Luong, come down; don't be stubborn."

She laughed and shook her head.

He finally gave up, looking very disappointed. He turned around and swam on his back toward the other side of the small river. There, he got out of the water and went to a group of men who stood there talking. Moy felt bad for disappointing him. She watched from across the river as Ming and his friends pushed and shoved at each other, like children having fun. Then they ran into the jungle and disappeared from her view. She sat on the rock, feet kicking in the water again, feeling happy.

On the streets of Kompong Kol, everyone smiled as each family made its way to the common kitchen for their last meal together. Ming, Chan, and Moy sat at a long bench with many people at the table. Moy sat facing her big brother. Ming's family had a large bowl of banana-tree-and-fish soup that they ate with white rice. Today was a special day, so the Khmer Rouge let everyone eat white rice.

Moy stirred her spoon around in the soup bowl, looking for a fish. She found one and dropped it into her big brother's rice bowl.

Keem

She didn't know she was feeding him his last meal.

"Why you no eat it yourself?" Ming asked.

"Elder must eat more meat." She looked up.

Ming choked up, his face turning red, and his shoulders shaking. Every muscle on his face laughed, and his beautiful black eyes sparkled. Chan rubbed his back, because his mouth was full, and it took a while before he could swallow the food. People who sat at the same table with them told Ming he was lucky to have an adopted little sister who loved and respected him that much. Moy loved him more than some blood brothers and sisters loved each other.

Everyone laughed harder when a father slapped his son's head and yelled, "This unlucky one shove all the meat in his own mouth. He no think of his old father! You hear what that child say to her big brother? And he younger than me!"

"Moy, you want to be my little sister?" a couple of people asked her. They looked, and sounded, serious.

"That Chinese child very respectful," people whispered to each other at the tables around them.

"Moy, you want me for a big brother?" some men asked her.

"I already have my big brother, Ming," she told them as she looked at her big brother's smiling face.

"Chi Minh no good. I better than him. Come, be my little sister," some of the men told her.

"I happy with my big brother, Ming." She didn't understand why the Cambodians were making such a big deal out of it. This was how Keem and Wong taught her to respect her elders. And Ming was six years older than her.

In Wong Lai's family, at the dinner table, Moy always looked for large pieces of meat that she would pick up with her chopsticks and drop in Grandpa's rice bowl first.

"Grandpa eat meat," she would tell him. Then she would find another piece for Ma, because Ma was younger than Grandpa. Or she picked up vegetables for Grandpa and Ma.

"Ma eat vegetable," she would tell Keem.

"Eat it yourself," they would tell her. Keem and Wong did the same, telling her to eat more. It was their way of telling each other of their love and respect. And some nights, when she ate more than usual, both Keem and Wong emptied the rice from their bowls into Moy's.

"Grandpa and Ma eat it yourself." Moy would try to give the rice back.

"Grandpa full; you eat. Why you cook so little rice tonight?" Wong would ask Keem as he put the rice bowl and chopsticks down.

"Ma full. You eat more and grow up fast, fast. I cook less rice because we have leftover every night," Keem replied.

"If we have leftover then we have leftover. Cook more rice for Moy to eat!" Wong would snap at Keem for her poor judgment.

* * *

"Go find your own little sister. No try to steal my little sister from me," Ming told the people at their table, making everyone laugh. He gave half of the fish back to Moy. She gave it back. Then he gave it to his wife. He couldn't stop smiling while eating.

People talked to each other, from the left and right and all around, about Ming's Chinese little sister. She respected and loved him very much. They wished they had a little sister like his. Moy made Ming a respectable man. And he smiled, so happy and carefree.

"Want it?" he asked, while eating his last meal.

"Pretty," Moy said, staring at the large, silver watch on his big wrist. It had a red circle above a green circle inside it. And it had a small circular dial near the top. It also showed the date, in black. On the outside of the watch, there was a red circle around the cover. A couple of months earlier, when Moy had seen this watch on him, she had asked, "Where is Grandpa's watch?"

He explained that their grandpa's watch was not working, and he had exchanged it with someone. He was sorry afterward that he had done it.

"If big brother happy with it, I happy," she told him, and he looked relieved.

She knew he told the truth. Wong Lai had a very expensive, silver wristwatch as long as she could remember. It was a Shamrock brand, with a white face and black date. It was always on time, never a minute late or early. But after they came to live in the jungle, that watch was never right. The master's health got weaker and weaker. And the life of that watch always followed its master's. That watch died countless times before their grandpa passed away.

"It too big for me, and it look pretty on big brother," she had told Ming.

"When you older and want it, I give it back to you." He had smiled, keeping his beautiful black eyes on her.

"I give it to Big Brother forever," she told him.

"You give it to me, forever." Ming had a masculine look of satisfaction and happiness.

Yes, the watch was his forever. He took an old, dying watch and exchanged it for a better one. He chose a youthful, healthy looking watch, to match his good looks.

* * *

That day was such a bright day. There wasn't a cloud in the sky. The sun was strong and bright, waiting…such a beautiful day, but so greedy!

On this day in 1978, Ming, Moy, and Chan left their house together. They walked, talked, argued, and laughed now and then as they went to meet their groups at the main common kitchen. Then Ming's family parted from each other. Ming went with his group, Chan went with hers, and Moy went to hers. There were a few thousand people standing in lines with their groups between a "baby mountain" and a small sugarcane field. Every group waited for its general to tell them where to go, then lead them there.

Moy had just gotten to her group and was standing behind her co-workers. She had just parted from her big brother only five short minutes earlier. Then a Vietnamese girl from Moy's group called out to her, "Buddy Moy, your big brother Chi Minh die." The girl looked somber.

"Buddy talk like crazy." Moy smiled.

"You dare laugh! I just tell Buddy, your big brother die. Buddy think I lie? They take big brother Chi Minh's body over there. Go and look," the girl pointed toward the men's side.

All the girls turned around and stared at Moy. Her smile became wider. She stepped out from her group and walked toward the men. A large group of men had formed in a circle, looking at something.

"Chi Minh's little sister here; let her in," the men shouted to each other. They stepped aside, making way for her.

She stood still and looked at the men. No one said anything. They just stared at her, looking shocked. She walked farther into the circle. Some men got up to their feet, not looking at her, and stepped aside.

Her smile gradually waned. Each puff of breeze washed it off her face, slowly. Moy stood behind three or four men who were on their hands and knees. She listened…

"Bite his heel!" one man yelled, and another man bent down and bit Ming's heel.

"Bite harder!" someone shouted.

Keem

The man bit Ming's heel so hard his head shook from side to side.

"Pull his ears! Give him pain, and he'll wake up!" someone shouted.

Moy looked at Ming, but she didn't really see him. Time went by so slowly; then finally she saw her big brother Ming.

He wore a black, long-sleeved shirt; long, black cotton pants; and a pair of black, ankle-high boots, which he always wore. He lay on the earth, his long legs straight out. His long arms were spread out, palms facing heaven. His eyes and mouth were half open. And his beautiful black eyes weren't twinkling anymore. Instead, they were dull and gray looking. Even the small, round, black birthmark on his left cheekbone didn't make him look handsome anymore.

Moy went to his side and sat on her heels next to her big brother. She picked his hand up, but it slipped through her fingertips. His hand just slipped out of her hands, hit the earth, then lay there. She sat and stared at that hand. She had tried to push her big brother Ming away when he was alive. But she loved him with all her shattered little heart. Now that he was dead, she reached for his hand. Perhaps Ming didn't want her to touch him now that he was dead. He knew she loved him, and he wanted to keep it that way. Moy couldn't cry for him that day. Maybe someday Ming's little sister, Moy/Luong, might cry for him.

This was the first time she had touched Ming's hand. She wanted him back, and held onto him tightly. But he was dead to her world. Perhaps, when his hand slipped from hers, it was his way of saying good-bye to her. Maybe it was his way of telling her his new world was not where she belonged. Perhaps he didn't want her holding onto his warm hand and feel it getting cold. He wanted her to feel warmth in her hand and remember him that way.

Perhaps Ming wanted her to remember the laughter and happy times they had had together. Perhaps it was his way of telling her she must let the dead go, and she must go on with her life. Keem, Wong, and his world wasn't hers. The dead and the living are in two different worlds. Just remember their warm, loving smiles, and the laughter they had shared with her.

She picked Ming's hand up again and laid it next to his body. Then she folded her hands on top of her lap. She kept her eyes on his handsome face. The longer she looked at him, the more of a stranger he became to her. Her big brother Ming had beautiful black eyes. This man lying there had dull, gray eyes. Strange—she felt no pain, emptiness, or fear like she had felt when her ma, Keem Lai, was taken from her. She felt nothing. She heard people whisper the awful words again, "She too scared to cry. Pity her!"

"She has only a big brother, now he died. Her heart is broken; she can't cry. Pity her!"

"Pity the Chinese child!"

She just sat there staring at her dead brother. Then she looked up and saw Chan, smiling. Chan had just arrived, and the men made way for her. Chan's smile faded away little by little when her eyes locked with Moy's. When Chan reached Ming's side, she stood there and stared at her husband. She sat down slowly, looked at Moy, then looked at her husband again. She didn't say a word. She just looked at her young, handsome husband. Then she stared at Moy, sitting on the opposite side. Wordlessly, Chan tried to close Ming's eyes and mouth for him, but he refused. One by one the men left, leaving Moy and Chan with Ming's remains lying between them.

Moy looked up to heaven. It was a clear and beautiful blue sky. All three people Moy had cared for and loved had died on days with clear, blue skies and bright sunshine. Were Wong, Keem, and Ming trying to tell her something? If Moy was capable of thinking at that moment, she might have asked, "Why are you doing this to me?" She saw her family die, one by one, in front of her.

Keem

Later an army truck came. A couple of men picked up Ming's remains and laid him on the truck platform. Moy and Chan had Ming's body between them. The girls sat on their heels, unable to do anything but stare at him. Then they looked at each other. They took Ming's remains to the hospital, where the men took his body from the truck and laid him on the ground in front of the hospital's entrance. There, both girls had their beloved Ming between them again.

"Buddy Big Brother, please help my husband," Chan begged the Khmer Rouge doctor, who was about Ming's age.

"Buddy's husband is dead. Buddy no see him?" one of the Khmer Rouge doctors shouted at Chan. He stood above Ming's head without any respect, like he was not brought up by a mother or father, but like he was just a black ant.

"Who is he?" another doctor asked.

"Chi Minh," someone answered.

"What? Chi Minh die?" The doctor sounded shocked.

Moy looked up and saw a doctor, younger than her big brother. He looked sad! He didn't say anything as he stared into Moy's eyes.

"That one is Chi Minh's little sister," a young Khmer Rouge told the doctor. He carried a long gun on his shoulder. He was younger than Moy.

"Chi Minh's little sister," the doctor mouthed aloud and nodded. The kind doctor sent the boy to the common kitchen to ask for a cow wagon to take Ming's remains away.

* * *

Two cows pulled a wagon with Ming's remains on it. Two men walked next to the cows, and Moy and Chan walked behind the wagon. The men whispered to each other. They couldn't believe Chi Minh just died like that. They went on whispering about him, but Moy couldn't hear what they said.

Moy was simply tired. Very, very tired for a young girl of her age. She was just…tired.

Everything was going too fast! It took them about thirty minutes to reach the jungle area where they would bury the body. Chan and the men dug a grave for Ming. The grave was only about two feet deep. Then the men stopped digging. They put the shovels down and turned toward Ming's remains on the wagon.

"*It not deep enough!*" Chan yelled, horrified. She stared at Moy with big eyes.

Moy walked to the edge of the grave and stood there. She stared and stared at the long, deep footpath that was to be her big brother's grave. She couldn't speak.

"If you want it deeper, you dig it yourself," the first man told Chan.

"We love Chi Minh. But I no want to be here when the sun go down. I no want to be here when the human-wolf come out!" the second man told Chan.

"The human-wolf too hungry for human's heart; I want to keep my heart where it is!" the first man looked scared.

"We no want to die yet, no," the second man told the girls. He looked and sounded frightened.

Moy watched the men carry Ming's remains from the wagon and lay it in the grave. Moy stared at her big brother's remains. His eyes and mouth remained open. His back was on Mother Earth's chest, just like his adopted Ma Keem Lai. *Like mother, like son. So stubborn! Neither one willing to close their eyes and mouths*, she thought.

Moy stood close to the edge of the grave and watched.

Chan and the two men pulled black dirt into the grave, shovel by shovel. The first dirt fell in slow motion onto the face of the man lying in the grave. Moy woke up and stood watching. The men threw black dirt on her big brother as he lay in a two-foot-deep and six-foot-long hole. She kept her eyes on her big brother Ming's face, watching black dirt fall on his handsome face, in his dull, gray eyes, and into his ears. She watched as black dirt fell on top of Ming's perfect nose, then rolled into his mouth.

"*Stop, stop, stop!*" Chan screamed. She unbuttoned her black, long-sleeved shirt. She knelt and brushed dirt off her husband's face; then she covered Ming's face with her shirt. She looked up and stared at Moy with big eyes.

Moy stared back. She said nothing. Then she looked at Ming's remains. She couldn't see his face anymore. Chan's shirt covered from his face down to his large, powerful chest. *His chest will not rise or fall again, ever,* Moy thought, watching. More and more black dirt was thrown on top of Ming's remains. Each grain of dirt thrown in pushed Ming deeper into the arms of Mother Earth. Moy looked up and saw Chan throwing dirt on her husband's face. Moy looked back down. Ming's face was now almost blanketed by black dirt. Then his face was gone underneath his wife's shirt and dirt, just the tip of his nose still peeking up. Moy looked to the left, just in time to see the tip of Ming's black boots before they were buried. She whipped to the right immediately, looking for her big brother Ming.

She blinked only once—just once. And her big brother Ming's face and body were gone forever. Gone…he was gone.

Moy just stood there at the edge of the grave, staring. Ming refused to get up and climb out of that two-foot-deep hole! No matter how hard she stared at the grave, he wouldn't get up and get out. Then she heard each grain of dirt that was thrown into the grave, sounding like a rope that lets go when a big, shape knife beheads a prisoner's head. Suddenly, everything went very fast. It took the men and Chan only a few short minutes to fill up the grave. No one said anything. Everyone just turned away from the grave and walked out of the jungle. Moy never looked back. They could all hear the wolves calling for each other behind them.

* * *

When they reached the common kitchen, it was dark. The men, Chan, and Moy ate their dinner in silence, and then they went home. That night, Chan asked Moy to share Ming's bed with her. Throughout the night, Moy wanted to get up and go to her big brother's small, folding army bed. She didn't want her big brother to come home, wake her up, and tell her to go sleep in the small bed. However, something kept her from getting up and going to the small bed. Every time she wanted to get up, it was like someone told her, "Lie down and go back to sleep."

She couldn't sleep. Whether she was too worried that Ming might walk in any second and wake her up or it was Chan's loud snoring next to her, Moy tossed and turned throughout the night. She couldn't close her eyes. She couldn't think. She just lay in bed and stared at the darkness until morning. At eight or nine the next morning, she sat in an army truck half loaded with long sugarcane going to Head Tiger, where her group was. She walked into the grass house, picked a spot, put her little clothes bag down against the wall, lay down, and closed her eyes. She went to work that same afternoon. She heard a lot of whispers about her, and her big brother's sudden death. That didn't bother her.

Moy heard rumor from some adults *about that day*, when Ming died.

Ming had stood behind his co-workers and then he leaned slowly, sideway, fell down, and died. But earlier on *that day*, Ming had seen a group of men meeting under a small tree on his way home. He had stopped to ask what they were meeting about and could he join them? No one answered. But he sat down in the circle with them and then the men disappeared into thin air, before his eyes! He got scared, got up and ran.

Some people believed when you saw a ghost or ghosts, never run; if you run they'll take your soul.

Most people wouldn't want to walk alone on that road or go near it. Moy went to see that *tree and area* many times when the children were back in Kompong Kol again. She didn't know what kind of tree it was. It was about as thick as the size of her thigh, ten to fifteen tall, on the side of the dirty road.

* * *

Later, Moy talked, laughed, and smiled more. Strange as it might seem, she felt freer and happier than she had been before. Perhaps her carefree heart came from the knowledge that Ming was not mutilated to death by the Khmer Rouge. It was heartache to lose her big brother, but Ming died from a natural cause. He was finally free from this evil world, this hell on earth. Ming was no longer living in fear, wondering and worrying when the night would come that the Khmer Rouge would take him to the jungle and have him at their mercy, knowing what he knew, and how he had seen mutilated human remains. Wondering when it would be his turn to have his heart pulled out or get beaten to death by the Khmer Rouge. Now he was free from all those fears.

When Ming was alive, he and everyone who lived in that sugarcane field were more like human-chickens, living in a coop. None of those human-chickens knew when their necks would be grabbed from behind and they would be pulled out of the cage. The real chickens were luckier than the human-chickens. The real chickens got their throats cut only once, and quickly. Or one quick sweep of a knife or ax got their heads off, and they died quickly. However, the human-chickens wished a million times per second for a quick death, not to get played to death slowly by the black ants/Khmer Rouge.

* * *

Moy heard a story about the former commander of the Khmer Rouge from Kompong Kol. She had never met him. She saw his little brother, who was about a year younger than her. She didn't know him. Moy remembered one day when she was talking to a boy about something and someone yelled at her to get away from him.

"That dog is a traitor," someone else told her.

The boy lowered his head and walked away. His dark skin looked sickeningly gray. The smile on his face looked frozen. The story of his family had Moy shaking in fear for her big brother Ming when he was alive. The boy's family was taken by the new group of Khmer Rouge. The blank ants/Khmer Rouge had raped the mother in front of the brothers, forcing them to watch. Afterward, the Khmer Rouge got a long stick and shoved it from the lady's privates all the way through her head. The older brother screamed and cried as he watched his poor mother raped, mutilated, and killed by his own people. Then the Khmer Rouge mutilated him slowly to death in front of the boy. They were going to kill the boy, too, but they didn't. Everyone in the sugarcane fields heard his story.

Every few weeks, the Khmer Rouge took the boy somewhere for a couple of days. Then he returned looking more and more like the walking dead.

"Dog, come here; dog, go over there," the Khmer Rouge called to him.

Sometimes, Moy saw the Khmer Rouge kick that boy. He always had that frozen smile.

* * *

Ming was a large young man. He lived on borrowed time, one second at a time, until he died of natural causes at the age of twenty-one.

"I'll die, too, when I twenty-one," he had told Moy when he first took her to live in the sugarcane fields.

Moy had the strength to go on after Ming's sudden death because some days she felt happy and satisfied. She had stood up to Vulture and stared him down. And this new group of Khmer Rouge took Vulture's authority away. First, they made him a captain of ten men. Then they took his title away because he worked too slowly. Currently, he stood behind a civilian captain! Moy was the small captain of her group. Every morning, she would look toward the men, about twenty feet from her. She would stare and smile at Vulture. He looked a little scared and always looked away from her. Why didn't the Khmer Rouge kill this one evil man?

Perhaps Buddha wanted Moy to defeat the evil man again. She was standing tall, but Vulture hung his head in shame.

Now he had a taste of his own threats. His wife might get raped in front of him. He might get cut in half and have his heart pulled out, chopped into small pieces, fried with pig oil, and eaten with rice, by his people. Nothing was worse than living in fear!

Moy watched and stared at the girls who had picked on her and made her cry. They fell low, one by one, before her eyes. Moy's former general, who had ordered the thirty whips on Moy, was now standing behind someone else, and her group was next to the men. One day, she hesitated before she walked out from her group, head hung low to stand in front of everyone, sick. She must have felt Moy's stare. She looked toward Moy, and their eyes locked. Moy smiled. The former general looked away quickly. That Khmer Rouge's daughter and Girl had always picked on Moy and made her cry. Now the three of them were all in the adult groups, their heads hung low in shame for working too slowly!

Sometimes, Moy talked and laughed as she led her group to work. As she walked, she stared at Vulture, the former general; Girl, that Khmer Rouge's daughter; and the girl who got Moy the thirty whips.

"Buddy Moy, why buddy so happy?" some girls would ask.

"I look at them." She thrust her chin out toward the men and women's groups.

"Them? No look at those dog! Thank you, Buddha! Thank you!" the girls would snarl. They were terrified of Vulture's whips, and they had been whipped at their former general's orders.

If people knew what went on inside Moy's mind after Ming's death, no doubt they would say she had gone crazy. Moy's mind was like a TV recorder, playing different clips of images. She didn't hear voices, but she knew who said what in each clip. It was like a movie. Perhaps she *had* gone crazy. Maybe her mind wanted something beautiful for her to hold onto, giving her the strength and will to go on living.

14

Different Flashbacks from Childhood

In her mind movies, Moy saw herself as a baby, as a little kid, and as a younger child.

"Moy walk to Ma," Keem coached her baby in Teochew. She sat on her feet, holding her hands out to her baby.

"Moy come this way; walk to Grandpa." Wong smiled, sitting on his feet. His fingertips almost touch Keem's. They had the baby within their arms' length.

Moy babbled happily and baby walked slowly toward her ma. She screamed in delight as she grabbed onto Keem's shoulders. Then she turned around and walked back to Wong's arms. They both beamed with pride, telling her how well and far she could walk.

Grandpa had baby Moy on his lap, with his arms around her. He chewed on a rice noodle, then put it in a spoon with pork noodle soup juice and fed it to her. Moy waved her little hand up and down excitedly and babbled to Grandpa.

"Puppy like noodle. Grandpa give puppy more noodle." He smiled handsomely as he fed her more noodle soup.

When Moy was no more than three years old, they were visiting Phnom Penh. She sat on a dark wooden bed, inside the mosquito net, rubbing her upper right arm and crying. Someone had pinned her because she wet herself. Grandpa reached for her and carried her around the house.

Moy sat on the floor in a large room, chatting to herself. Then she got up. She had a long towel on the floor in front of her. She rolled the towel up, one end at a time, and then she folded it in half, like Ma had taught her.

"Grandma, I play with my doll." Moy stood in front of the wooden bed. She looked at a large, unsmiling woman.

The overweight woman fanned herself with a heart-shaped, light brown fan made of leaves. Her shiny black hair reached below her ears and round face. "If you have doll, then play with it and quiet! I bore listen to you!" she snapped sharply, staring hard at little Moy.

"Grandma, where Grandpa?"

"He go die somewhere. Where else?" She stared harder at Moy.

Moy lowered her head, her eyes rolled left and right, and then she cried.

"He go buy thing. Where you think he go? I hate it!" The woman didn't move from the bed.

Moy sat on the floor and played with her towel doll, quietly. She wiped away tears with the backs of her little hands. She had dolls from three inches to two feet tall at home, in Siem Reap.

"Don't let her eat the rice away," the woman told a young, teen-aged girl.

Moy's lips trembled as she looked at the people eating at a large, round table. Later, Moy stood in front of a door. She looked up and around, and asked, "Fourth Uncle, where Grandpa?"

"Get out of the way. I don't know." A man walked in, the door closing.

Keem

Later, Moy stood in front of the door again. She looked hopeful and asked, "Second Uncle, where Grandpa?"

"I don't know; walk aside." He looked at her.

"I want Grandpa," she told him.

"Grandpa come home soon. Don't stand near the door." He smiled and walked in.

Later, the door opened again. Moy shouted, "Grandpa, Grandpa!" She held her little hands up.

"Puppy, you scare Grandpa to death! Why puppy cry?" He picked her up.

"Grandpa not go die somewhere. Puppy want Grandpa." She wrapped her arms around his neck.

"Not smart; why you say that?"

"Grandma say, 'He go die somewhere. Where else?'" she sobbed aloud on his shoulder.

Grandpa yelled at Grandma for saying such words to a child. Grandma told him Moy lied, but he said a child of that young age only repeats what she has heard. He asked Moy if she had eaten any rice yet.

"Grandma say, 'Don't let her eat the rice away.' I want Ma, Grandpa. I want Ma." Moy cried harder.

Grandpa told her not to cry, that they'd go downstairs and eat pork noodle soup. He brought a bowl of soup and fed it to her slowly. Then he brought a bowl of sweet nuts soup in ice and fed that to her.

"She can hate me all she want, but she can't beat or starve my child! I will not give her another penny! You will not give my money to her again. My sad child, Ma love you." Ma cried as she held Moy in her arms and paced around the house. She yelled at Grandpa some more. "You will not take my child to that witch's house again! My sad child, my flesh, my heart, my life." Ma showered her with kisses.

MOY

Moy remembered that the first face she saw when she was a baby was Grandpa's. And the first word she heard was spoken by him: "Moy."

Baby Moy turned around. She looked at a handsome, smiling face, and then she screamed and cried. She looked back and stared at a beautiful, unhappy face. Then Moy heard the first sentence spoken by Keem, "It is Ma. Don't be afraid. Ma love you." Ma smiled.

Then Moy wrapped her cuddly arms around Ma's neck and cried. Ma rubbed Moy's back and soothed her with silly words.

"Not smart to shave off your beard now. You know she in a stranger state," Ma said.

"Puppy, it is Grandpa. Puppy no recognize Grandpa?" Grandpa smiled and reached for her.

Moy stared at him. Then she swept her hand left and right, pushing his hand away. Wrapping her arms around her ma's neck, she cried harder.

"No make my child cry; go somewhere else! You know she in a stranger state, and you have to shave off your beard now."

Moy had on a brown-and-white-plaid, long-sleeved shirt and matching long pants. She sat on Grandpa's lap, wrapped in his arms, looking tired. She turned her face into Grandpa's chest, away from a spoonful of noodles.

"Puppy no want noodle? Puppy make Grandpa unhappy if puppy no eat."

"Why Moy very quiet today?" Uncle Noodle asked.

"Puppy has fever; she no feel well," Grandpa told the owner of the noodle shop.

Baby Moy stood on a chair next to Grandpa while he was eating noodles at a large, round table. Moy slipped and fell from the chair to the ground. She screamed at the top of her lungs. Grandpa looked upset. He picked her up, held her in his arms, and bumped her up and down gently.

"No cry. No cry. Puppy no cry. Grandpa love you. Grandpa love you." He bumped her a little harder in his arms, making her scream aloud.

Uncle Noodle got so angry at that chair that he picked it up, threw it down, and kicked it. Then he gave her a new chair to stand on and a glass of sweet iced milk to drink. This time, Grandpa kept an arm around her. She baby talked to Grandpa and rubbed her head.

"Grandpa know it hurt. Grandpa love puppy. No cry."

"Mama," Moy cried and reached for her.

Ma sat in the middle of the platform of their five-and-dime shop at the open market.

"What happen? Why my child cry?" She took Moy from Grandpa.

Grandpa told Ma that Moy fell off the chair. Ma got mad and criticized Grandpa for his carelessness. He had let her child fall and get hurt, and Ma cried for Moy's pain. Ma wrapped a towel over her shoulder and around Moy. Moy played with Ma's nipple under the towel and sucked on Ma's milk.

"Grandpa, look. It rain!" Moy ran in and out of the little shower. She laughed, hopping up and down excitedly.

"No run! You slip and fall. Puppy like this hotel and play with rain?" Grandpa smiled very handsomely. He sat on his feet, holding on to her.

"Yes! I like play with rain." She ran out of his arms and played under the shower, screaming in delight.

"Puppy hungry?" Grandpa asked, looking at her.

"Yes." She tripped but didn't fall, as he held onto her little hand.

"Walk careful. Walk careful. No fall!" He picked her up and held her in his arms. "Puppy hurt? No cry. Grandpa love you." He looked at the foot she pointed at.

"Grandpa, I want Ma." She wrapped her arms around his neck, crying on his shoulder.

"We go home soon. Puppy no cry. Grandpa love you." Wong always took her with him when he went to Phnom Penh on business and holidays, after Keem stopped breastfeeding Moy.

Keem walked in the dark street to the movie theater with Moy in her arms. Moy poked at the tip of her ma's bra and giggled.

"You think it too pointy?" Ma asked, giggling.

"Yes!" she laughed and poked at her ma's bra some more.

"Child, walk careful. No fall." Ma had Moy on her feet, holding onto Moy's little hand.

"Ma, carry me." Moy stood in front of her ma and held her hands up.

"Puppy walk little more. Ma's arm still ache." Ma rubbed her arm.

Outside the crowded Chinese theater, Keem looked so embarrassed. Her bra was too pointy, a wealthy lady with her child. She held Moy in front of her, telling her daughter not to poke at the tip of her bra.

"Big Sister (or Aunt), you bring your child here to see movie," people greeted her with warm smiles.

"Yes, Big Brother, Big Sister," or "Yes, Aunt and Uncle. You come to see movie?" Keem returned their greetings.

In Cambodia, most of the rich and middle class Chinese and Cambodians dressed in their best clothing to go to the movie theater. If they dressed poorly, people were embarrassed to sit next to the poor people, saying, "Bad luck!"

Keem

"It doesn't matter who we sit next to, rich or poor. They human, and they eat rice like us. No different! We must not forget where we come from," Wong and Keem always told each other and the family.

Moy stood on a large chair inside an airplane. She asked Grandpa a million questions about everything.

"Grandpa, what this?" or "Grandpa, what that?" or "Why?"

"Puppy no ask so many question. Grandpa bore!"

"Why Grandpa bore?"

"Puppy ask many question."

"Puppy like ask question."

"Good child no ask many question," he told her.

"Grandpa, puppy is good child." She stepped on his lap and wrapped her little arms around his neck.

"Yes, puppy is good child. Now sit down." He picked her up and sat her on the large seat next to him.

Moy stood on a chair at a large, round table at Uncle Noodle's shop. She was crying and shoving the spoonful of noodles in Grandpa's hand away. "No!"

She wanted the whole bowl of soup, and chopsticks, from Grandpa. He gave them to her. Holding the chopsticks in both hands, she twisted the chopsticks around and wrapped the rice noodles on them.

"Blow on it first; it hot. No bite too big. Bite little at a time," Grandpa coached her.

"Uncle, you teach Moy well how to wrap noodle on chopstick," Uncle Noodle praised him.

"I no teach her. I not know she know how to wrap noodle like that herself." Grandpa looked happy. He walked around like a proud peacock with little Moy in his arms. He told Ma that Moy made him very happy.

"My child very smart, good child!" Ma smiled, breastfeeding Moy under the towel.

Moy sat on a chair in the small kitchen in Pailin. At that time she was eleven years old. Her infected feet were in a metal bucket filled with a witch doctor's medicine.

"Grandpa, I no feel good," Moy whispered, hanging her head low.

"Why? Moy!" Grandpa screamed and grabbed her shoulders.

"Grandpa, I no feel good." Her head leaned on his strong arm.

"Moy, what wrong? Moy?" He picked her up in his arms and carried her to a small folding bed. "Moy, talk to Grandpa. Moy."

Later, Ma came home and looked very worried. She asked, "What wrong with my child?"

Grandpa told her Moy had her feet in the bucket of liquid medicine from the witch doctor, like she had every day for the last few months. Then she went limp after she told him she didn't feel well. It was late at night, and Moy got worse. But they couldn't leave the house, or they would get arrested by the police. Grandpa told Ma to ask their next-door Cambodian neighbor for help. The Cambodian man worked for the government, so he had some authority over the policemen. Ma carried Moy in her arms to a doctor's house. It was more than an hour's walk, and they got stopped a few times. Their neighbor told the policemen they had to take a very sick child to a doctor.

Moy didn't have any strength to move, but she heard people talking, and she listened.

"Why you wait until about to throw this child away, then you bring her to me?" the doctor yelled at Ma. Keem didn't speak Khmer very well but did her best, begging the doctor to save Moy. The doctor opened Moy's eyes. He looked young and angry.

Keem

"No yell at her; pity her. Her child very sick," a woman with long black hair, wearing a flowered sarong, whispered to the doctor.

"Sick? This child near death; then she bring the child to me! I not know what to do. You give this child witch doctor's medicine. Take this child to the hospital. If this child live to morning, then she live," the doctor told Ma.

"Moy, child. You hear Ma, Moy?" Ma kept whispering to her as she carried Moy in her arms and walked to the hospital. Ma sat on a chair next to a small hospital bed and watched her.

Moy had an IV drip placed into her veins. The bag was next to the bed. She heard everything going on around her but didn't have the strength to move or talk. She was not sleeping; she just kept her eyes closed. She knew the nurse came to check on her. Ma picked Moy's hand up and held it in hers, and Moy listened to her ma's prayers throughout the night.

"Grandma, Grandpa, don't let anything happen to my child. Your powerful spirit must come to help my child. My child is my life, my flesh, my heart, my pulse. Don't let anything happen to my child. Pity me, Grandma, Grandpa. Pity me. You must save my child. My child is all I have. You must help me save my child."

Sometime toward early morning, Ma woke her up. "Moy, child, open your eyes and look at Ma. Make Ma happy." She looked tired, but relieved. "Child, Ma go home to change clothes and tell Grandpa not to worry. Then Ma come back. Don't let anything happen. Ma come back fast, fast. Puppy go to sleep."

Then later, "Moy, wake up. Ma come back. Ma buy sweet milk for child to drink." Ma looked tired but very happy. She helped Moy sit up and gave her the sweet milk to drink.

Moy turned away from the small cup.

"Child drink a little more and make Ma happy." Keem held the cup to Moy's lips.

Then later, Ma called to Grandpa, "Dad, puppy come home."

"Moy, child, you come home!" Grandpa took Moy from Ma's arms. "Moy open your eyes; look at Grandpa and make Grandpa happy." He looked worn out, but he smiled handsomely.

Ma and Grandpa looked very happy. The house smelled of burning incense.

Little Moy stood behind a door. She looked around as it opened, then shouted in delight, "Grandpa, Grandpa!" She ran around him as he walked into his wife's house in Phnom Penh.

"Puppy, you scare Grandpa to death! Dead! Why you naked? Let me hit your butt." He reached for her and tapped her backside gently.

"No. Grandpa must not hit puppy." She pushed his hand away.

"Why puppy naked?"

"Puppy just shit over there," she pointed toward the small bathroom, then led him there.

"Dead! Why you shit here and not in the toilet." He got a can of water and washed it off the area next to the four-foot-tall water tub.

"Puppy still small. Puppy no want to fall in the toilet; then Grandpa has no more puppy to love."

"This one full of problem," he complained.

"This one has no problem." Her littler finger pointed skyward.

"Enough, enough. Sit down and Grandpa bathe you."

"Grandpa must not bathe this one," she told him.

"Why?"

"Grandpa's hand smell bad. This one no like."

"Why my hand smell bad?"

"Grandpa hit this one butt. This one butt has shit." She pointed at her backside.

"Dead! There is shit on my hand!" he shouted.

Laughter came from his wife and children in the main room.

Keem

"Let me hit your butt again!"

"No. Grandpa must not hit this one butt again." Moy wiggled away from him.

"Not smart. Good child not keep say, 'this one,'" he coached her.

"Puppy is good child, Grandpa."

"Yes, you a good child. Let Grandpa wash your butt, then bathe you."

"Grandpa must wash hand with soap first. Smell good, good, then bathe puppy."

"This one only heaven have!" He laughed aloud. There was more laughter from his wife and children in the main room.

Moy walked side by side with Keem, in Pailin.

"A year or two more, you and I can walk with our arm over each other shoulder," Ma told her. Mother and daughter sat next to each other, eating Cambodian fish noodle soup.

"Ma, enough! No more, Ma!" Moy laughed and pushed Ma's hands away.

Keem pinned Moy under her leg and tickled Moy. Ma laughed as her fingers wriggled left and right over Moy. Moy went crazy, wriggling under Ma's leg.

"Ma, my stomach hurt. No more!"

"I tickle you more!" Ma's face was red from laughter.

"Ma, I can no laugh anymore. I pee in my pants!" Moy pushed her hands away.

"You pee your pants, I tickle you more!" Mother and daughter laughed together.

Moy was a choppy little kid. Her hair was cut short like a boy. She was all naked. She tried to run away from Ma. Ma smiled beautifully as she grabbed onto Moy's upper arm and turned her around. She had Moy facedown on her lap.

MOY

"No, no!" Moy screamed and cried, her choppy hands waving madly and her feet kicking.

"Crazy child," Ma laughed.

Moy screamed louder when she felt something cold pushed inside her butt.

"All done." Ma put her down. Ma protected her face with both hands from Moy's small, angry fists. "Sinful, sinful hit your own Ma!" she laughed.

"I shit it out!" Moy yelled, hopping up and down on her feet.

"No. You shit it out, I hit your butt." Ma couldn't stop laughing.

"I shit it out!" Moy walked backward, then sat on her feet. She pushed and pushed on whatever she had inside her. Then she got up on her feet, saying, "I shit it out." Her tiny finger pointed at the little drop on the floor.

"You!" Ma made a grab for her.

Moy ran toward the doorway and shouted in delight, "Grandpa, save me!" She grabbed onto Grandpa's leg, swung behind him, and hung on for dear life.

"What happen, puppy?" He rubbed her head.

"She push ice in my butt!" she complained.

"Not smart!" both Ma and Grandpa told her, as they smiled.

"You must not call your Ma 'she.' Respect your Ma," Grandpa coached her.

"Ma push ice in my butt," Moy repeated again.

"It medicine, and she shit it out. Let me hit her butt." Ma tried to reach for Moy, but Grandpa pushed her hands away.

"Grandpa, carry me." Moy held her hands up.

"No carry her. Her butt not clean," Ma told him.

"My butt clean, clean. See?" Moy showed him her little behind.

"All right. Let's go. Grandpa wash your butt for you." He held onto her hand.

Moy screamed and ran in front of Grandpa when Ma tried to reach for her. Grandpa had a long rope attached to a small metal bucket that he lowered into the water well. He pulled the bucket up and sat it down next to his foot.

"Sit down on your feet and Grandpa wash your butt for you." He poured water from a large metal bowl on her small back, his bare foot wiping left and right on her backside. "You are wet; let Grandpa bathe you."

"No, I bathe myself," she told him. He gave her a small cup, but she pointed at the large bowl in his hand. "I want that."

"No, it too big."

"I want, I want!" she whined, hopping up and down on her feet.

He gave her the bowl.

She held the bowl in both hands and dipped it into the bucket for some water that she then threw over her back. Grandpa tried to help, but she refused, instead getting water all over him. He got mad and held onto her hand as he spanked her backside. She couldn't run away. She cried and dipped water out of the bucket to throw at him.

"What you crazy old person and crazy child do?" Ma asked, leaning on the door frame and laughing.

"She throw water on me!" Grandpa complained.

"Ma, Grandpa pee in his pants," Moy cried and laughed, pointing at Grandpa's wet navy-colored, long pants and white, short-sleeved shirt.

"You crazy grandpa and crazy grandchild," Ma laughed.

Grandpa smiled handsomely, looking somewhat embarrassed. Moy giggled. Then they all three laughed, very happy together at the back of their house in Siem Reap.

"She sleep?" Ma asked.

"She sleep long time ago," Grandpa replied.

"Sad! Your eyes still bright, bright." Ma smiled and rubbed Moy's back.

Baby Moy smiled, her chin resting on Grandpa's shoulder.

"She not sleep yet?" he asked.

"Her eyes still open big, big. Grandpa carry you around the house all night and you still no sleep. Quick, close your eyes and go to sleep," Ma told her.

Moy babbled happily.

"Why puppy very quiet tonight; she has fever?" Grandpa sounded worried.

"No. Her forehead feel cool. Your eyes bright, bright." Ma played with her, and Moy giggled.

"Go put on your clothes, before she give you trouble." Grandpa walked away from Ma.

"I go put on my clothes. No give me trouble." Keem played with the baby.

"Go put on your clothes; no bother my grandchild." Grandpa turned around, and Moy screamed in delight.

"Give me my child, and you go take your bath." Keem tried to get Moy back.

"No." Grandpa and Ma went into a game of tug of war over her, making Moy laugh.

"You have milk? I have milk for her." Ma had her hands around Moy, who was in Grandpa's arms.

"You cheat!" Grandpa shouted with laughter, and Ma laughed with him.

Ma sat on the bed and breastfed her. She sang softly and rocked the baby slowly to sleep in her arms.

* * *

Keem

Those were some of Moy's childhood memories from as far back as she could remember, and they played slowly for her, like movies. That is what made her smile and laugh every day.

How could she remember all those conversations and events since she was a baby, and before she could talk? Perhaps she had gone completely crazy and imagined things and words from so long ago. Or maybe Buddha took pity on her, and blessed Moy with a strong mind so she could remember and relive memories as a little girl surrounded with love from her ma and grandpa again, helping her forget the horror while she lived under the Khmer Rouge claws, so that she could go on. One day, she might get out of this hell on earth and see the bright sunlight again.

1965
Big Angkor Wat

My third stepsister, Papa/Grandpa, Má, and me in Ma's arms.
Ma always got her hair done for Chinese New Year,
and she drowned me in jewels!
I was a year old.

15

After Ming died, there were handfuls of men offering to take his place. Moy just smiled. None of them looked or sounded like him. She wanted a friend to replace the big brother she lost, and she found one, from adult Bike One, in Head Tiger. This one woman looked somewhat like Ming. She had a round face, high cheekbones, and thick lips. She was educated in French and English. Moy went to see her every Sunday night, sitting next to her and listening to the women talk. This woman told Moy her mother had died when she was a little girl, and the Khmer Rouge killed her father. She had a stepmother, a brother, and a little sister. Since their stories were similar, she wanted Moy as a little sister. Moy agreed and went to meet her family in Kompong Kol, during Cambodian New Year. Moy felt the stepmother was not a nice person, but she liked the big sister, so Moy told Chan about it.

Chan didn't want Moy to have a relationship with that woman, because Chan had argued with her a while ago. "That woman is a bad person," Chan told her.

Moy didn't care. She spent two nights in Chan's house. She liked her big brother's small, folding army bed. But Chan didn't want to keep it and gave it away. She neither looked sad nor lonely. She showed Moy a black and white picture of Ming. He looked about thirteen or fourteen years old and wore a white shirt. That was the only picture Chan had. Moy didn't ask for it. Chan told Moy she had dreamed about Ming crying that he knew he died.

"I will die, too, when I twenty-one." How did Ming know?

Let's say he had a gift, more or less like Keem.

* * *

"Last night I dream Grandpa cry. He know he die," Keem told Moy seven days after he had passed away.

It was also seven days after Keem Lai went to heaven that Moy dreamed Keem was standing in front of what might have been a bridge. She was crying, brokenhearted, and Moy looked at her ma from a couple of feet away.

"I die," she told Moy. She just stood there and cried until Moy woke up in the morning.

The Chinese and Cambodians believe that when a person dies with so much love left for his or her loved ones, like Keem had for her daughter; or when they die young and suddenly, like Ming, their souls will hang around until they find justice. And, like all the other souls, seven days after they died, their souls would walk across a bridge from the living to the other side. Then the souls walk down to the river to wash their faces, hands, and feet. Their flesh falls off, and only then does the soul of an individual know that he or she has died.

* * *

Moy spent a night at her new big sister's family's house. She just wanted to have a good time, while the Khmer Rouge was being kind and giving people three days off from work for the Cambodian New Year. Every morning, people had their breakfast at seven o'clock. This was the first time since Moy went to live in the sugarcane fields that the Khmer Rouge had given them breakfast! After breakfast was

Keem

a meeting. The Khmer Rouge told people to work harder, like they hadn't already been. Then it was lunchtime. People ate white rice with large pieces of pork, beef, or chicken and had many more foods like sweet rice cake and iced water! People joked and laughed with their family and friends.

Moy and a couple of other people laughed when they overheard some Khmer Rouge telling each other, "Ice grow on tree." Almost all of the Khmer Rouge were illiterate.

One day after the meeting, Moy stopped in front of a small common kitchen on her way home. From the street, about thirty feet away, she looked at some men sitting on the long benches on one side and women sitting on the other side. Three Khmer Rouges stood behind a long table, calling people's names. A man and a woman came out, one couple at a time. They stood facing each other and exchanged their scarves, then wrapped them around their own necks, in front of the Khmer Rouges. Then everyone clapped their hands. Moy couldn't hear what they said. Then the meeting was over, and Moy heard something like, "Marry..." then, "Success, success, Communist Cambodia!" The Khmer Rouges shouted and everyone repeated after them, three times. Some of the men and women looked happy, but most looked shocked, sad, and scared.

Since Moy didn't understand what the meeting was about, or why the men and women exchanged their scarves, she just started to walk on. Then she heard a shout behind her. She turned around and watched. A lot of women coming from that meeting were crying while the men walked next to them. One man chased after a woman, saying, "Little Sister/Sweetheart, no cry."

"No call me Little Sister. I not your wife!" the young woman shouted at the man. He tried to keep up with her angry march.

"Onka marry us," he tried to explain.

"I no want to marry you!" She cried harder.

Moy stepped aside to let the unhappy newlyweds pass.

Just then, another man came running from the other side of the street, toward the couple. He rooted to the spot and stared at the woman. The husband stepped up quickly and stood next to his new wife.

Then the wife saw the other man. "Big Brother/Sweetheart," she said. Her face lit up like a beautiful full moon. Then she wept in her hands and howled in pain.

Moy couldn't help watching and listening to this heartbreaking scene.

"I not know Onka give her to me," the husband explained to the older man.

"You marry her?" The older man looked like he wanted to die.

"What you want me to do, when Onka marry us? Now she my wife, and I love her!"

The wife cried harder and fell on her knees. The husband tried to help her up, but she yanked her hands away. The older man took a step closer. Moy was afraid the two men were going to have a fistfight and get killed by the Khmer Rouge.

"You know I want her," the older man shouted.

"You want her, but Onka give her to me," the husband shouted back.

"I no want to be your wife!" the woman shouted.

"Onka marry us. Now Little Sister is my wife." The husband looked miserable.

Moy had no idea she was jumping so hard she nearly lost her sarong. Suddenly, the husband, wife, and the older man all turned around, stared, and shouted, "You no have work to do?"

"No. No work. Today is New Year Day." Then Moy left the unhappy people to stare after her.

Keem

Before Moy left Kompong Kol, she had a fight with Chan. She didn't like it when Chan told her she couldn't have a new big sister. Then, a couple of months later, a girl came from Kompong Kol and told Moy that Chan was going to marry her next-door neighbor. Moy's blood boiled. Her big brother was in his grave for just a couple of months, and Chan wanted a new husband. *Sad!* Moy thought. That's what Keem and Wong would say if they were there; then they would shake their heads.

Moy couldn't think about Chan without getting angry. She couldn't talk to Chan and didn't want to see her. And Moy got closer to her new big sister. Then one day, the new sister told Moy her family had been selected to go and live in another town, working on a farm. She wondered if Moy wanted to go with her family.

"Yes," Moy answered without thinking.

Perhaps Keem's spirit wanted Moy to get out of the human chicken coop—now. She knew danger was coming closer to Moy, and this was the only chance for her to escape. Moy didn't feel comfortable with her new family. However, she was not afraid to leave the sugarcane fields.

Before Moy left the sugarcane fields, she told a few girls in her group and big sister Pat. Big Sister Pat was a Khmer Rouge from the south-side salt mine. She was the kindest of all the Khmer Rouge. She believed that if people worked hard, they needed to eat more. When Moy got sick in the field, Big Sister Pat took turns with her second-in-command, carrying Moy in their arms to get home. Big Sister Pat was light-skinned, her face sort of pinched, with a small chin. Her second-in-command was also a nice Khmer Rouge, a full head shorter than Big Sister Pat, but darker skinned. The two women always smiled at the children, men, and women under their command.

The next morning, Moy went to Kompong Kol to see Chan. Moy asked for her gold and clothes back. They got into a big fight. Chan asked Moy why she was doing this and told Moy, "Your big brother very angry with you and ashamed of you, if he here."

"Big brother not here. He no angry with me." For the first time in months, Moy accepted that Ming was gone from her world. She took the gold and clothes and gave them to the stepmother for safekeeping. The stepmother smiled like a hungry shark.

The next day, Moy's new family was like all the other families. They waited all day on the other side of Kompong Kol, the human chicken coop's headquarters. The Khmer Rouge all carried long guns as they went around having tête-à-têtes with people. At about three or four in the afternoon, the army trucks came and took people away. Before the Khmer Rouge let each truck leave, two or three of them would hop on it. They were trying to catch runaways.

Moy sat on a truck that was headed toward Battambang, and they were on the highway for a long time. When they arrived at the small town of Sneung, the commander was there to greet them. They walked a couple of minutes from the main highway into their town. Moy's family went to live in a large house/temple, like the one in Head Tiger at the sugarcane fields. This house/temple was smaller than the one in Head Tiger. There were about fifteen to twenty steps to reach the top. Inside the house, the floor was beautiful, dark-brown wood, and there was just one large room. An elderly Chinese couple lived in the right corner, near the entrance. Their daughter-in-law and grandchildren lived on the left side of the entrance.

Moy's family lived at the back, behind the elderly couple. Moy's family had a curtain around a little corner, like a bedroom. The stepmother and her children slept on a bed. Moy slept on the floor like the Chinese family in front of them. The next day, the stepmother told

Keem

Moy to sleep outside the curtain, because she was the oldest. That didn't bother her. She hadn't felt she belonged to this Cambodian family since she had first met them. Why had she chosen to come with them? She had no answer. But perhaps Keem's spirit helped her pick this new sister for a reason. The big sister went with her group to work in another town, not by choice.

Moy couldn't be happier, living in a house with Chinese people who were Teochew, like her! But she had a first taste of her own medicine that she had forced down Ming's throat when he was alive. She couldn't speak Teochew anymore!

"You a Teochew person and you no speak Teochew? You what kind of Chinese?" the elderly Chinese woman criticized her.

"Grandma, Black Shirt not let me speak Teochew, only Khmer," Moy tried to explain, in Khmer.

"You speak Khmer with Black Shirt. You speak Khmer with Khmer. You speak Teochew when you come home! You no speak Khmer to me. You speak Teochew with me! Chinese must not forget Chinese. If you no respect yourself, who respect you? Sad, sad, sad!" Grandma shook her head and swept a finger furiously left and right in front of Moy.

The Chinese and Cambodian youngsters always addressed an elder as Grandma or Grandpa to show respect for their maturity.

Moy remembered she said almost the same thing to Ming whenever he tried to speak Teochew to her. She could speak Teochew, but poorly, like when Ming tried to speak to their Ma and Grandpa. Keem and Wong always shook their heads at his poor Chinese, like grandma was doing right now. If Ming was watching and listening to grandma lecture Moy, he would laugh. What goes around comes around! She felt hurt and disappointed with herself. Now she understood what Ming meant when he said, "I understand every word. I just can't speak like I want to."

Moy walked and looked around her block. Everything was different from the sugarcane fields. A large house/temple stood across from hers, along with three grass houses. Inside a small common kitchen there were three long wooden benches and tables, but no walls. A small grass house stood behind the kitchen. There was a tiny, but tall, house about three feet off the ground, facing the kitchen. There were more grass and wooden houses behind the other side of the kitchen. Moy's house was on the left of the kitchen, about thirty feet away.

At dinnertime, there were about twelve people eating in the common kitchen. Old and young, they ate white rice with soup that had meat and green vegetables! Everyone ate his or her fill. They ate, talked, and laughed, and the cooks told people to take the leftovers home or the food would get thrown away!

The Khmer Rouge, the human-heart eaters at the sugarcane fields, used to tell the workers there, "You lucky to work in sugar factory; we feed you. The people work at the farms, they have nothing to eat but dirt." So no one wanted to leave the sugarcane fields.

Moy ate and ate the rice with meat-and-green-vegetable soup. Then she asked an elderly cook if she could take some leftovers home. The elderly woman grabbed Moy's hand and dragged her to the stove, where she gave Moy a large bowl of rice and a bowl of soup. The elderly cook warned her that if Moy didn't return the bowls to her by morning, "If I see your face, I take your head and make soup with it!"

"No worry, Grandma. I clean them and give them back to Grandma," Moy laughed.

"Remember your word! It sinful lie to Grandma." The elderly cook shook a finger at her.

"I no lie, Grandma." Moy was very happy to have the leftovers for later.

"Remember, lie is a sin!" the elderly cook reminded her.

Keem

Moy walked away from the elderly cook with arms full of leftovers. She had liked her block the second she jumped off that army truck. Now she knew why.

When she lived in the sugarcane fields, sometimes Moy had daydreamed of eating a whole chicken. Some days tears rolled from her eyes as she daydreamed for a taste of meat or white rice with salt. Every day she ate corn, or small pieces of green bananas, or mung beans mixed with a few grains of rice. Since she had lived at that sugarcane field, she had rice to eat only about a handful of times.

Every time Moy saw a bird fly around in the sky, she had wished she was that bird with wings and could fly away from that sugarcane field.

* * *

For the first month, Moy worked with some elderly men and women in her block, across from her house. She sat with the elders around a large pile of dried corn, peeling off the kernels. The elders always teased each other and made Moy laugh. Then they laughed when they saw her laugh. Sometimes, she had no idea what she had said to make the elders laugh so hard, and they chased her away. They told her if they laughed anymore, they might die from laughing or pee in their pants.

Other times, she helped out in the common kitchen. She cut vegetables, banana tree, and fish or helped wash the pots and pans for the cooks. The two elderly cooks were very happy to have Moy around.

One day, the commander came to take Moy to the meeting in the main town, about five minutes from her block. There were four lines of houses on the left and four lines on the right. The houses were small, with bamboo walls and grass roofs. Each house was about three feet off the ground, with a small porch in front of each house. There were fifty or sixty rows of long wooden benches and tables under the wall-less common kitchen, on the left of the houses. Moy was shocked when she saw six- or seven-year-old boys and girls running around, playing with each other in the main town. She walked past a few people who looked much happier and more carefree than the people in the sugarcane field.

Inside the kitchen, a group of women were in the meeting. No one gave Moy an ugly look or hard stare like she often got at the sugarcane field.

"This Chinese child go work with you for now. She has no mother or father; look after her like your own child," the kindhearted commander of the Khmer Rouge told the women in the meeting.

The women smiled at her!

"Why you cry?" he asked. He looked about thirty, with dark skin, black hair, black eyes, and a long chin. He was handsome.

"Uncle good person; Uncle has good heart," Moy told him, as she wiped tears from her eyes.

"Buddha, pity her!" the women whispered to each other.

16

Moy and the women went to work in another town. They traveled in seven wagons; each pulled by two cows. Every woman was someone's wife, mother, and grandmother. Moy was the youngest in the group. The women whispered to each other that the stepmother was cruel to Moy. They didn't like the mean woman. The Chinese lady who lived in the same house with Moy had told someone, and the word got out.

Once a week, the Chinese lady's husband brought some fruit home for his family. They always shared the fruit with Moy's family. At first, the stepmother did share a small amount of fruit with Moy. She ate it by herself, outside the stepmother's curtain. Moy didn't know the Chinese family was watching. Then one day, the nice Chinese lady asked her, "Moy, your mother give you any fruit to eat?"

"No, Aunty," Moy told her in Khmer.

"Why your mother no love you like she love your little brother and little sister?"

"She not my mother, but adopted mother. I like her older daughter; she good to me," Moy told Aunty in Teochew after Grandma gave her a hard stare.

From that day forward, Aunty gave enough fruit to the stepmother for only three people instead of four. Aunty always gave some fruit to Moy directly and told her, "Go eat downstair; no let them see you."

Then one day while Moy was eating the fruit, the stepmother came from work and yelled at her, "Why you take my fruit? Bad child!"

"I no take Mother's fruit. Aunty give them to me."

"I no believe you," the stepmother shouted at her.

Moy didn't say anything, but Grandma was watching and listening from the common kitchen. Then she told her daughter-in-law about it. That made Aunty and Grandma angry, and they stopped giving fruit to the stepmother. Whenever Uncle brought the fruit home, either Aunty or Grandma would give it to Moy the next day, telling her to go eat it in the common kitchen, in front of the cooks.

"If she asks where you get the fruit, tell her, 'Grandma Cook give them to me,'" both Aunty and Grandma taught Moy.

Aunty was a tall lady, and Uncle was a large man. He didn't talk much. He came home once a week, spent one night, then left the next morning. Aunty made clothes for people in town and for the Khmer Rouge. Grandma and Grandpa were short. Grandpa hardly had hair on his head. Grandma's hair was all white. They hardly smiled, but they had good hearts. Aunty and Uncle also hardly smiled, but their hearts were always cheerful and kind to Moy. Grandma's family were not talkative people, but they observed everything around them. And these Cambodian women from Sneung were also kind to Moy. They looked after her like she was their daughter.

The wagons took Moy and the women to a long, red wooden house. They didn't have time to do anything when they got there. After their dinner, they bathed under the bright moon. Then they slept on a long platform with many adults. There were about two hundreds girls and boys also living in that house. They looked hungry and painfully thin and slept on the concrete floor or in their hammocks.

The girls and boys got up at around six in the morning. Moy and the women slept late. There were about twenty women in her group. Three women stayed home to cook for their group. Moy's group was there to pull the tree potatoes/yuccas. Some of the potatoes were over a foot long, the size of a baby's wrist, or a woman's ankle. The branches were well over seven to ten feet tall. If the potatoes were small, it was easy to pull them out, but if they were large, it was difficult. There were knuckle holes all around the branches, where the stumps came off. The leaves were shaped more like oak leaves. Those potatoes were best to eat when they first came from the ground. They would turn brown and bitter if they were kept too long.

The boys and girls pulled the potatoes on the other side from Moy's group. She wondered why they didn't cook some of the tree potatoes and eat them or just eat them raw. The tree potatoes tasted somewhat like sweet potatoes, but with thicker milk.

At lunchtime, a man with a cow-drawn wagon brought food in large pots for Moy's group to eat. Moy and the women sat under a large tree and ate their lunch in three small groups. Everyone had a plate full of white rice. Each group shared a large bowl of fish and banana tree soup. The driver ate with a group of women, and the women talked and laughed while they ate.

"Eat, Niece, eat! Niece very thin. We have a lot of food." A woman pointed at the rice and soup pots next to them.

"I eat," Moy smiled.

"You thin like monkey! Eat!" An elderly woman shook a finger at her.

Moy felt like a daughter and granddaughter to all these kindhearted women who didn't see her as a Chinese. They told each other, "Anyone's child is your own child. Anyone's grandchild is your own grandchild." These educated women saw Moy as a human being. She needed to eat when she was hungry, cry when she felt pain, scream when she was angry. She would need someone to care for her if she got sick. She needed someone to comfort her if she felt lonely. She would laugh if she was happy.

She ate and chattered along with the women. Now and then, the elders tried to kick her out of the group so they could have "old, old people talk."

"I no listen," Moy told them.

"Man, man spoil," an elderly woman started. Then she went on, "What man, man do? He only think about his penis!" She shouted angrily.

Everyone laughed. Some women laughed so hard they fell over the soup bowl and spilled it everywhere.

"Old Grandma, old Grandma, watch your word. A child here!" the red-faced driver shouted through his laughter.

"Ha. Moy, no listen to Grandma. Go away!" grandma told her and waved her off with a spoon and rice plate.

"No," Moy shook her head as she laughed like all the women, though she didn't understand what Grandma was talking about.

"Let her listen. When she marry, she know it anyway," one woman defended her.

"She too young listen to old, old people talk. Moy, go away!" Grandma tried to kick her out again.

"She not too young. Moy, you how old?" a woman asked.

"Almost fifteen."

"She marry tomorrow; let her listen!"

"If she not know what happen, she'll be scare when she has husband," another woman spoke up.

"Why this good for her to know? Man, man only think about their penis, nothing else!"

"Old Grandma!" the driver shouted through his laughter.

"It true," Grandma nodded as she went on. "You think at my age, my old grandpa not want me? Every day, he get home, he throw my sarong up…"

Keem

"Old Grandma, watch your word!" Everyone howled with laughter, tears rolling from their eyes.

"After he finish his business, he ask 'What you cook for dinner tonight?' I tell him, 'Your penis.'" She held her plate up.

Moy laughed so hard, she fell over like most of the women. Old Grandma laughed at her own joke, like everyone else. Moy sat up, wiped tears from her eyes, and kept giggling.

Then she just happened to notice a girl sitting alone under a big tree not too far from Moy. The girl looked left and right carefully, like she was afraid of something. Carefully, she put something in her mouth. Then her hands pulled on the grass and played with it. And she looked left and right again, about to put something into her mouth.

A man carrying a long gun came from behind the tree. He appeared suddenly, and he pulled the food out of the girl's hand. He shoved her shoulder, and she fell over on her side, crying, wiping tears off with the back of her hand. The Khmer Rouge said something, shook a finger at her, then kicked the poor girl so hard she fell on her face and her head bounced backward. Then he grabbed her arm, yanked her up to her feet, and dragged her behind him toward a large group of children.

"Khmer look down on our own people," a woman standing next to Moy whispered, sounding very sad.

What could that poor girl have had to get that kind of abuse? Perhaps she had a small bite or even a mouthful of the tree potatoes.

"Khmer kill our kind!" one woman wept.

Moy watched. The Khmer Rouge had that girl stand in front of all the other children. He said something. The children laughed and pointed at her.

Moy looked away. She knew what it was like to be hungry and abused by others. *Fight back! Don't cry. Don't let them see you cry!* she thought. Still, she knew each person must find her own way to cope with fear and abuse and go on living, like Moy had, and she hoped to see a better day soon.

"Girl, girl, let go back to work. Let not stay here and watch Khmer abuse Khmer. It break our heart and die!" Old Grandma shouted the order.

Moy looked back at that girl. Her head hung low as the children laughed at her.

"No look back, Niece," an elderly woman told Moy. Her hand rested on Moy's head as they both walked behind the other women to the far side of the potato field to pull more tree potatoes.

Moy didn't have to work hard. The women pulled one or two potatoes, then stood there and chatted about this or that. She didn't understand what the "old, old people" chatted about, but she smiled and laughed with them. Every now and then, one of the women would ask, "Right or wrong, Moy?"

"Right," she would saying, nodding.

"Niece must hold Aunt's feet a little," another woman told her. She meant that Moy must defend her or take her side.

"If I hold Aunt's feet, how can Aunt walk around?" Moy went along with the joke, bringing more laughter.

After two weeks working in the potato field, Moy's group went home. Later, the group got sent to work in another town. One day, Moy wanted a snack and found some long, green leaves. She boiled them in salt water and ate them, but then she couldn't stop hiccupping. The women tried to scare her to make the hiccups stop, but no matter what they said or did, her hiccups went on and on. Some of the women started worrying. They got up in the middle of night and got water for her to drink. Some older men and women whispered that Moy might be poisoned by something. Finally, an elderly Cambodian man, who was a witch doctor, went out in the middle of night. He came back with a bowl of water that was gray looking and told Moy to drink every drop; then he asked a woman to rub Moy's stomach.

"Dead! Her stomach hard like wood!" the elderly woman shouted. She sounded horrified but kept rubbing Moy's belly.

Moy threw up everything she had eaten, and the hiccups stopped. Some women helped her lay down. She closed her eyes and went to sleep.

But before she fell asleep, she heard people whisper around her, "This child has been poisoned. If we waited a little longer, she will die."

"Her stomach hard like wood!"

"Pity her much. Always hungry at her age."

In the morning, Moy felt weak like a baby. Food poisoning was no fun! When she got up with the rest of them, the women told her to stay home and sleep. The women from Sneung asked a couple of people from other towns, who had stayed home for some reason, to look after Moy. A few days later, Moy and the women went back to Sneung.

Shortly afterward, Moy returned home when she got an eye infection. It started with one eye, then both. Her eyes were badly infected, causing great pain in opening her eyes and keeping them open. She heard the elders whisper around her that they feared she might go blind from her eyes infection. They felt sorry for the Chinese child. But there was nothing they could give her or do to help her. She was scared and cried. She didn't want to be blind and not be able to see. She cried even more when the stepmother told her one morning, "It disgusting to look at your infect eye; they make me want to throw up." Then she went to work.

"No cry too much and hurt your eye some more. No rub or touch them, keep wash your face and eye. No cry because she speak ugly to you," Aunty told Moy.

Moy tried very hard not to cry, but she missed her ma and wished Keem was there. *If Ma were here, she would know what to do with my eyes. Ma would take all the infection and pain away. Ma, I want you! Ma, help me! I don't want to be blind,* she thought, terrified. She cried herself to sleep every night, longing to feel Keem's warm arms around her. Then one morning she woke up, and while sitting up suddenly remembered that Wong Lai's fourth son once had a fight with his friend. He got hit on the chest and had chest pain. Wong told his son to drink a baby's pee, that it would stop the pain, and it did.

"But you must not drink your own pee. It will break your strength," he also said. Baby's pee could be used like medicine; it was good for many things.

Moy also remembered that after her family lost their big house, business, and fortunes because of her third uncle's betrayal, they left Siem Reap in the middle of the night to go to Phnom Penh. There, they lived in a tiny apartment with another family, behind the palace. Keem and Wong made Chinese/Cambodian oil or orange cakes (fried rice cake with sweet mung beans inside) to sell on the sidewalk. At that time, Moy was five or six years old, and Keem taught her how to hold a long tray on her hip. Each tray held two hundred small cakes, on top of each other. It took Moy more than forty minutes to walk to the business district. She went from one or two in the afternoon to eight or ten at night, seven days a week. Sometimes, after she finished selling all the cakes, she would sneak in to see the Cambodian movies by grabbing onto some man's hands saying, "Uncle, let me in with you." Then she would duck her head, trying to hide.

The men always laughed and took her in with them. Moy would wait at the cheapest seats. Not many people wanted to sit up close to the screen, so the middle seats were the most expensive seats in any theater. After the movie started, she'd look for an empty middle seat.

Keem

One day, she was playing with an old bike when her left foot got cut on the rusty chain. Keem put the liquid red medicine on it, but Moy's foot kept swelling up. She kept going to sell the cakes until she could hardly walk. Then she cried and told her ma, "My foot hurt."

"Child, no cry. Help Ma one more day. We poor, and you must learn to deal with it. Wipe tear away and go sell the cake. Ma go help you sell them," Keem told her daughter in Chinese. The cakes would get thrown away if they didn't sell them, and they had very little money. Tomorrow, they would make fewer cakes so Moy could stay home.

Moy cried and hopped slowly, grabbing on to the tray of cakes in her hand and on her hip. She wiped tears away, like her ma told her. She hopped around and sold the cakes outside the movie theater. Then she went inside the noodle shops, mostly the bar areas.

"Uncle help buy my cake," she asked at each table, in Khmer.

"Little sister, why you cry and sell cake?" the men asked, laughing.

"My foot hurt, Uncle. Help. Buy my cake." She showed them the cakes.

"Dead! Why you come to sell cake when your foot swollen and hurt like that? Buddha, pity her!" The men looked at each other around the tables, shaking their heads.

"I poor, and I must help my ma and Grandpa," she explained.

"The Ma and Grandpa poor, and this small child must help. Pity her much. Let see, Uncle help. You guy come, help buy this child cake!" the men told each other, and some of them bought from two to twenty cakes.

"Little sister come here," a man at another table called to her. He bought fifty cakes and told his large group of friends that watching and listening to a small child help her family make a living made him feel ashamed and angry with his adult children. "Those unlucky one only eat the rice away and act silly, but not know how to make a living!" he complained loudly.

"And you buy the cakes for them to eat?" one of his friends asked.

"After they eat, then I kick them out, and the wife go with those unlucky one, too! I tell the truth! I very hot and angry!" he shouted, but his friends laughed.

"Why you stare at me like that?" one of the friends asked Moy.

"How many cake Uncle want to buy? Mr. Rich buy fifty," she told the friend who sat next to Mr. Rich.

The men laughed and teased that Mr. Rich should buy all the cakes for them. Mr. Rich said if he had children like Moy, they'd make him a billionaire. Mr. Rich's friends asked her, if they bought and ate her cakes, would they have smart children like her?

"I pray to Buddha, let Uncle have children smarter than me!" She looked toward heaven and prayed.

"Hear that? Your Ma teach you how to talk like this?" Mr. Rich laughed.

"No, Uncle, I born to talk. My ma say, 'You talk and talk. Your tongue never get tired!'" She shook a finger, imitating Keem.

Later, Moy saw her ma in front of the theater. Keem didn't do well selling the cakes. Moy traded her empty tray for a tray of cakes from her ma. Keem wanted her daughter to sit down somewhere, but Moy said, "No, I still little. People feel sad for me when they see my foot, and I can sell faster. Ma wait here for me."

"Like that, my child?" Keem brushed hair away from her daughter's face.

"Yes. We poor, and we must deal with it. Ma no cry. I go finish sell the cake; then we go home." She wiped her ma's tears away then went to sell the cakes.

The next day, Wong brought dry mushrooms home. His friends had told him to soak them in baby's pee overnight, then put it on Moy's foot, where the cut was, and let it "suck out the poison." It took a long time, but it healed her foot.

Keem

* * *

Moy just couldn't go around and ask for baby's pee, and she didn't know what to do. But then she went to pee and, without thinking, put a drop of it in her eye. It was pure fire! Though very painful at first, the pain gradually eased away. Then she treated the other eye and had the same reaction. She treated her eyes a couple of times each day, always careful to wash her hands and cheeks after each treatment. She didn't wash her eyes until bath time, in the evening. It took a long time, but slowly the infection went away. All the elders were surprised and happy for her. When they asked, she told them what she did.

"That Chinese child very smart. She know how to take care of herself," the elders told each other.

On one of the Cambodian holidays, about thirty children came home for two days. The goodhearted commander came to take Moy to meet Momb, who was the girls' general. The commander told Moy she would go with Momb after the holiday to work with the children. She liked Momb right away, and Momb liked her. Momb was light-skinned and round-faced, with big black eyes and black hair. She had a small, black birthmark on one side of her lip. She was taller and wider, and a few years older, than Moy. For those two days, Moy and Momb were always together, one Chinese and one Cambodian. Each would follow the other around.

One day, Momb took Moy to the tree potato fields to pull potatoes. Then they cooked and ate them in the field. Moy was afraid of getting caught by the commander/uncle. She didn't want to get kicked like that poor girl had been, and she told Momb about it.

"Uncle good person. He no say anything or do anything. If he see us eat potatoes, you know what Uncle say?" Momb looked very serious and leaned toward her.

"No." Moy leaned away as she took a bite of a potato.

"If Uncle see us, he say, 'You hungry? Good. Eat, eat until you full. Eat!' Why you so scare?" Momb laughed, looking at Moy carefully.

"I no scare; I no want Uncle angry with us." Moy bit and chewed on the potatoes.

"Uncle is Khmer Red, but he good person. Uncle no happy if he see people in our town go hungry. We very lucky have Uncle for our commander," Momb told her.

"Yes! Some people very mean. They no give food to anyone to eat, and make people work very hard," Moy told her new friend.

Momb told her she liked this Khmer Rouge from the north. They wanted people to work hard, and they let people eat. Some other groups, like the south side, were mean. They worked people to the bone and starved them to death. At the sugarcane fields, it was the south-side Khmer Rouge who were nice. Big Sister Pat was from the south. It really meant nothing where these Khmer Rouge came from. Some of them were kind, and some were mean and evil.

Momb told her that Uncle/commander was the second-in-command of their block. The south-side Khmer Rouge had stripped his title and authority as commander of the town. The town of Sneung was ruled by a woman from the south. She made people work hard and wouldn't feed them.

"She no good, but she away right now, and we only have Uncle. All of us afraid she might hit Uncle away. When she come back, we go hungry again. I hate her!" Momb looked very angry when she spoke about the woman from the south. She would smile whenever she spoke of the kindhearted commander. Her smile became wider as she stared at Moy, then said, "Tomorrow you go with me! You no call me or anyone Buddy. Just call me Big Sister Momb, and call everyone else by their name. No Buddy. I no like Buddy. Tomorrow at ten o'clock, I come and get you. We take some tree potatoes with us, yes?" Momb asked, and they giggled.

"Yes," it was nice to talk and smile with Momb.

Momb and Uncle/commander were Cambodians, but they were nice. They were brought up properly by their good and educated parents. Whether their parents taught them or they taught themselves, they looked beyond a person's language, underneath a person's clothes and the different languages people speak around the world—Chinese, Vietnamese, English, or any other language—to see that each of those people is a simple human being. Momb and Uncle were educated, and they understood that. But that evil Khmer Rouge Vulture and Girl were not.

17

The next day, Moy and Momb had an early lunch at the common kitchen, and then they were on their way to their group. Moy had her small clothes bag with her. The two girls walked through the main block and out into the jungle, where the footpath was just large enough for two cow wagons to go through. The girls walked and chatted about this or that and laughed now and then. Then Momb said they should stop. They picked up three small rocks and made a stove and fire at the side of the footpath. They boiled the tree potatoes in Momb's small metal pot, and then they each wrapped some potatoes in one end of her scarf. They walked, talked, and ate at the same time.

After close to a two-hour walk, the girls entered a small village in the middle of the jungle with about twenty houses of grass roofs and walls. The houses surrounded a wall-less common kitchen with five to ten rows of long wooden benches and tables.

"Come to my mother's house," Momb told her.

"Big Sister Momb's mother live here?" Moy was surprised Momb's mother didn't live in Sneung.

"Uncle tell me go to Sneung and get you." Momb pointed at her. Then she added that she liked going to Sneung to see her older sister, who always cooked tree potatoes for Momb to eat. Before they entered a small house, Momb turned around and told her, "No tell my mother, yes?"

"No tell your mother what?" Moy asked.

"Mother, I come home!" Momb shouted and smiled at Moy.

"Yell, yell, yell like baby!" Moy heard the complaint from inside the house. She walked in behind Momb and saw a tall, thin woman sitting on a wooden bed, three feet off the ground and which occupied most of the house. All their belongings were pushed to one side of the bed, against the wall, and they slept on the other side. About two feet from the bed was a tiny hallway.

"Good!" The woman's smile became wider when she saw Moy behind her daughter.

"Aunt," Moy lowered her eyes and head with respect for her elder. It was the Cambodian custom and expected of her.

"Look at this child! Speak like lady! You, yell, yell like baby!" Momb's mother shook a finger at her.

"I love Mother very much!" Momb hugged her mother around the waist.

Moy giggled, but she felt like crying. *I want to hug Ma and Grandpa like Momb is doing, but Ma and Grandpa aren't anymore*, she thought.

"Look! You no embarrass? Look at her. She younger than you, but like a lady." Momb's mother smiled and playfully pushed her daughter away.

"Now you know why I want to go to Sneung and no live here with my mother." Momb made faces at Moy and they giggled.

Shortly afterward, the girls left the village. Momb was a general and had to be at the camp before the other girls. Moy and Momb walked past a small pond behind the village. Momb told her the villagers used the water from the pond for cooking and bathing. After the girls walked past that pond, the jungle closed around them. They walked on a small footpath and made so many left and right turns that Moy lost count.

Later, the girls reached their home. The tall house had no walls, just the white, standard metal roof and the concrete floor, at ground level. There were hammocks tied this way and that way onto the many large, round wooden poles. Small piles of dry brown grass were here and there, and small clothes bags lay on the concrete floor. There was a small pond across from the house, and the blue sky looked at itself cheerfully in the pond. Small and large trees, tall grass, and bushes surrounded the wall-less house.

"They faster than us! Come," Momb complained as she pulled Moy toward the two empty wooden poles at the edge of the house. She helped Moy tie a brown rice bag to the poles for use as a hammock.

The house reminded Moy of something—a house and area like this where she had been before. But she couldn't remember where. About fifty feet away from their house was a small shelter covered in coconut leaves. Momb told her Group Two lived there. Moy was in Group One. Some days, the children's commander had Group One and Group Two work together. They grew pumpkins, corn, mung beans, and rice.

Later, Momb took her to a pumpkin field about twenty minutes from their house. There was row after row of inch-long, green pumpkin vines shyly peeking out of the ground. On the other side of the field, some pumpkins were the size of a baby or an elephant's head. The skins on the small, young pumpkins were green and soft looking. The older, larger pumpkins were light pink or dark orange and tough looking. Some of their leaves were big enough to wrap around Moy. The pumpkin leaves had many pointy angles along the edges. The pumpkin vines were everywhere. Some vines were light green, and some were dark green with silver fur all around.

The girls broke off two handfuls of tips from the hairy pumpkin vines, and Momb picked a small, young, green pumpkin. The girls wrapped these in one end of their scarves, and then they went to the peanut field. The foot-tall peanut bushes were about a hand's width around. Momb told Moy not to pull the whole bush out, or Big Sister Heng, the children's commander, would yell at them. So they only pulled one or two stems from each bush. Moy sat on her feet, like Momb, and pulled the peanuts. The peanuts came out with dirt dangling from the roots. Moy watched as Momb tapped the dangling peanuts on her palms to gently knock the dirt off. Then Moy did the same. Each girl wrapped the peanuts in another part of her scarf to take home.

By the time Moy and Momb got home, the other girls were there, each with a small cooking stove formed by three little rocks. The girls talked and laughed while they cooked their pumpkins or peanuts. They stopped chattering when they saw Moy standing next to Momb. Moy's black outfit was a gift from the Khmer Rouge at the sugarcane field. Most of her clothes from Pailin were old and torn. The girls from Sneung wore whatever colored clothes they had. They whispered to each other about Moy's black outfit and black sandals, like Momb and their commander wore.

A large woman, very light-skinned, got up from her hammock and smiled. Momb was busy making a cooking stove with three rocks, and she told the commander that Uncle wanted Moy to come here to work with them.

"Very good." Big Sister Heng's smile was friendly.

Moy lowered her eyes with respect for this kindhearted woman of the Khmer Rouge. She had a feeling she had met this woman somewhere before.

"She very shy," the girls whispered. They wondered if Moy was going to be their captain.

"Little Sister, you come from sugar factory?" Big Sister Heng greeted her in a soft voice.

"Yes, Big Sister." Moy kept her head low.

"What you have there?" she pointed at the mounds hanging down in Moy's scarf.

Moy told her peanuts and pumpkin vines. Momb told Moy she didn't have to tell Big Sister Heng anything, that she knew Momb liked to eat.

"You follow the big stomach. She always eat and eat; never stop," Big Sister Heng complained. Moy returned her smile.

Moy and Momb helped each other wash and cook the pumpkin and vines in salt water. They boiled the peanuts in a different pot. The two girls shared the food with Big Sister Heng. Moy thought that was their dinner, but at six o'clock, three girls brought a large pot of white rice and a large pot of banana tree soup with fish for about sixty girls. They ate their fill.

When Moy lived in the sugarcane fields, sometimes people drank rice soup. They couldn't find the rice to chew on, just water to drink, and they had to work all day and night.

* * *

After dinner, most girls took their shirts off and tied their sarongs above their chests, or kept their pants and shirts on. They went to the pond across from their house and took their bath. The silver moonlight was all the girls had to see by, and they had fun bathing under the beautiful silver moon. Millions of little stars in the dark sky twinkled down upon the giggling girls, who ran back and forth, dipping water out of the pond with their small metal bowls or pots, then tipping the water over their heads. One hand held the bowls or pots of water over their heads, while their free hand rubbed their hair, face, chest, arms, or legs. Some girls threw water at each other, laughing. A few girls screamed as they slipped into the pond. Some girls laughed and some girls yelled that the water in the pond was for cooking and drinking, not for swimming. After their bath, the girls sat around in their hammocks or on their homemade grass mats and chatted, until Big Sister Heng told them to go to bed.

That night, Moy lay in her hammock and stared at the full moon. It was bright, and millions of little stars twinkled down at her. Then she heard a wolf cry and another wolf answer. Suddenly, a gun was fired! Moy jumped in her hammock, and memories flooded back like it was yesterday. It was not this place or this wall-less house. It was in another town, almost two years earlier, when Keem Lai and Wong Lai were alive, and they lived at the French Farm. There were a lot of coconut trees, milk fruits, oranges, pineapples, and bananas. (The round milk fruits have very thin, green- or dark-red-colored skin, are soft and white inside, and sweet.)

Moy remembered that awful day. Her memories played back slowly, like a movie. The headman from their block came and took her away from Keem and Wong. The headman grabbed onto Moy's hand, and she fell as he dragged her out of the house on her side, back, or face. Moy tried to grab onto something and her skin blanketed Mother Earth, who drank Moy's blood when the headman yanked Moy around like a little puppy. Wherever she touched, she left a trail of blood from her small hand or infected ankle, and tears from her frightened eyes. She cried for her ma to help, but a Khmer Rouge had his arms around Keem to keep her from following her daughter.

Wong looked horrified when he saw Moy's blood and tears. He sat at the edge of their bed, watching helplessly as tears dripped from behind his thick eyeglasses. He was too sick and old. He couldn't get down and help her. He just sat there, watching helplessly, and cried in silence. Perhaps he begged Buddha in heaven to help his young, innocent granddaughter.

Keem's tears could have filled an ocean. She cried and screamed in horror as she watched her only child dragged, like a piece of raw meat by a mad dog, out of their house. She wanted to run to her daughter and save Moy from the abuser, but Keem was imprisoned inside the Khmer Rouge's strong arms. Keem screamed loudly, like she wanted to open the door of heaven for Buddha to look down and see the injustices being done to her little daughter. How could any man drag a hurt and helpless child like that mad dog headman did?

That toothless headman took Moy to the children's group. The house where they took her was like this one. Her brown-rice-bag-hammock was tied to the poles at the edge of that house, just like right now. Back then, she looked at the full silver moon and tried to think of a way to get home to Ma and Grandpa. She cried from missing her ma, longing for Keem's warm arms around her. She stared at the bright full moon and stars. Then she heard a wolf cry and the gunfire. The bright full moon and the twinkling stars had been putting Moy to sleep with an aching heart, and a storm of tears washed her face then, like it was doing now. Back then, she had hoped to see her ma and grandpa again. Now, there was no hope for her to see or feel Keem's or Wong's warm arms around her again—ever. Moy would get up tomorrow and face another sunrise inside the freedom…cage.

The next morning, the girls got up at seven, roused by Big Sister Heng's soft shouts. After the girls came back from washing their faces and mouths, Big Sister Heng took them to work. The girls carried bent shovels on their shoulders and walked fifteen or twenty minutes to a large, open field. The land was already plowed, and the small holes were ready. Big Sister Heng gave each girl a can of corn seeds.

Moy wrapped the corn seeds in one end of her scarf, like all the girls did. Each girl had a row to work on. Moy's left hand held onto the mound of corn seeds in her scarf as she used three fingers from her right hand to pick up three or four corns seeds and throw them in each hole. Then she swept dirt back into the holes with her feet, tapping gently on top before moving on, planting more corn, like all the girls were doing. When she finished her row and looked back, all the other girls were only halfway through with their rows. She didn't know what to do. She went to ask Big Sister Heng if she wanted Moy to help the others, and the commander couldn't have been happier.

"You work very fast!" The kindhearted woman told Moy to rest first, then help the others if she wanted.

Moy thanked her and went to sit under a small tree. She heard the girls whispering to each other that Moy was very shy, worked very fast, and called everyone Buddy. Their remarks made Moy feel good. She got up and helped the girl who worked next to her. From that day on, the girls liked her and wanted to work next to her.

One day, Momb was not herself. She yelled at everyone or anything that moved. After lunch, Moy tried to cheer her friend up and called her over. Momb walked toward her, asking, "What?" at the top of her lungs. She sounded very angry about something.

"I tell Big Sister something." Moy patted the spot next to her.

Momb sat down. The other girls were resting close by.

Moy told Momb about a movie she had seen a long time ago. She remembered very little; she was just trying to cheer Momb up. Soon, all the girls formed in a circle and listened to the story. Group One and Group Two were all together. From then on, Momb frequently made Moy tell her stories.

"I no remember any movie." Moy would tell the truth, trying to escape from telling a story.

"Make it up; I no care. You stay right here!" Momb pointed at her.

One day, Momb and Group Two's general, a Khmer Rouge's daughter, fought to have Moy in their group. Momb shouted that Moy is in Group One, not Group Two. The Khmer Rouge's daughter shouted back, "You want listen to the story, and I want listen, too!"

Big Sister Heng had to step in between the two generals before a fistfight broke out. Moy tried to be a peacemaker by telling the two generals she would work with Group One that day, and the next she would work with Group Two. Momb wouldn't speak to her. Those days, Moy was in good spirits and made funny faces at Momb until the older girl laughed. Then they became friends again.

* * *

One night, Moy was startled awake by a wolf cry. The jungle was very quiet, and the girls were dead asleep. Moy looked around and saw small, round, bright flashlights everywhere around the wall-less house, just a couple of feet away from the sleeping girls. Moy looked carefully, and saw the bushes and leaves moving ever so slightly. Some of the flashlights blinked as they seemed to move closer to the house—and her. Then Moy heard some girls whimpering softy.

Without thinking, Moy shouted, "Scream!"

Everyone screamed as loud as she could. They were scared stiff, and some girls sobbed aloud.

"Hit something and make loud noise!" Moy shouted.

The girls rushed around, grabbing their metal spoons and rice plates to hit on them. Every little bush and leaf moved as the bright flashlights turned around and ran away. That was one large pack of wolves! The girls and Moy almost got eaten alive by them. Later, a couple of Khmer Rouge showed up and spoke to Big Sister Heng. They laughed and fired a few shots, then told the girls not to worry before they left.

A couple of weeks after planting the corn, the girls moved to the small village where Momb's mother lived. The girls lived in an open field, without a roof or wall. Moy cut a large pile of dry grass and put it under a small tree to use as a bed. She learned from watching the other girls who were doing it. The girls had come to work at the rice paddies, where golden-skinned rice grew on two-to-three-foot-tall stalks.

Keem

Every girl had a three-foot-wide area where she would work, half bent over, to grab the plant and cut it with a sickle. Then she would grab the plant and twist it close to where the rice was. Using the stalks like a rope, she tied an armful of rice stalks in a pile, and left them to dry in the sun for a few weeks. Then either another group of children or the older people would take over. Each person would pick up a pile and swing it on a piece of board to make the rice come off the stalks. Then another group would use grinders to remove golden skin, yielding brown rice. The brown rice then needed to be ground gently to get the brown skin off, turning it into white rice.

As Moy worked, she swept the sickle from her right hand around the plant, then pulled toward the right to cut. She was the slowest at cutting, and soon she had half of a paddy to herself! And the other girls had each left a little area on both sides around Moy for her to do, too. Big Sister Heng yelled at them for picking on poor Moy. She told the girls to get back in the field and help Moy at the end of the day. Despite cutting slowly, Moy nearly lost her third finger once when the sickle slipped from her hand and she tried to catch it. It cut her fingers in an *L* shape.

One cold night, Moy had trouble sleeping under a small tree. She sat up and rubbed her arms to get warm. Moy watched a girl not far from her as she got up from her grass bed, then crawled in between the folded pile of grass. This way, the bottom half of the grass was her bed, the top half was her blanket. Moy followed the girl's example. It was much warmer than a real blanket, but it itched! Still, she got a good night's sleep after a long day of hard work in the rice paddy. Sometimes it rained all night, and the girls would sit under the trees in the rain and wind, because no one could get any sleep. Then they had to work the next day.

When their work at one rice paddy was done, the girls moved on to the next paddy where, again, there was no shelter. This time, Moy got smarter. She cut a lot of dry grass, and then she used thin vines to bind them to two long sticks and two shorter sticks. Using a big rock, she hammered a couple of larger sticks into the ground; then she tied the two long sticks with the dry grass onto them. Now she had two walls. One wall was lower than the other at the top, so they formed a roof and wall. Then she added a third, smaller wall at one end. She made a little door, tied up with vines, that she could flip up and down. Everyone laughed at her, but she didn't say anything. She went out and found more branches and laid them inside her little house. Then she placed a lot of dry grass on top of the branches. Now Moy had a soft little bed, inside her own tiny house! She was warm and dry inside her shelter, while the other girls sat in the rain and wind, shivering in the cold. One night it rained very hard, and something cold, like ice, woke Moy up.

"Moy, let me come in and sleep with you."

"If you come in, where I sleep?" It was dark inside, and she couldn't see who the girl was. Outside, thunder and lightning screamed.

The girl got mad and pulled a wall off. Moy got up and shouted angrily, and put the wall back again. She heard Big Sister Heng yell at the girl for picking on Moy. The next day, while Moy ate her lunch, she heard Big Sister Heng tell the two generals that Moy was very smart, and that they should make shelters like she had. Big Sister Heng let the girls have the afternoon off to make shelters. Big Sister Heng and the two generals shared a larger shelter.

Moy's group got a new captain, and one day Moy didn't feel well, so she asked to stay home. The captain refused. She told Moy to go to work. When Moy felt hot and cold, she called out for help before falling slowly to the ground. Some girls screamed for others to help Moy. Four girls carried her to a large tree and put her down in the shade. All the girls yelled at the captain for making Moy work when she was sick.

This was not the first time Moy had had a fever. She had had fevers many times when she lived in the sugarcane fields at Head Tiger. Everyone else would go home to their families, while Moy was sick at the hospital shelter for females, where everyone slept in two long beds. A Khmer Rouge nurse would give everyone the same medicines, made from tree bark, and thin rice soup with salt to eat. Moy missed going home to see her big brother many times, but he always sent word through the girls. When Moy got better, he would ask her to come home and see him if there was a meeting in Kompong Kol. One time when she was not sick, but just tired and wanting to sleep and eat, Ming showed up.

"Why you no go home and visit me?" He sounded worried.

"I tired," she told him.

"Why you tired? You no like me?" He looked hurt.

"I lazy." She kept her head down.

"Has someone abuse you? Has someone want you to do something you no like?" he asked.

She didn't answer, just played with her fingers.

"I can no help you if you no tell Big Brother what make you unhappy." Ming sat at the edge of the long wooden bed she shared with all the girls.

She refused to look at him. She wanted him to go home. She didn't want Vulture to see them together, since he might hurt her big brother.

"You no want to talk, no talk. I can no help you." Ming got up and walked out of the house.

Moy felt hollow. Later, the girls yelled at her for being difficult and giving Ming a hard time. The girls told her she was lucky to have a big brother who loved her. That evening she felt bad when she saw Ming eating alone in the common kitchen. When she went over and sat next to him, he looked surprised. He told her he had asked for two days off so he could come to Head Tiger to see her.

"Hungry?" he asked.

"I already eat."

"I ask, *you hungry?*"

"Yes. I no want Big Brother have trouble with Khmer Red." She played with her hands.

"Go get your spoon. Go," Ming told her.

Moy got her spoon and came back. He had a large plate of rice mixed with corn for her, and they shared the banana tree soup with fish. He told her not to worry what the Khmer Rouge thought, that he was a visiting guest, so Khmer Rouge had to feed him. He wanted to share his food with his little sister. If Khmer Rouge didn't like it, he would stop eating and let her eat his share. The Khmer Rouge did come and ask what they were doing. Ming told them he had come to visit his little sister, who he hadn't see for a long time because she had been sick. He said he gave her more food to get her strength back, so she could work harder for Onka. He smiled handsomely as he told her, "Moy eat more and work harder for our Onka." But his knee bumped gently against hers under the table.

She lowered her head and ate her second dinner faster. After the Khmer Rouge were gone, and they had finished eating, she asked Ming where he would sleep that night. Ming said he would sleep on the table in the common kitchen and go back to Kompong Kol the next morning, with the cow wagons.

Can I Have Another Smile?

The sky was blue
The sun was bright
You were eighteen
I was twelve
When I ran
From your first smile
Then I had nothing
But the clothes on my back
Grandpa and Ma
Had left me
And I felt naked
You melted the ice
From my heart
And embraced me
With your warm smile
You warned me
When I was thirteen
It won't be long
Heaven will call for you

Sky light! Sky bright!
My eyes had no sight
My life had no meaning
Now you're twenty-one
And you ran from my smile
The sky was blue
The sun was bright
Now, you ran from my smile
My big brother Ming
Can I have another smile?
Your little sister
Moy

By

Luong Ung-Lai

June 23, 2012

MOY

* * *

Moy lay under a tree, half asleep and half awake with her fever, tears rolling from her eyes. She wished her ma and grandpa were there to take care of her. She heard the girls criticizing the new captain for being mean to Moy. Moy remembered Big Sister Heng had taken Moy in her arms and shouted for the girls to help her. Now Big Sister Heng woke her up and asked, "Moy, how you feel?" She sat on her heels.

"I hurt," Moy told her. In Khmer "hurt" can mean pain from an injury, like a cut, or just that you are sick.

"No sleep too much or you no get better," Big Sister Heng told her.

For the first time, Moy took a good look at Big Sister Heng. She was around five foot three or five foot four, heavyset, very light-skinned, with black hair, black eyes, and a sort of large, flat face. But her face was friendly, full of understanding. She looked almost like the same woman who had sent Moy to the hospital at the French Farm. That's when Moy had run home, and a few months later Wong and Keem passed away.

"Sleep now," Big Sister Heng smiled and told her.

A few days later, the Cambodian stepmother came to see Moy. The old woman sat next to her and talked for a few minutes. Moy wept, but the woman showed no love or concern for her. She was *cold,* and her voice held a tone of dislike, almost hatred. Moy remembered when she lived in town and the stepmother worked at the river. She sent fish for her two children every week, but not once did she send a small fish for Moy. Even when she returned from the river, she never gave any fish to Moy. Whenever Moy wanted an extra fish for dinner, she went

Keem

to help the cooks in the kitchen. The cooks were happy to give her a couple of fish for lunch or dinner. It made the stepmother angry when Moy had fish to eat.

"Give me the fish!" the stepmother would demand.

Sometimes Moy gave in to the stepmother's demand; other times she didn't. Then she learned to ask the cooks if she could eat the fish in the kitchen instead of taking them home.

"Yes, Grandchild. You cook fish here and eat here. Then go home." The cooks looked at her with pity.

At the thought of it all, Moy cried harder.

"Cry, cry like baby!" the stepmother complained. She told Moy she was lucky to have her as a mother who loved her like her own child. She said she had left her own children in Sneung and come to see Moy when she heard Moy was sick.

At dinnertime, Momb brought a bowl of rice and sweet-and-sour fish soup for Moy to eat. Momb said her mother asked her to share the fish soup with Moy. She thanked Momb and her mother for their kindness but said she was not hungry at the moment and wanted to save the food for later. Then the stepmother came back from dinner with the girls and saw the food at Moy's side.

"You no hungry?" she asked.

"I not hungry now, but—" Moy didn't even get the last words out.

"You no throw away food. Let me see," the stepmother reached for the food and ate it!

Moy looked away in disbelief. Momb and some of the girls looked angry and disgusted with the stepmother. When the stepmother went back to Sneung, Momb stormed over immediately, hands on her hips, and shouted, "I never see a mother like that one!"

"She is not my mother; no yell at me," Moy shouted back and cried.

* * *

Keem would have starved herself and died for her daughter, which she did. One day, the Khmer Rouge gave her a couple of pieces of sweet sticky rice cakes to eat, but Keem had saved them for Wong and Moy instead.

"Good to eat?" Keem asked, watching Moy lick her fingers.

"Good." Not once did Moy think to share a bite of the cake with her ma.

Later, Wong told Moy that Keem didn't eat any, that she had saved every bit for them. Moy felt guilty for the rest of her life. Sometimes, Moy cried at the thought that Keem was sure Moy would share the sweet cake with her, but she hadn't and disappointed her ma. *I wish I could have been a better daughter for Ma*, she thought.

"In future, if your Ma give you food to eat, remember to share with her," Wong taught her.

* * *

Momb asked why Moy called that Cambodian woman mother if she wasn't. Moy told Momb the woman was her adopted mother. Moy cried herself to sleep.

Some time during the night, Big Sister Heng and Momb came and forced a couple of spoonfuls of rice soup into her. Then they covered her with a blanket. Sometimes Moy was cold and shaking, other times she was hot, but she never called for help. A few weeks later, the girls moved to another area. Big Sister Heng asked the wagon's driver to make room for Moy to sit on the wagon because she was too sick to walk.

18

The brown walls of the long school building were made from wooden boards. It took the cows pulling wagon a couple of minutes to reach the school from the highway. Moy was the first girl in the building, where all the doors were gone. The Khmer Rouge didn't like doors or walls. But for some reason, they had kept the walls of this school building. A concrete floor, metal roof, and four walls. It was like living in heaven!

When Moy worked in the sugarcane fields, a lot of times they didn't get off work until ten o'clock at night. Often, she and the workers slept in the fields or on the roadsides, even through pouring rain, thunder, and lightning. People would sit under any tree or bush they could find. Most people, like Moy, sat in the pouring rain, wet and cold. Countless times, Moy woke up in pouring rain but went back to sleep. She was too tired for rain to keep her awake.

* * *

Now, Moy and the girls welcomed their new home with warm and happy smiles. Moy picked a spot next to the entrance, lay down, and went to sleep with a smile. She and the girls lived in that school building for a couple of weeks, and Moy slowly got better.

Then one night, everyone was awakened by a very loud noise.

Keem

"It a bomb," Moy whispered to her neighbor. She had been listening to the gunfighting and bombs being dropped now and then from far away. The other girls were all either dead asleep or listening like she was.

"You talk like crazy; it no bomb." The girl barely got the last word out before the explosion from another bomb shook the earth, rattling the roof. The girls sat up straight. Almost immediately, there an explosion from another bomb that sounded like it was right in front of them. Moy fell over on her side, knees under her chin, arms and hands wrapped around her head. It felt like the roof was blowing away, and fire lit up the sky, as if heaven opened a door and embraced the girls. Inside the school building the air was bright red. No one could hear her own screams. Silence, silence—suddenly! The girls flew out of the school building, stood in front of the entrance, and cheered! They stared at the black sky as, every now and then, it again turned light before going dark pink.

"Vietnamese drop the bomb. They come to help us!" some of the girls shouted.

Moy watched from her bed. She didn't go out like the other girls. She was burning up with fever again. She remembered one time when she lived in the sugarcane fields at Head Tiger, she had been sick like this. She got better and stronger, and then the fever returned. During those weeks that she stayed home sick, a couple of people got killed each day by lightning strikes. As they swung their long hunting knives or bent shovels up and down, lightning would strike them dead! Between thirty and fifty people were killed.

For some strange reason, the Khmer Rouge didn't want people to be killed by lightning strikes. They told people to drop their tools and walk away because of rain, thunder, and lightning. Sometimes people got the whole day off from work. And the Khmer Rouge had healthier human hearts to eat later.

"Keep one, no gain; take one out, no lose," they reminded people daily.

* * *

Nowadays, Moy heard gunfighting and bombs dropping all day long. The rest of the girls still worked at the paddies while she stayed home sick. About a week after the first night of bombs being dropped, the girls came home with pale faces and large eyes; some looked in shock and were crying. A bomb had been dropped in a rice paddy and killed a group of boys and girls working next to Moy's group. Later that day, the Khmer Rouge came to see Big Sister Heng and told her that bomb was meant for Khmer Rouge. But the children in the paddy were dressed in black, and the Vietnamese mistook them for the Khmer Rouge.

Big Sister Heng left with the Khmer Rouge to "meet with Onka" for two days. She returned one late evening and told the girls to go home. When Onka needed them next, this time the whole family would go together.

By then, Moy had gotten better and stronger. She had been on her feet for the last few days. So she walked and ran on the highway with the other girls to get home. And she listened to the sound of bombs dropping like thunder. They would be followed by the softer sounds of gunfighting. It was like music to her ears, the music of *freedom*. She looked far away. Red bullets flew back and forth midair in the midnight sky. The black sky would turn light, then dark pink or red, and it was beautiful! *Heaven has about bombed hell on earth away!*

Moy didn't notice that she ran so fast she left the others behind. She thought she was the only one on the road. She and the girls went in different directions to their houses, and it took her a while to get home. When she neared her block, the main highway was crowded.

Keem

People on the street looked scared and worried as they searched for their children. Some families formed in groups with other families, talking and laughing softy.

An elderly woman saw Moy and asked where the children were. Moy told her the girls were coming from the school building, that Onka had let everyone come home. Then mothers or fathers asked her where their sons or daughters were, and Moy told them she didn't know where the boys were, or that she didn't know their daughters or sons.

"Niece!" someone shouted.

Moy was about to climb up the stairs at the tall house she used to share with the nice Chinese family. She turned around and saw Momb's mother, and Moy shouted, "Aunt." Moy ran to hug her.

"You see Momb?" Momb's mother looked worried.

"Momb stay in school, Aunt. Big Sister Heng say Onka will meet with all generals." She heard the Khmer Rouge tell Big Sister Heng that Onka would not let the generals like Momb go home. Onka would train Momb and the other generals to fight the Vietnamese. But Moy didn't tell her that.

"You not know if they let Momb come home?" Momb's mother looked like crying.

"No, Aunt. No worry, Aunt. Momb will come home soon." Moy didn't know why she lied.

"Your face white like ghost. Niece sick?" She held Moy's face between her hands.

"Yes, Aunt."

"Go up and sleep." She added, "If Niece live through the Viet…" she smiled beautifully as she trailed off.

"Yes, Aunt." Moy knew what she meant.

They had to be careful with what they said. The Khmer Rouge were still in power in Sneung. Moy heard people whisper that Phnom

Penh, the capital of Cambodia, was taken by the Vietnamese weeks earlier. However, the Khmer Rouge wouldn't give up fighting. The Vietnamese had to fight for one town and one city at a time. People prayed in silence for their Vietnamese rescuers to save them from their own people, the Khmer Rouge.

Moy heard a Cambodian man say it would be better to live with the Vietnamese than the Khmer Rouge. The Khmer Rouge let word slip that the Vietnamese would have everyone's head on picket fences. They would cut people open, take their intestines out, and shovel dry grass into their hollow bodies, but that news didn't bother most people, especially Moy, who had heard worse in what the Khmer Rouge had done to their own people.

She now lived in the same house with the same Chinese family and a new Cambodian family. The stepmother had moved to another town on the other side of the highway to live with the big sister and new son-in-law. Most people in Moy's block didn't like the stepmother for being so mean to Moy. Later, Moy met the big sister and her new husband, but Moy didn't want to live with the mean stepmother again. Moy told her big sister what the stepmother had done, and she told Moy, "When I a little girl, she tie me up to the window all day. Sometimes, she kick me on my head or whip me with my father's belt. Other times, she whip me with small stick until I black out. Sometimes, she pull my hair and tell me if I tell my father, she hit me more."

"Big Sister no tell your father?" Moy felt bad for her.

"No. I never tell my father. He think she love me and I love her."

"I see Big Sister love her. You always call her 'Mother' and smile at her. You no want to stay in Kompong Kol without her? Big Sister always listen to her and say 'yes' to everything she say." Moy didn't understand why the big sister wanted to live with someone as mean and evil as the stepmother.

"She the only mother I have." Big sister sounded very sad.

Keem

"Big Sister's mother is dead," Moy told her. This woman was not her mother. *Her* mother would never tie her to the window all day, kick her in the head, or pull her hair. Her mother would never whip her with the father's belt or small sticks until big sister blacked out.

She looked at Moy strangely. Then her sorrow melted away slowly, and she smiled, "Thank you. Thank you very much, Little Sister!" She wiped her tears away.

"No problem." Moy smiled back. She remained in her block. Sometimes, she wasn't sure what she did was right, but she remembered Keem and Wong always saying that if Moy wanted to do something and she thought it was good, then she should "be brave; go and do it!" They always encouraged her to follow her heart.

* * *

One day, in Sneung, the Khmer Rouge had a big meeting. Even the babies were there, in the middle of the highway. They ordered people to go up on a mountain to look for enemies that Onka knew lived there. They were afraid the Republic Soldiers would come to town and kill everyone. But everyone prayed for the Republic Soldiers and the Vietnamese to win the war and free them from the Khmer Rouge's claws.

"No talk to them if you see them. Come get us, and we take care of our enemies," the Khmer Rouge told them.

The next morning, Moy went to the large common kitchen for her share of food, like everyone else. But no one thought to take water! Everyone met on the highway, then went to the jungle as a large group. Halfway into the jungle, the group broke up—a family here, a couple of people over there, a person on the left or right. Moy and some others saw a man walk out of the thick woodland in front of them. He had no hair. His black pants and shirt were torn. He was a walking skeleton. His large black eyes were round and lifeless. His cheekbones stuck out. He walked slowly, swaying left and right, looking more dead than alive. As he walked toward Moy, she could see a body walking, but the man himself was long gone. That man was either from the adult Bike One or an escaped prisoner of the Khmer Rouge. Some women wept as the living skeleton walked into the thick jungle and disappeared from the crowd.

"Khmer torture Khmer; very embarrass!" people whispered as they made their way slowly up the mountain.

People searched very hard. They chatted as they hunted for mushrooms on their way up the mountain. The white and black mushrooms were everywhere, under wet grass, under blocks of wood, and around some trees. People picked them and wrapped them in their scarves, carrying them on their shoulders or around their necks. People shouted loudly for their children, who were walking right next to them. The mothers, fathers, and grandparents told the children to sing and shout as loudly as they could. They wanted the Republic and the Vietnamese soldiers to escape before the Khmer Rouge could get them.

By noon time, no one talked or smiled. The sun was strong and hot, and there was no water anywhere on the mountain. The mountain was large. It took Moy all morning to reach the top. The trees did help ease the heat, but Moy's throat was on fire. Her mouth felt like dry sand had sucked all the moisture out, and her tongue hurt. People stopped for their lunch near a small pool at the top of the mountain. It was the only water.

The pool was about two feet deep in the middle. People had to either drink the water and live a little longer, or die from thirst. Moy stood at the edge of the pool, watching some people kneel around the edge, dipping their lips into the water to drink. Then without any thought, she knelt, scooped up water in both hands, and drank and drank.

Keem

The water looked like strong tea because of the black mud under the water. Four dark gray water buffalo weren't happy. The selfish creatures turned their large heads around and stared angrily at the humans who drank their bathwater, with their dark yellow shits and pee in it. The selfish creatures said, "*Mmaaa!*" loudly at the humans. Two water buffalo stood up and wagged their tails furiously left and right. Then they flopped down on their sides angrily, turning the tea into coffee, and let out another angry, "*Mmaaa!*"

"I'm dead! I drink water buffalo shit and pee!" some of the men and women cried and laughed at the same time.

"Khmer Red no want give us food to eat. And this unlucky water buffalo angry because we drink their bathwater with their shit and pee. Buddha, pity us human!" A man in his late thirties next to Moy laughed and shook his head.

"I'm dead. I'm dead," some people laughed as they knelt at the edge of the pool to drink.

Others shook their heads. "No look at the shit. No think of the pee. Just drink and live."

"Those unlucky buffalo make the water black, now no one can drink it. Buddha, pity us human!" some people screamed. Most overlooked the dark yellow drops of shit in the water and just drank quickly before it turned black again.

Moy would never forget the taste and the smell of that buffalo bathwater. At the time, she didn't smell or taste any difference from the water she drank every day. She just drank her fill. But afterward, she smelled and tasted it. She didn't worry too much about it. She just wanted to go home and wash the taste from her mouth with clean water.

Moy's life had been like this. She climbed up a couple of mountains, worked up there, then climbed down and went home. When she drank that buffalo bathwater, she lived; otherwise she would have died from thirst. She could either keep going and living by climbing each and every mountain when she faced it, or stand still at the bottom, saying, "I'm tired of climbing mountains," then lay down to die.

She never thought about the size and height of each mountain she faced. She just climbed up, then climbed down, from mountain to mountain, hoping she might reach a golden mountain where she could stand tall at the top. Moy fought so hard to live, but not for glory. She lived to honor her beloved Ma's wishes.

"Child, in future I give you good day." Those words were Keem Lai's dying wishes for her little girl. *That wish carried Keem's love, and it lived inside Moy's soul, heart, and mind forever after.* Now that Keem was a spirit, she still loved and looked after her daughter.

Moy knew this in her heart.

* * *

After lunch, people climbed down the mountain. Moy and some others saw old grass mats near a cooking stove made of three rocks. Some kids found an old scarf and showed it to their parents.

One mother yanked it out of her children's hands and tied it around her hips. "My scarf!" The mother smiled. People laughed and walked on.

Whoever got in town first ate first. Moy didn't get home until seven or eight at night. After dinner, she went to the small pond behind her house to bathe, then went to bed. Her mouth still had the taste of the buffalo's bathwater. She felt like throwing up every now and then, but nothing came up. She had a stomachache and headache and was hot and cold. She felt like dying, but she slept through her sickness.

After that day on the mountain, no one went to work, and the whispering began. Moy heard people say the Khmer Rouge had planned to execute everyone on the mountain that day. But because the people

Keem

didn't go up as a group like the Khmer Rouge wanted, they couldn't run around and shoot one person here and one person there. When their plan fell apart, the Khmer Rouge returned to town and told the cooks to get food ready. Two weeks later, the Khmer Rouge tried it again, but this time no one went to the meeting.

19

One day, Moy went to the tree potato fields. She was surprised to find most of the potatoes were gone. She pulled a couple of potatoes the size of a small arm, and then she heard a whispered, "Niece!"

She looked around, saw no one, and thought she must be hearing things. Then she heard it again, "Niece!"

"Who is it? Come out and let me see you," she shouted, thinking, *I'm not afraid of ghosts!*

It was not a ghost, but close to one. A man came out from hiding under the potato branches and leaves. Moy refused to move from her spot as he walked out from under the shadow. He had no hair, his clothes were too big for him, his cheekbones pointed out, and his eyes were surrounded by two big holes. He looked like wet tissue paper covering a handful of sticks. He couldn't stand up straight and was half bent over. His bony hands held his pants up. There was dried blood and dirt on his face and feet. He stood there, looking helpless and frightened, his eyes large and dull. He was a walking skeleton.

Moy could see his pain, hunger, and helplessness. She felt sorry for him, but this was not the first time she had witnessed this kind of suffering. Her grandpa, Ma, and Moy herself had been through the same thing.

"Uncle," she greeted the stranger.

"Niece, Uncle beg for a mouthful of potato to eat."

Keem

"They not cook."

"No worry; Uncle can eat like that." He pointed at the long, brown-skinned tree potatoes in her hands.

"Uncle no eat that. It root and very hard to chew. Uncle give it to me. I give this to Uncle. Exchange it with me." She pointed at a potato's root in his bony hands, and she held a long potato out to him.

He stared at the root in his hands, looking embarrassed. Then he smiled and threw it away, taking the long potato from her with both hands. He didn't bother to peel the bitter, dark brown skin off; he just bit, chewed, and swallowed.

Without thinking, Moy told him the commander in her block was a good man, and that he should go talk to the commander and get a place to live. She watched as he bit into the long potato with his broken teeth. White potato juice ran down from the corners of his mouth, and he licked it off every now and then. He looked up and stared at the long potatoes in her hands. She gave him all of them.

"No stare at people eat. Not nice to watch them when they hungry. No embarrass them," Keem taught her daughter when she caught Moy staring at poor people eating the pork noodle soup left in the bowls at the pork noodle soup shop.

"I go home now," Moy told the stranger.

"Niece no tell anyone Niece see Uncle here?" He looked and sounded worried.

She shook her head. "I no tell."

"Thank you, Niece. Uncle give Niece good and long life," he said, wishing her good fortune.

"Yes, Uncle." She smiled and went home empty-handed, but she felt much happier.

A few weeks later, Moy was happy to see the man eating dinner in the common kitchen with everyone else. He had new clothes on, a house to live in, and good food to eat! She didn't want to embarrass him by talking to him, and when he saw her, he didn't say anything, either. Their eyes met, then looked away quickly.

As each day went by, the gunfighting between the Khmer Rouge and the Vietnamese was getting more intense. There were also more bombs dropped, and they were getting closer to Sneung. The Khmer Rouge let word slip that the Vietnamese would cut people's throats if they got their hands on them, so everyone moved their families to the small village where Momb's mother lived.

People put their clothes and whatever belongings they had in sarongs, scarves, bags, and boxes. They used tree branches as carrying sticks to tote the bags, one in front and one at the back. Some people carried large bags on their heads, or pushed the wagons that carried their belongings heading for the village. But it was too small! There weren't enough houses for everyone, and each house was shared by two or three different families. At night, most people slept on the common kitchen's floor. For a week or two, no one did anything but eat and sleep. A few people listened to the news on a radio, while everyone else was on the lookout for the Khmer Rouge.

"Vietnamese just come in to Battambang!" the excited men, women, and older children went around and whispered to the lookouts.

"Thank you, Buddha! Thank you!" Everyone cried and laughed at the same time.

"Vietnamese come closer to Sneung now!" the whispers went around again.

The cooks slaughtered a pig, a cow, and chickens to cook, and everyone ate them with white rice. The townspeople continued listening to the news on a radio, while young children played around them. There wasn't any sight of the Khmer Rouge.

One night, a meeting was called and Moy listened to the arguing.

"What we do here?" one woman asked.

Keem

"We here because we no want Vietnamese kill us," someone answered.

"Who say the Vietnamese will kill us?" a man sitting next to Moy asked.

"Khmer Red," someone shouted the answer.

"Who is Khmer Red? How many people Khmer Red kill? They kill my husband and he Khmer like them," an elderly woman shared her story. She was standing in front of a house, leaning on the wall. No one said anything. She went on to add that if the Vietnamese wanted to cut her throat, she'd let them. "But I no want the Khmer Red dog come and cut my throat. I Khmer like them." She waited then walked away from the meeting in silence.

Everyone began talking at the same time. The adults kicked the children out of the meeting, but Moy didn't move from her spot. No one said anything to her. She just sat there and listened. Some people were afraid the Vietnamese might cut their throats like the Khmer Rouge told them, but most people didn't believe the Khmer Rouge. The question was why did the Khmer Rouge want everyone in this small village? No one had an answer, so they all went home. Later that same night, a man came running into the village and woke everyone up.

"Vietnamese come in Sneung! They bathe without clothes on, and they sing in the pond!"

Moy was all eyes and ears, excited. She ran in and out of the house she shared with a Cambodian couple she called Aunt and Uncle.

The townspeople called for a meeting immediately. Everyone agreed to go to Sneung and face the Vietnamese. However, some people wanted to wait until morning, and others wanted to leave right away. The family that Moy stayed with wanted to leave immediately, like most.

So it was around twelve or one in the morning when, once again, everyone picked up their belongings and this time left the village.

MOY

The small footpath was crowded with people, and their whispering, laughter, and chatter filled the air. The sky was tinted light and dark pink from bombs dropping and bullets passing back and forth from far away.

Moy remembered one day when her grandpa had talked to her ma about war.

"When you walk in the jungle, no walk in front or back, stay in middle. If something happen, you can hide," Wong told Keem.

Now everyone waited on the footpath inside the jungle, about fifteen or twenty minute's walk from Moy's block in Sneung. Some people slept on Mother Earth amid the sounds of bombs dropping and gunfighting. Some people just sat there and listened to that same music, like Moy. They waited for a man to come back from sneaking into Sneung to see if it was safe for them to go. He came back and said they should wait until sunrise, then go into town. Hopefully, the Vietnamese wouldn't shoot them on sight, mistaking them for Khmer Red.

The sun had just peeked out from behind the mountains, and the sky was colorful. Some people were still sound asleep. Suddenly, someone from behind shouted, "Run! Khmer Red come from behind! They come for us. Run!"

No one needed to be told twice. People picked up their belongings and ran. Some people screamed and cried, waking their loved ones. Some people didn't bother with their belongings. They just grabbed their young children in their arms and ran. The children screamed and cried in their parents' arms or ran next to them. In the madness and confusion, families got separated.

"Mother? Father?" some confused and scared young children cried as they stood there or ran around searching for their parents. Some parents also ran around, crying and screaming their children's names.

Keem

"Mother, Father, where are you? Mother, Father, no run away from me!" A few children jumped up and down, hands fanning for their parents. Some adults grabbed the children's hands and told them to run now and find their parents later.

Moy grabbed her small clothes bag and ran next to the Cambodian family she stayed with.

"Moy, run. Child, run!" the Cambodian woman shouted.

"All the short life, Khmer Red!" the woman's husband cursed, his young son crying in his arms. He grabbed their bags with his free hand. His wife ran behind him. Then she fell over, with her daughter in her arms.

"Aunt!" Moy cried and ran back.

"Run! Niece, run. No worry about Aunt. Run!" she shouted.

"No, Aunt! Get up, Aunt!" Moy screamed and pulled the woman's arm to get her up.

But she lost her balance halfway up and fell over again, with her daughter still in her arms. The crowd ran around them.

"*Get up!*" Moy shouted, as she tried getting the woman up on her feet.

"*Get up!*" Her husband ran back and pulled her up. Between her husband and Moy, they got her on her feet. The little girl screamed her head off in her mother's arms. Then they ran together. Luckily, there were people behind them.

Parents grabbed their children's hands and shouted at them to run faster. The young children ran and cried. Some mothers cried and fathers cursed every bad word they knew. People fell left and right on the crowded footpath. Some people ran past or around them. Others stopped to pull them up; then they ran together.

People at the front were greeted by Vietnamese guns pointing at them when they reached town. The Vietnamese soldiers shouted at people, but the Cambodians didn't understand what the soldiers said.

Some Cambodians tried to tell the Vietnamese that the Khmer Rouge were behind, and chasing them into town. The Vietnamese didn't understand Khmer. In the madness of confusion, the Vietnamese fired their guns skyward, silencing everyone. Time went by slowly. Finally, a man in front yelled and pointed behind the terrified crowd, "Khmer Red come from behind. Khmer Red!"

The Vietnamese looked at each other and whispered among themselves.

"Khmer Red come. Khmer Red!" A man kept screaming and pointing behind the crowd. The crowd pushed forward from the back, toward the Vietnamese guns.

"Khmer Red!" the crowd shouted, pointing backward. Even the children joined in.

Finally, the Vietnamese understood, and one of the soldiers shouted something. Most of the soldiers took off running past the crowd, toward the jungle. People pointed behind them as the soldiers ran by.

Moy was shaking from the run and the guns pointed at the people in front of her. A few soldiers stayed in town, and they guided people to a tall house across from where Moy used to live with the nice Chinese family. Children and women were crying from fright. The soldiers tried to make up for their mistake, carrying the young children on their backs for the mothers. Some young soldiers carried the belongings for elderly women and men. A young soldier carried a thin, elderly Cambodian woman in his arms, looking confused and sad as he walked past Moy. Everyone was quiet. The Cambodians just stood there and stared after him.

"Vietnamese carry Khmer in his arms. But Khmer kill Khmer! Pity! We very embarrass!" the Cambodians whispered and shook their heads.

The soldiers told people to stay under the tall house across from them. At lunchtime, the soldiers gave them white rice and cans of food, the same food the soldiers ate. Now that the soldiers understood this crowd was civilian; they were friendly. Moy watched as some soldiers tried to talk to the Cambodians by using their hands and body language. The children giggled, and the soldiers smiled and laughed with them. Some soldiers ran around, chasing after the giggling children. Children wrapped their arms and legs around the soldiers, and the soldiers would laugh and shout to their brothers in arms to help them. Some soldiers had so many children wrapped around them, they looked like children's happy trees! No one could see the soldiers, just the children's arms, legs, and backs. Everyone laughed about the children's happiness as they played with the soldiers.

The small group lived with the Vietnamese soldiers for about two weeks. As each day went by, more soldiers and civilians came into Sneung. The main highway was crowded with hundreds and thousands of people who stopped or went on by Sneung on their way to Battambang or other cities and towns. People carried bags of their belongings on their shoulders, in their hands, or on the wooden wagons that were pulled by two cows, oxen, or dark-gray water buffalo. (Those selfish creatures! They didn't want to share their shit-and-pee bathwater with people, selfish creatures!)

People of all ages smiled on the crowded highway. They welcomed a new life and freedom, given by the Vietnamese and Cambodian Republic soldiers. *Finally, the sun rises again.*

People came from all over to Sneung, and in Moy's block she saw many people from the sugarcane fields. She saw the young woman who had been married to the wrong man by the Khmer Rouge. Now she walked next to the older man, the love of her life. They smiled and chatted happily as they walked past Moy. Then Moy met a children's nurse from the sugarcane fields. The young woman told her that shortly after Moy left, the girls in Bike Two were sent to the adult Bike One. And the young girls got picked off by men, like candies chosen from a bowl by hungry children. All the men had to do was go to the Khmer Rouge and order this girl or that woman for a wife, with or without the woman's family's permission. The Khmer Rouge were the bosses. Moy had been married off along with most of the girls in her group. But at the time, she was miles away and didn't know a thing about it!

The Khmer Rouge were angry and embarrassed when Moy was not at the wedding ceremony. They were short a bride, and they went looking for her. They were told Moy had gone to the farm with her mother. The nurse didn't know who the man was who asked for Moy's hand. Moy had an idea who he was, though, and she couldn't be wrong.

* * *

After Soeun ended Moy's fistfight with Lee, Moy never forgave him. He cheated her out of a few more hairs from Lee's head for calling Moy a "Chinese rag." Then he threatened to slap her and tell Ming on her. Moy remembered one day when Soeun had a fever, and he asked her for help. She refused. Ming looked at her with disapproval and told her she should help. She stared at Ming's face, then looked at Soeun's large back.

"I go help!" she told Ming cheerfully. She even borrowed a "scratching coin" from someone. Ming stared at her as she marched by, smiling.

"If I you, I not let her come near me," he laughed and shouted over to Soeun.

The Chinese and Khmer liked to use a "scratching coin," or a spoon, to scratch their backs, chests, and arms if they had fever or didn't feel well. They believed the scratching would bring out the fever and make them feel better. Moy dipped the coin in water and scratched Soeun's back. She started light-handed and Soeun praised her gentle scratching.

Keem

But soon she had him hopping up and down on his backside, screaming that she was taking his skin off.

"Uncle go ask Khmer Red help. They scratch gentler than me," she told him.

He yelled at her to take it easy on his back.

"Yell, yell, like baby." She pressed the coin harder on his back.

He moaned and groaned, wiggling around under the scratching coin. She told him there was a houseful of women where he could ask someone else to help him. He didn't.

"I hurt (sick) before, but I hurt more now. Buddha, Buddha, she take my flesh out! No man want your little sister for a wife. She so mean; she take my flesh out!" he complained loudly to Ming, getting everyone laughing.

Ming lay on his back, laughing and kicking his feet like a little boy.

Moy also remembered when she lived in Kompong Kol, she went to visit Ming one day. She was close to his house when she heard, "No! She too young. No." It was Ming talking to someone. He sounded angry, "I say no, and I mean no. What you not understand about no? My little sister is too young!"

Moy stood in front of the door to watch. Ming was on his feet, going nose to nose with Soeun.

"Why you very greedy and mean?" Soeun looked and sounded angry.

Ming was just an inch or two shorter than Soeun, but just as large, and much younger and still growing.

"You stay here," Ming pointed at her and said. Then he pointed toward the door. "Soeun, go home!"

Soeun was angry and looked from Ming to Moy. She was afraid the men might get into a fistfight. If he dared hurt her big brother, she would be all over him.

"You very greedy. I go and ask Onka," Soeun shouted.

"Then I fight you. Get out of my house, now!" Ming pointed toward the door.

Soeun stormed out of the house angrily. Moy turned and stared after him.

"Moy, get in here, now!" Ming yelled.

"Big Brother," she greeted as she walked past him. She went to sit on his small folding bed.

Ming just stood there staring at her. His anger melted away slowly, and he smiled, then asked, "You fight Soeun for me?"

"I no afraid of Soeun. I fight Soeun for Big Brother," she told him.

"You only this tall and you want fight Soeun for me." He held his hand up around his stomach, showing how tall she was.

"I small, but I strong, and I fight Soeun for Big Brother," she told him, and then they laughed.

20

One morning, Moy and a woman were talking about something. They were under the Vietnamese soldiers' house, watching a group of Vietnamese walk a long line of prisoners toward, then slowly past, them. Two long ropes, tied on the fifty or sixty Khmer Rouge's upper arms on both sides, kept them in a straight line. Another long rope tied the prisoners' hands to their backs, on both males and females. The Khmer Rouge tried to hang their heads as they walked by their own civilian people, but the Vietnamese used their guns to lift the prisoners' chins gently up.

Moy stared at each prisoner's grim face and dull eyes. The Khmer Rouge looked scared and defeated. Some of them appeared to be hurt, hungry, and thirsty, and they couldn't walk straight. The civilians stood on both sides in silence as the prisoners moved by.

"Before, Khmer help Khmer. Now Khmer stand here and watch Vietnamese take Khmer prisoners. Difficult! Difficult!" a woman standing next to Moy wept.

Strangely, Moy didn't see a Cambodian Republic soldier anywhere. She only saw the Vietnamese soldiers fighting the Cambodians for the Cambodians, every day and night.

About two weeks later, the Vietnamese offered to take people to any city or town they wanted. A Cambodian family that Moy stayed with at the small village had come from Siem Reap, where Moy was born, and she planned to go back with them. On that day, they were waiting for the Vietnamese army trucks to take them there, and Moy felt very anxious.

When Keem was alive and Moy acted like a wriggling worm, Keem would yell, "You can no sit or stand still. Wriggle around like worm eat your butt! What wrong with you?"

Well, there wasn't a worm eating her butt, but something was! Moy felt she must go across the main highway, to the other side of town, and see the stepmother—and she must go right now! Moy told the Cambodian woman she'd be back in time to go to Siem Reap at noon. There were hundreds of people on the main highway toward Battambang, and some people rested on the side of the road. Moy was already on the other side of the highway when she heard someone shout, "Moy! Moy!"

She looked toward the caller. It was Paula, Pon's grandson, who was a year or two younger than Moy. He was on his bike. She ran to him and asked where her adopted Cambodian mother and father were. Before Keem Lai took her last breath, she had told Moy to go live with Pon's family. Paula told Moy his grandparents were at the back, behind them.

"You want to see them?" Paula asked and got off his bike. Then he walked with her to his family.

Much later, Moy believed that on that day, her ma's spirit chased her across the highway to meet Paula. She believed Keem's spirit didn't want her daughter go to Siem Reap, because then Moy wouldn't escape from Cambodia.

"Grandma, Grandpa, look. Moy here," Paula shouted to them.

"Moy? Buddha, Buddha, she still alive! Grandpa Pon, look. Moy still alive!" Pon's wife shouted in surprise to her husband.

Pon came from the other side of the cow wagon. He had a bowl of rice in one hand, a spoon in another.

Keem

"Moy? Child, you still alive!"

"Mother, Father," she greeted them.

"Child, you not thin like other! You eat yet?" Pon asked. He looked shocked that Moy was still walking and breathing.

"Not yet," she replied.

"Come, come eat." Pon grabbed her upper arm and pulled her behind the wagon.

While they ate, Pon told her that they thought she was dead when they didn't hear anything from her for two years. She did go see them, after she went to live in the sugarcane fields. Moy wanted to visit her ma's grave, but when she was close to the grave area, she suddenly got scared. Perhaps Keem's spirit didn't want her daughter inside that jungle again. So Moy went across the stream to see Pon and her ma's jewelry and spent the night with them.

Pon told her they were worried about her after not seeing her for so long. They asked if she wanted to go to Battambang with them, and without thinking, she said yes. But it was more like someone *told* her to say yes. After lunch, she went to tell the Cambodian woman she had found her adopted family and was going to Battambang with them. The Cambodian woman was happy for her and praised Moy for remembering Keem's wishes. Moy cried as she said good-bye to the kindhearted woman.

"Niece is good child. Buddha go with Niece. Aunt will miss you." The kindhearted woman hugged Moy, then sent her off to her adopted family.

* * *

Moy walked with Pon's wife at the back of their wagon, which was pulled by two cows. She didn't tell Pon's wife what happened to her in the sugarcane fields. To Moy's shock, Pon's wife told her Moy's third uncle had gone to the French Farm after she left with Ming for the sugarcane fields. He had gotten the news that his father, Wong Lai, and big sister, Keem Lai, had died. Then he went to the sugarcane fields for Moy, but the Khmer Rouge chased him away because he didn't have a pass. He went back to the French Farm for two or three days, then finally went back to his wife and children in Battambang.

Not all of them were killed by Black Shirt, like that Chinese man told me, Moy thought. She cared very little about her uncles, and she wondered why he had come looking for her. It wasn't as though he loved her. He used to hit her head with his knuckles when she was little. *Ma and Grandpa's jewelry. That's what he was looking for.* Moy knew but kept the thought to herself.

Pon's wife sounded angry and happy at the same time when Moy told her that Ming had died.

"He dare come and demand for your mother's gold!" She told Moy. One day, Ming had shown up and demanded Pon return all Keem and Wong's gold to him. They didn't give him anything, because they weren't sure if Moy was still alive.

Moy didn't know that Ming had gone back to see them.

They walked and talked, like the hundreds of people on that main highway to Battambang. Moy heard bombs dropped now and then. Some were dropped far away, and others sounded like they were right in front of them. Everyone would scream and cover their heads, lying flat on the ground. And the gunfighting between the Khmer Rouge and the Vietnamese never stopped. All over the highway were small and large holes made by bombs. Human blood painted the center and sides of the highway. Moy saw body parts on both sides of the road, but she looked away and walked on, like everyone else. They were walking on a road that had been slowly built up with their mothers', fathers', brothers', sisters', and children's blood.

Keem

In her short fifteen years of life, Moy had known and walked the road between Battambang and Pailin. That road led her, and many others, to a living hell on earth—it led some to heaven. Now this same road would lead her to either another living hell, or to a new future. Only time would tell.

The crowd on the road kept pushing forward. Some people stopped to cook a meal or take a nap. People ate lunch while listening to gunfire and bombs being dropped. Moy heard people saying that some families were killed by bombs right on the highway she was walking on. Once in a while, she saw bloody victims being carried in hammocks by their family members. Victims were missing one or both legs or arms, and blood was everywhere, dripping from the hammocks. Some victims couldn't even moan. Moy saw people covered in blood, lying on the side of the highway as family members cared for them. The children of one woman, who was covered in blood, were holding onto her hands and crying, "Mother, Mother no die. Mother no run away from me."

"No, child, Mother no die. Please, help look after my children," she whispered weakly to anyone who tried to help her.

"Pity her much," Pon's wife whispered. She and Moy didn't stop to help.

Moy remembered how she had cried and shouted almost those same words when Keem was taken from her.

One night, a family stopped next to Pon's family. Moy listened to a little girl screaming in pain. She was no more than seven years old, and one of her legs was missing. A large cut on her small cheek was so deep, Moy could see the white bone.

"Hurt much! Mother, help me!" the child screamed, large tears falling from her swollen eyes and face. She tossed left and right on Mother Earth, trying to escape her pain.

"Child, no cry. Mother not know what to do." Her mother looked helpless as she tried to calm her daughter down. She couldn't even cry for her child's pain. She looked terrified of losing her daughter, but there was nothing she could do.

"It hurt, Mother. Kill me! Mother, help me! I no want to live. Mother, kill me!" The little girl couldn't stop screaming.

This was the price the young and the helpless must pay for the greed of some men to rule a country. This earth is large enough for every man, woman, and child to share. However, it is not big enough for a couple of greedy dictators to rule the lives on this land, turning the cities to mountains of fallen stone and rubber, backyards to graveyards where human remains piled up in gardens and rivers were filled with human blood.

Some place on that main highway between Battambang and Pailin was painted with that little girl's blood. What could anyone do? They had to keep walking, over her young and innocent blood, to hell or to heaven. Who cared? It was her blood, not theirs! How many people would remember this little girl? Not many. Certainly not those Khmer Rouge who had started this war and hell on earth.

Moy lost count of the endless days she and hundreds of other people walked toward Battambang. She slept when the sun was down, got up and walked when the sun rose. The sounds of gunfights and bombs dropping was her music. It was such a pity, she thought, when a new baby had been born and slept on the blood-covered road, like Moy. Then again, whoever said war has pity and mercy?

* * *

Moy's family stopped in front of a Buddhist temple, like many families, for the night. There were some wooden houses along the highway, on both sides. Her family slept under the coconut trees.

Keem

When morning came, many people wanted to remain right where they were, close to Battambang. Moy's family liked the area and stayed there. People found a small area and made shelters for their families out of whatever material they could find. Dry brown grass, palm leaves, coconut tree leaves, anything to have a small roof over their heads. At night, some people slept under their cow wagons. During the day, they hung around it. Pon's family had a double wooden bed that they surrounded with three walls, then covered with a roof made of coconut tree leaves. Pon's daughter, Small, and her family also had a small shelter covered with coconut tree leaves.

As soon as shelter had been built, most of the men took off to hunt for the rice the Khmer Rouge had hidden in the minefields. That killed many people.

When Moy lived at the sugarcane fields, she heard of people disappearing every day. Now she knew what had happened to some of them. People who went to the sugar factory for sugar and sugarcane found human fingers, arms, legs, heads, eyeballs, thumbs, toes, faces, and other body parts inside the black sugar tank.

"It a human's head in my bucket! I see something big, big, I think it black sugar. I pull it out and wipe it clean; it a human's head, from neck up!" a man told Moy's family when he stopped to spend the night on his way home.

"Human's eyeball, finger, and a human's face in my bucket," a woman who lived next door to Pon told everyone. She died two days later.

Well, sugar is sugar. Sugar is sweet, whether there are human parts in there or not. People took whatever human parts they found, threw them away, then took the sugar home and ate it! How many people were killed, mutilated into little pieces, then thrown in that tank by the Khmer Rouge? Hopefully, they were already dead and weren't killed in such an unspeakable way as to be mutilated alive by the Khmer Rouge.

* * *

Nowadays at home, some women, the elderly, and children made rice cakes, rice-noodle-and-fish soup, sweet banana soup, and many more homemade goods to exchange for rice. Rice and gold were used like money. "You give me gold; I gave you rice."

The little town had a tiny store around the Buddhist temple. As each day went by, the store got larger. More people were doing business, buying and selling everything—clothes, shoes, food. Some people continued to search for rice, and if a family had cows or oxen, the children took care of them.

Moy was happy to help Pon's daughter, Small, make rice-noodle-and-fish soup to sell. She was not happy to take care of cows in the fields with Seron, Small's son.

"Moy, pull!" Seron shouted from the other side of the small, muddy lagoon.

"I pull! But it no want to come!" Moy shouted angrily.

The cow wanted to go one way, and Moy wanted to go the other. She was no match for the cow in that fight. Moy sat in the muddy water that looked like coffee with cream, her legs parted and hands pressed deep into the mud in front of her. That no-good boy was laughing at her. He sat on the back of his cow, nice and dry on land.

"I no like feed this cow! Seron, help me," Moy shouted over the lagoon.

"You feed your cow." Seron was slim and very dark-skinned, with a long, thin face.

"It no like this water," she told him. She saw cows all the time but had never dealt with them.

Keem

"No pull rope left and right. Pull straight, straight, if you want cow to go straight. Pull left go left, pull right cow go right," the nine-year-old boy taught her.

Moy had no idea what she did to make the cow almost walk over her, forcing her back to sitting in the muddy water again. Then that ugly cow rested her long, heavy neck on top of Moy's head.

"Go away," she yelled, pushing the cow's neck away.

She struggled to get up, but kept falling in. The mud was too slippery. Sometimes, she fell on her hands and knees. Other times, she went face first into the muddy water. Lifting her face out of the muddy water, she screamed. She was nose to nose with that hateful cow.

"What you look at?" Moy snapped.

The cow stared at her with its beautiful light-brown eyes. She got up on her hands and knees. The cow was only a foot away from her. Moy and that cow were in a war of stares, eyeball to eyeball. Moy took a good look at that cow. She was white, with big and small black spots all over her body. A rope was tied around her neck, instead of going through her nose, because the top part of her nose was missing. That was where people controlled a cow by pulling a rope through its nose, left, right, or straight. This cow had her own free will. But she had endured great pain for her freedom when the top of her nose got cut off. Still, she went on living, one minute at a time—or a second at a time, like Moy did. She never knew when she'd get killed and eaten by humans.

"You ugly," Moy told the cow, and pushed its face away. She didn't know why she said it. Perhaps Moy felt ugly herself. The top of that cow's nose was missing, and Moy was very sick, but she didn't know.

Seron laughed at her mischief as Moy kept on trying to pull the cow across the muddy lagoon, but it wouldn't move.

"You eat mud water, not grass. You abuse me, you go hungry," Moy told the cow. Then she went looking for clean water to bathe in.

That evening when Moy got home, Small yelled at her for not feeding the cow. For some reason, that cow refused to go to the other side of the lagoon to eat, and her stomach was flat. Seron had fun telling everyone what happened to Moy and her cow at the lagoon. He was Small's second husband's son. His father had been killed by the Khmer Rouge in 1977.

Paula, Small's first Chinese husband's son, was good-looking. Now Small had a third husband, a Khmer Rouge, and their baby was on the way.

"Father, I no like cow. I not know how to take care of cow," Moy told her adopted, silver-haired father that evening.

"Child, no cry. Why child cry like baby?" Pon sounded angry.

"I no want to take care of cow. I want to stay home and help Big Sister Small."

"Then talk like grown up, not like baby. No one torture you," Pon told her.

There! I did it! No, no one abused me except that cow! Moy thought. A couple of weeks later Small had that cow killed and sold the beef. Moy ate some of the beef soup with the family. And she broke a front tooth by biting on a bone in the meat.

Moy didn't sleep in the double bed inside the house with Pon, his wife, and Paula. She felt uncomfortable. Paula was a big boy of twelve. So she slept outside, on the cow wagon platform under the coconut trees. When it rained, she went across the street and slept on a small grass mat under a tall house next to the Buddhist temple. All her belongings remained with Pon. Then one day, Pon's wife told Moy she had used some of Keem's jewelry to exchange for rice. Moy said that was all right. There were ten people in Pon's family, eleven with Moy, and the rice went out fast. But later, Moy found out that Pon's wife had gambled away the necklaces and rings that Keem and Wong had worked tirelessly for and saved for their beloved Moy.

Keem

"I lose your mother's necklace at card game," she told Moy.

Moy said nothing, but she was not happy. Her Ma's necklace was gone.

Pon's wife continued to use Keem's jewelry ruthlessly, exchanging it for rice to feed her family and gambling for her own pleasure. One day, she told Moy with a grim face, "I lose your Ma's necklace in card game again."

Another necklace from Ma gone? Moy was fed up! "Mother no take my ma's gold to play card game again. My ma keep them for me. No more game with my ma's gold!"

"Why child so greedy?" Pon's wife looked like crying.

"Play no more game with my ma's gold," Moy told her, then walked away.

A few days later, Pon's wife came to her. "I can no help myself. I lose your Ma's bracelet."

"I take back all my ma's gold now." Moy was angry, and stared hard at the old woman.

"Child still too young to keep the gold yourself. Mother swear Mother will not play card game again. Trust Mother, good child? I love you like my own blood child! Let Mother keep them for you." The old woman seemed remorseful.

"Play no more card game with my ma's gold," Moy warned her.

"No more card game! Mother swear to child," the old woman told her.

21

"You eat too much. Go find your own food," Small told Moy.

"Buddha! Why so mean!" Pon's wife stared at her daughter's smiling face. Small always smiled.

Moy said nothing. She did as she was told. She went out and found her own food. At that time, she would go to the pond next to the Buddhist temple, and carry large buckets of water home for her adopted parents' bath.

"She better than our own blood daughter; she a good child. Pity her," Pon and his wife told each other.

Moy told Pon not to use any more of her ma's gold to exchange for rice, since she would no longer eat with them.

"You let your own mother and father go hungry, good child?" the old couple asked her.

She told them there was a lot of rice in Small's house, and they could eat that.

It was about three months after the Vietnamese had overthrown the Khmer Rouge, and some people had found a way to go back and forth to the Thai border, where they bought sarongs, shirts, pants, different kinds of canned food, and candies from the Thai people, then brought them back to Cambodia. It was the best time for Moy! She had no problem finding her own food. She didn't use any of her ma's gold to make a living. She walked back and forth, looking at everything in the

Keem

open market on the street around the Buddhist temple. She saw a large table about a foot off the ground, covered with new clothing, cakes in plastic bags, and candies. Moy asked the businesswoman if she could buy a bag of candies to sell and pay her later. It cost eight cans of rice for a bag of a hundred pieces of candy.

"Aunt, I orphan and I live with Grandpa Pon's family. Sell it to me cheap, cheap," Moy complained loudly until she got the candy for six cans of rice.

She bought two bags of different candies and borrowed a large plate from the businesswoman. Then she took the candy to the other side of the store. She sold ten pieces of candies for a can of rice. Moy was Keem's Lai's daughter! She earned four cans of rice per bag of candy.

Sitting on her feet, like all the business people at the open street market, she sang out, "Candy! Candy! Buy candy. Only one can of rice buy my candy."

Her first customer was a Cambodian boy. "I can buy your candy for one can of rice?" His eyes were as large as an elephant's head, and his chin almost rested on his toes.

"Yes! One can of rice, but I not have many candy. They go fast!" She pointed at three piles of candy she had put on the plate.

Word got out quickly. For just one can of rice, people got ten pieces of candy to eat! Within a week, Moy was selling four to five bags of candies per day. She would mix two or three different kinds of candies in different piles on the plate. Some people bought two piles of candy at a time. Everyone in the market nicknamed her Little Sister Candy.

Now she had the money (rice) to buy anything she wanted to eat. She bought white rice, pork or beef fried with green vegetables, and soup for lunch and dinner. A bowl of pork noodle soup cost four or five cans of rice. She ate it every day! One morning, Small saw her eating in the shop, and said, "People hungry, have no rice to eat. You dare buy pork noodle soup to eat."

"It my rice. If I have rice to buy pork noodle soup to eat, then I buy. I no eat with Big Sister," Moy said, shutting her up. Moy continued eating.

When Moy got home that evening, Small's parents repeated what she told them Moy had done and said some very unkind words to her. Moy shut them up with a couple of pieces of candy. Then she remembered they had given her only two pieces of candy to eat after they returned from the Thai border where they had bought new clothes and a lot of food.

Moy asked Pon's wife if she had used Keem's gold to buy all those things.

"Yes, but mother bring candy for you." Pon's wife always looked guilty when she got caught using Keem's gold.

"I no want mother to use my ma's gold anymore," Moy told the old woman.

"Why child so greedy? Mother love you more than my own blood daughter," Pon's wife would say, looking sad and hugging Moy.

One day Moy met a Cambodian woman whose husband was the commander at the French Farm during the Khmer Rouge. He was *that commander*—the one who dragged Moy facedown on the ground out of her home. The woman told Moy her third uncle lived across the river. Two days later, her third uncle showed up and took Moy back across the river with him. He was sad and older, his carelessness gone. His daughter had died, but he had a new daughter.

His wife told Moy that almost five years earlier, they had felt something wrong and didn't get on the boat with the oldest—fourth—uncle, the third and youngest aunts, and Grandma going to Vietnam.

Moy's second uncle's wife chose to go to Vietnam with the others. They didn't know what happened to the people on the boat, but

Keem

her second uncle lived somewhere around the river with his young daughter.

Moy lived with her third uncle and his family for about two weeks. Everyone around there used the coffee-and-cream-colored water from the river for cooking, bathing, and washing their clothes. They also shit and peed in the river. Human waste floated around, and the fish got fatter. Then they got eaten by the happy humans! Everyone drank and ate someone else's shit and pee!

Moy felt no love from her uncle and his family. Sometimes he looked at her strangely, like he first felt hate, then pity. Perhaps he wondered why Moy had lived when his daughter died. She didn't feel comfortable living with them, so one day she picked up her little clothes bag and told her aunt to tell her uncle she was leaving. Before Moy went back to Pon, her aunt took a couple of pictures from Moy of Wong's family.

A couple of months after Moy's family settled near that Buddhist temple, there was talk of a larger store in a town called Rock Cow. It was closer to the Thai border. Pon's family moved there, like many people. Moy paid ten cans of rice for Pon's wife to take a Lu-Mo (I'm not sure if I spelled it correctly)—a motorbike taxi with three to four seats for six to eight people. Pon's wife said she'd walk and Moy should take the taxi herself, but Keem had taught her daughter well.

"Mother older than me; take the Lu-Mo," Moy told her.

Pon's wife looked guilty, but still very happy, to take the taxi. And Moy walked with many men, women, and children on the highway toward Pailin. She stopped once in a while and bought water to drink, and stopped only once to buy rice to eat. Her bare feet hurt from the long walk on the hot concrete. The sky was clear, and the sun was bright. Sweat dripped from her head nonstop. She sat under a tree, resting, remembering when Pon's wife had given everyone the same amount of sweet cake to eat when she came back from the Thai border. That was why she walked and let Pon's wife take the taxi.

It took Moy all day to walk to Rock Cow. This was her first time there, while Pon's family had gone back and forth. Small lived in town for a while, selling beef. Moy got to Rock Cow when the sun was almost down, and Seron and Paula were playing in the street. She greeted them, then walked to their new home inside a large, old, wall-less building with a concrete floor and white metal roof.

People slept head-to-head and feet-to-feet. There was hardly an empty space anywhere, with a couple hundred people living under that one roof. When Moy walked into the building, the first things she smelled were the human odors of sweat, blood, and shit, along with mud, fish, and some other scents she couldn't name. The mosquitos were everywhere! As soon as she walked in, mosquitos landed on her ears and cheeks. She swept them away with both hands. Moy was the mosquitos' dinner all night long. Still, she gave her old, small mosquito net, which had belonged to her grandpa, to Pon and his wife. They were older than she. She only slept with Pon's family that one night.

The next morning she noticed there were no Vietnamese in Rock Cow, only Cambodian Republic soldiers, just as there were only Vietnamese soldiers at the Buddhist temple. Considering the bad blood between the Cambodians and Vietnamese, it was safer if they lived in different towns. After the Vietnamese saved them from the Khmer Rouge, some of the Cambodians still called them "Vietnamese rag." How's that for a thank-you?

The first morning in Rock Cow, Moy walked and looked around the market. It was large and new, with a concrete floor and no roof, built by the Cambodian Republic's government. In the first half of this new store, people sold sarongs, shirts, and pants, hanging from the two-wheeled wagons or lying on the concrete floor. Some people sold

Keem

candies, canned foods, rice, and cakes in plastic bags off large plats or wagons. Everything came from Thailand.

In the second half of the store, toward the back, mostly women and children sold cooked rice, pork or beef fried with different kinds of vegetables in large pots, sweet banana soup in large bowls, and sweet rice cakes off small, homemade tables. This store was like the one from the good old days, before the Khmer Rouge destroyed everything.

Moy smiled and wondered what she should do for a living, but the decision was made for her.

"Little Sister Candy, over here!" a businesswoman shouted and waved like mad to get Moy's attention. She was the same woman who sold the first two bags of candies to Moy when they lived near the Buddhist temple. The woman and her husband couldn't have been happier to have Moy as their business partner again, and they respected her. The young couple had told her to call them "Big Brother and Big Sister." This time, Big Sister didn't go check on Moy, like she had at the Buddhist temple, making sure Moy didn't run off with her candies. Now both husband and wife would come to ask, "Little Sister Candy want Big Sister get you more candy?" or "Little Sister Candy want Big Brother get you more candy or cake?"

Every day, the young couple let Moy pick her own candies. "You take only three bag? Take more! Take as many as you want!" they would complain.

"I have no rice to pay. I just take three bag."

"No worry, Little Sister. You sell, then pay later. Big Brother and Big Sister trust you," the young couple told her.

* * *

"No take what you not need. If you do, you will owe people," Keem and Wong taught Moy when she was a little girl.

When Keem and Wong were alive and living in Siem Reap, they trained Moy to do business before she could speak properly. They had her put white or brown sugar, black pepper, or MSG in small plastic bags. Then they had her sit on a little chair and sell them from a large plate in front of their five-and-dime shop at the open market, for one ning per bag. Moy kept the plate on a round bucket she could keep the money in.

"Buddha! Look at this small child, very smart. She know how to buy and sell!" People would smile at her, then look at Wong and Keem with respect.

When she got tired of selling, she would take the plate back to Ma and Grandpa. Keem or Wong would ask, "How many bag you sell? How much money you have? And how many bag you have left?" They trained her to count when she was very young, showing her different bills in a variety of colors and teaching her the value of each bill. They instructed her in giving back the proper change, using real paper money to play with her.

If she had the correct amount of money, she got to go out and play. If she was short of money, Grandpa made her sit down and count from one to one hundred. If she miscounted somewhere, Wong made her start again from the beginning. Poor little Moy would sit there counting and crying.

"What you must do, if you no want to count and go play?" Wong or Keem would ask.

"I look," she would say. She lowered her chin whenever she told them she had done something wrong.

"Look what?" They had her stand in front of them as they questioned her.

"I look at thing good, good." Moy looked left and right, showing Grandpa and Ma that she would be more careful.

Keem

"What you must do when you make a living?" Keem and Wong never yelled at her, but they did give her a look of disapproval if she was short of money. They wouldn't help her or try to catch the people who stole from her, either. They let her learn from her mistakes.

"I no play around when I do business. I look good, good," little Moy told them. She ran her business for half an hour or an hour each day; some days her training took longer.

Every evening, Wong and Keem sat in front of their house reading the newspaper. Most of the time, Wong had Moy sit on the ground next to his chair and count. Moy eyed a small whipping stick next to his chair while she counted and cried. He always made her recount from the beginning if she miscounted. She would cry harder.

Sometimes Keem came to her rescue, criticizing Grandpa. "Count and count. She go crazy and not know what she count anymore. You worse than prison guard! My sad child!" Keem would pick her up.

"Mama!" Moy arms wrapped around her ma's neck, and she cried on Keem's shoulder.

"Grandpa very mean. Let Grandpa eat rice by himself tonight. We go to the store and eat fry noodle. Puppy like fry noodle?" Keem hugged her tighter and carried her to the store.

They sat at a round table, and Keem ordered the large rice noodles fried with beef and green vegetables, feeding it slowly to her little daughter. She was always happy when Moy ate a lot. Sometimes Keem would say, "Let Ma feel your stomach." She would press her hand gently around Moy's belly, sometimes shouting, "Sad! Why my child's stomach still soft, soft? Ma no feed you today? Sad, sad, sad." Keem would do anything to get her daughter to eat more. "Child eat more and grow up fast, fast." After the fry noodles, sometimes Keem bought cold sweet nut soup (a rich people's food, like the fry noodles) for her daughter to eat.

Keem had had Moy sleep in the double bed with her since the day she was born. Now Moy slept outside on the old train platform, under the beautiful silver moon and twinkling stars. Strangely, there were no mosquitos out there, about thirty feet away from the old building. She had the whole platform to herself. Every night, she lay on the platform and stared at the moon. She missed her ma and longed for Keem's warm arms to wrap around her.

"Ma, where are you? Help me, Ma!" She would cry herself to sleep.

* * *

At that time, Small was the richest person in Rock Cow. She sold beef for a living and made a lot of money/rice and gold. She had moved with her four children to a small shelter covered in coconut leaves next to the market, a couple of minutes from her parents and their other two adopted daughters in the common house. Shortly afterward, Moy watched and listened to the strangest things that kept happening to Small and Pon's family. Someone was stealing their cows from the fields, and bags of rice were taken from under Small and Pon's heads when they slept at night. Then one day, Seron and Paula came home crying because their cows had run away.

"It like something startles them. They run and run. We can no catch them," the boys told everyone.

Later, two more people sold beef next to Small, and no one wanted to buy her beef anymore. Small salted the beef and dried it in the sun, but the beef got stolen. Then another bag of rice was stolen out from under Pon's head. Days later, Small cooked a very large pot of beef soup that she was going to sell, but it was taken from her house. These strange things kept happening. Small went mad and yelled at everyone. Finally, she gave up on the beef business.

Keem

Moy and most people wondered about those things. A little bag of rice was one thing, but a five-hundred-pound bag of rice would take two or three people to lift out from under their heads.

They must be sleep like dead! But not my business, Moy thought.

Moy might have been homeless and without a family, but she had her little business that made her about the richest person in town. Business in Rock Cow was better for her because more people lived there. People paid one can of rice for ten pieces of her candy, so now she had the money to buy whatever she wanted to eat, three times a day. She liked the rice wrapped in banana leaves; it smelled wonderful! She would buy beef or fish soup, or green vegetables fried with pork or beef, and eat it with rice. Most people in the market respected her, and a lot of people tried to adopt her. She just smiled and walked away. By then everyone, even the soldiers, called her Little Sister Candy.

She was happy during the day with her business. But she was lonely and cried herself to sleep almost every night. One night, as she lay on the old train platform staring at the full silver moon, she suddenly burst into tears. She rolled over on her side and wrapped her arms around herself.

"Ma, where are you? Come help me, Ma." She cried until there were no tears left. Then she lay on her back and stared at the twinkling stars and beautiful full moon.

Suddenly, a heavy rain came down on her. Perhaps Keem's spirit heard her child call and went to help.

Moy couldn't get up fast enough to run into the old building. Water dripped from her hair and clothes. She went to Pon's bed area of three boards and sat there playing with her fingers. Then she heard voices from a large group of men sitting on their feet in a big circle not far from her. She got up and walked toward the group. They were listening to a radio. She stood behind the men and listened to bits of what the Khmer broadcaster was saying. "Cambodian civilians go to Thai border. Americans help children who no have mother or father. American doctor…sick…United States…take Cambodians to America…freedom…go to school…United States…" Then the news ended.

I want to go to America! Moy thought, straightening up like a needle. She went back to the old train platform and went to sleep.

The next morning, she asked Pon's wife for her ma's gold. She said she was going to leave Cambodia and go to the Thai border. Pon and everyone laughed at her and called her a stupid girl.

"You want to kill yourself?" one toothless old man asked her.

"I want go to Thailand," Moy said. She lowered her head.

The elders told her many people got killed on the minefields. She argued that some people came back with clothes and food, but the elders said only forty people out of a hundred came back alive. They said the Vietnamese, the Khmer Rouge, and thieves were all waiting to rob and rape women along the way.

"You want them rape you?" someone asked.

"I want go to Thailand. I no afraid to die. If I stay here I might die. If I go I might die. I no want to wait and die here," she replied, then went to the market and bought two packs of rice wrapped in banana leaves and a bowl of beef soup with vegetables. After breakfast, Moy went to Small's house and said to Pon's wife, "Mother, I want Mother give my ma's gold back to me."

"What gold?" The old, toothless woman was cold as a dead fish. She looked at Moy like she had no idea what Moy was talking about.

"My ma's gold necklace, ring—"

"I no have your gold," she cut Moy off in a harsh tone of voice.

"Mother has my gold. When my ma died, I give all my gold to Mother to keep them for me." Moy felt cold from her head to her toes, inside and out.

Keem

"You eat them all! You not remember? You eat with us for four month." The toothless woman's face was hard.

Moy felt as if someone held a sharp knife to her heart. She took a good look at her adopted mother's round face, long chin, short black hair, and black eyes. The holes in each of her ears had grown larger than Moy's thumb from the large gold earrings she wore.

"What you look at?" the old woman demanded.

"I look at Mother's face." Moy had no more respect for this woman, nor did she feel sorry for her.

When they lived near the Buddhist temple, Pon's wife yelled at and cursed him for sleeping with a younger woman. He whipped her with his belt and sticks larger than his fingers. He whipped and whipped until he was exhausted. She lay on the ground, hardly able to move or whisper. Then Pon whipped her again after he got his strength back. No one dared interfere, or he would whip that person, too. His wife spent weeks in bed, burning up with fever and whimpering every time she moved.

At that time, Moy had watched from behind someone and cried. She was afraid Pon might kill his wife. Now, Moy felt nothing toward her. "I eat with Mother's family for two month. I no eat all my ma's gold."

"You eat with us for four month," the old woman shouted.

"Now is four month! Your daughter not let me eat with you since we live near the Buddhist temple," Moy shouted back, tears falling from her eyes.

"You dare yell at me? You have sin, and you will go to hell!" The toothless woman's eyes got larger, and her face became hard.

"I live in hell for five year; I no afraid of hell. I want my ma's gold back, *now!*" Moy took a step toward her.

"You eat all your gold," Small spoke up and smiled sweetly.

"I very small; I no eat all the gold away." Moy took on Small now, too.

"Small, but an old head," Small replied, always with that vulture's smile.

"Big Sister Small very right. I an old head; that why I remember you still have my gold. I no go to temple like Mother and Big Sister. *Now, give my ma's gold back to me*," Moy demanded.

"We not have your gold!" both mother and daughter shouted.

Moy wouldn't leave the country without her ma's gold, but she didn't know what to do. She walked to the market, crying. People stopped to stare at her. They had never seen her cry. She was always happy, sing-songing and calling out, "Aunt, Uncle, Big Brother, Big Sister, Little Sister, Little Brother, buy my candy. I sell them cheap, cheap. Come buy."

She walked past the first part of the store and was about to enter the food section when someone called out to her, "Little Sister Candy, why you no sell candy today?"

She turned around and saw a young soldier. A long gun hung from the gun belt on his shoulder.

"Why Little Sister cry?" he frowned and asked.

Moy told him almost everything, and she couldn't stop crying. He just stood there and listened.

"If this truth, then I take you to meet Mr. Big." He meant someone who has authority. "Come with Big Brother. I tell you which Big Brother you go talk to." He gestured for her to follow him.

22

They walked up toward the main highway. A white concrete house stood on the right corner of the main highway and a small street to the market. A few brown, wooden houses were close to the white house. All around, in front of the house, soldiers stood leaning on walls, and a few soldiers here and there were talking. A few feet away, Moy stood behind the young soldier. He turned around and whispered, like he was afraid someone might hear him. "Look there." He pointed to three men in gray uniforms and black boots, sitting on a long wooden swing.

"Yes." Moy looked at the backs of the three men.

"Little Sister, go talk to that big brother sit in the middle." The young soldier pointed.

"Who is he?" she asked.

"Little Sister not know? That big brother is Mr. Governor. Go talk to him. He will help Little Sister. Go," he said, fanning her off with both hands.

"Big Brother come with me?" She looked at him.

"Little Sister go first. Go!" He fanned her off again.

Moy walked to the front of the house, then just stood there waiting. One by one all the soldiers stopped talking and looked at her with great interest.

"Why Little Sister come here?" one of the three men sitting on the swing asked.

"I come to talk to Mr. Big," she said and pointed at the man sitting in the middle. (In Khmer, "Mr. Big" or "Mr. Big Brother" is a kind of respectful title, like Sir.)

"Me?" He sounded surprised, smiling and pointing at his chest.

Everyone laughed aloud, then stopped when they saw her teary face. The men looked uncomfortable. Moy stared down. Some soldiers shifted their feet around. Finally, the governor cleared his throat and stood up.

"What Little Sister want to talk about?" he asked.

"I come to complain against Grandma Pon's family." Moy looked at the tall man through tearful eyes.

Some of the soldiers' chins dropped slowly. The tall governor stood in front of her, unable to speak for a couple of seconds. Then he asked, "What Little Sister just say?"

"I charge against Grandma Pon's family," she sobbed aloud. She was not afraid of the governor or any of the men around her.

The governor observed her for a minute longer, then told his men to go away. The two unarmed older men on the swing remained, looking somber.

"Come with me." The governor led her into the house.

The house was one large room, with a big desk facing the entrance and a few chairs next to the walls. The door was missing. The governor went behind his desk and sat down, telling Moy to get a chair and come sit next to him. Moy sat at the side of his desk, her head lowered in respect.

"Why Little Sister charge against Grandma Pon's family?" the governor wanted to know.

"I want my ma's gold back. But they no want give them back." Moy couldn't stop her tears from dripping onto her hands and lap.

"What gold?" he asked.

"During Khmer Red, before my ma die, she tell me if she die, she want me take Grandpa Pon and his wife as my mother and father.

Keem

When my ma die, I no want anything. I just want my ma back. Ma tell me, 'Tell no one about the gold.' But Grandma Pon see the gold, and she take them from me. She say, 'I keep them for you.' Now, she no want give them back to me." Moy sometimes sobbed aloud as she told him the whole story.

He listened without interrupting her and was silent at the end of the story. Then he asked, "How much gold you have?"

"Ma have a lot gold. We have close to about a kilo of gold."

"Look at me," he ordered.

Moy looked at him, and he observed her. He was about twenty-five or thirty years old, with a long, handsome face, dark skin, black eyes, black hair, and a perfect nose. He looked good in his gray uniform, like a fighter.

"Now, tell me the story again," he told her.

"My ma know Grandpa Pon because he walk his cow by my house every day. Later, he give little food to my family. Then he help bury both my grandpa and my ma's body. When my ma die, I give Ma's necklaces, rings, earrings, and bracelets; Grandpa's rings; and my necklaces, rings, earrings, and bracelets to Grandma Pon. She say I still too young and not know how to keep the gold. I give everything to them to keep for me. Now, she no want to give them back. She say I eat them all." Moy paused, looked at him, then asked hopefully, "Mr. Big Brother help me?"

He looked at her long and hard. Then he got up and pointed at her. "Stay here." He went outside and shouted to one of his men. Moy's eyes followed his back. A soldier ran up and stood at attention in front of the governor for a moment, then took off. The governor said something to the men sitting on the swing, and all three men peeked at Moy. Then they whispered to each other, looking somber. The governor came back and sat behind his large desk again.

"My soldier call you Little Sister Candy. Is Big Brother right?" he asked, smiling.

"Yes, Mr. Big." She lowered her eyes.

A few minutes later, Pon's wife came into the house, followed by two armed soldiers. Her face was pale. The governor didn't get up, but he welcomed her with a smile. "Grandma Pon come in; sit here," he said. He pointed at a chair on the other side of his desk, facing Moy. One of the two soldiers was the young soldier who had taken Moy there.

"Out!" the governor pointed at the two soldiers. They stood at attention, turned around, and walked out of the house.

"You! You dare charge against me!" Pon's angry wife shook a finger at Moy from across the desk, standing halfway out of her chair.

"Grandma Pon, no angry with this child. Grandma Pon, this child say you have her ma's gold. Right or wrong?" the governor asked.

"I no have her gold. She has no gold. She lie to Mr. Governor," the toothless woman told him.

"I have!" Moy looked at the governor, and he smiled.

"This child say she give her gold to you to keep for her after her ma die," he spoke through his laughter.

"I no have her gold." She smiled at Moy from across the desk.

"Mother have my gold. I give you my gold to keep for me. Mother take my ma's necklaces and bracelets and go play card game and lost them!" Moy shouted.

"No yell! Talk. No yell, and no lie. Grandma Pon, you have this child's gold?" he asked again.

"I lost them!" she shouted loudly, then covered her mouth quickly, her hands shaking.

The governor froze in his seat. Then he leaned slowly forward and folded his hands on top of the desk. He turned toward the old woman and asked, "Grandma, you have this child's gold?"

"Before I have, but Khmer Red take them all before the Vietnamese come in." For the second time, she covered her mouth quickly.

"When?" he asked.

Moy just sat there listening and staring at her.

"Before, before…" She tried to remember something, then just shouted loudly, "When the Vietnamese come in!"

The governor looked at Moy. His face was hard, and he asked in a harsh tone, "How much gold you give to Grandma Pon?"

"Close to a kilo." Moy kept her eyes on him.

"What kind of gold?" He wanted details.

"My ma had three sets of big, big gold necklaces, rings, earrings, and bracelets. Grandpa had two big, big rings. I have three sets of big, big gold necklaces, rings, earring, and bracelets. And the baby necklaces, rings, bracelets, and ankle bracelets belong to me. My ma and I have many mismatched necklaces, rings, earrings, and bracelets."

"When you give this gold to Grandma Pon?"

"I give them to her the same day my ma die, June 18, 1977, between three-thirty and four o'clock."

"Little sister remember the date, month, year, and time?" He leaned back sharply, like someone had slapped his face.

"I remember my grandpa die on June 8, 1977, in the morning. My ma say number nine no good, eight better. My ma die on June 18, 1977, at three in the afternoon. Then I give my gold to Grandma Pon." Moy wiped tears away with the backs of her hands. Then she straightened her shoulders and tossed her chin up. She stared the old woman in the eyes and said, "If mother want to keep my gold, keep them. I give my gold to you, like say, 'Thank you.' Your husband come and help my grandpa because he sick. Thank you. When my ma sick, you, your husband, and your daughter come and help me. After my grandpa and my ma die, your husband help bury them. Thank you.

"If I owe you anything in the past life, I now pay you all back. I owe you nothing, and you owe me nothing. I owe you no more 'thank you.' You owe me no forgiveness. But I want my ma's ring back. Big

Sister Small wear that ring yesterday. You want the gold? Take them and keep them! I no want them. But remember, my ma and my grandpa give them to me. You want them? I give them to you. But today, I want my ma's ring back. I give you everything, but I no give you my ma's ring. *I want it back today.*

"If I know how to write, I'll write all of this in a book, and let people read and know what kind of person you are—and what I am!" Moy told her.

The old woman looked ashamed for a quick second. The governor was speechless. Time stood still. Finally, he turned toward the old woman and asked, "Grandma Pon, you have this gold?"

"I…I lost them on the road when Vietnamese come in. I put them in the rice bag and we forget to take them," she told him.

"Grandma Pon, you lie. This child have those gold, yes?"

"She has, but she eat them all. She eat them all! She eat a lot!" the old woman shouted.

The governor laughed. "Grandma, this child very small. She can no eat all one kilo of gold in four month. One kilo of gold can feed all of my soldiers for five or six months. You know how many soldiers I have? Just in Rock Cow, I have three hundred soldiers. Now, where is this child gold?" He sounded angry now.

"I no have her gold!" the old woman screamed. Her face got paler as each second went by.

"You answer me three times. And each time, you give me a different answer. At first, I think this child lie to me. Now I know she tell me the truth. People like you not know how to tell the truth, no. You lie to this child, and you lie to me. Where is the gold?" His tone was harsh.

"My family eat them all." She lowered her head.

"Ten people eat all one kilo of gold in four month?" He sounded angrier.

"Yes." She didn't dare look up this time.

"My soldier tell me this child buy her own food from the store to eat every day. She eat by herself morning, afternoon, and evening, right?"

"Yes," she whispered, keeping her head down.

"Your daughter take this child's gold to buy and sell beef in the store, right?"

"No! Yes!"

"Grandma Pon, yes or no?"

"Yes." Her nose was almost resting on the governor's desk now.

"Look up, Grandma Pon! I want to see your face!" For the first time, he yelled, his hand coming down hard on the desk.

The old woman jumped and looked up slowly.

"Old, old grandma like you, they go to temple, pray to Buddha, and wish to do good thing. But an old grandma like yourself, you lie to this child. You trick her and take everything from her. People who steal and gamble go to jail. You know that?" he asked.

"Mr. Big," Moy called for his attention.

He looked at her.

"I no want Mr. Big take Mother Pon to jail, no. I only want my ma's ring back. I give everything to this mother, but not the ring. I want it back today."

"Little Sister want to do this?" He looked at her strangely.

"Yes." She turned to Grandma Pon. "From today on forward, I owe you nothing. You and your family owe me nothing. We equal. But Buddha will give justice," Moy said, staring at the old woman from across the desk.

The governor opened his mouth to say something but changed his mind. He turned to the old woman and told her, "I give you one hour. And I want to see this child's mother's ring. If she come and tell me you not give it to her, I will take you and family to jail. Hear me, Grandma Pon?" he demanded.

"Yes, yes. I feed her like feed an alligator," she shouted as she rose from the chair.

"Yes, Mother right. You feed an alligator. If Mother no eat with an alligator, Mother would starve to death! You eat my ma and my grandpa's gold that they give to me. Mother, you eat an alligator's money. Mother is more an alligator; not me," Moy told her.

The Cambodians believe alligators don't know their owners or caretakers and, given the chance, would eat them.

The governor laughed aloud and mumbled something that sounded like "smart." Moy got up from her chair, but he reached over, grabbed onto her upper arm, and told her to sit down.

"You go," he told the old woman. He and Moy watched her walk out of the house.

Moy overheard the two men sitting on the swing yelling, "Unlucky and disgusting old grandma. Lie and steal from small child! What kind of old grandma you? Very disgusting!" They spat on the ground as the old woman walked by.

"One kilo of gold is a lot of gold. Little sister want to give all that gold to them?" the governor asked. Now his smile looked sad.

"Yes."

Moy thought he wanted to argue further but changed his mind. He told her kindly, "Come see Big Brother if they no give the ring back to you."

"When I get my ma's ring back, I go to Thailand." She shared her dream with this good man.

"Go by yourself?" His eyes got big.

"Yes! I go by myself and follow the sell people," she told him.

His eyebrows went up, but he didn't argue.

"Mr. Big, can I go?"

"Yes, go," he waved her off.

Keem

Moy stood up in front of his desk. She looked at this young governor's kind face, then lifted her hands, palms facing and fingers pressed together under her chin, and bowed. "Thank you, Mr. Big."

He smiled and showed her his respect by standing, too. Then he walked side by side with her out of the house. Now she was on her way to the Pons' house to get her ma's ring back! And she would be on her way out of the freedom cage!

Moy was halfway home when she saw Pon's wife with the two soldiers who had taken her to the governor's office. The young soldiers told Moy the governor wanted the old woman to wait for her.

"Mr. Big help Little Sister, yes?" the young soldier whispered.

"Yes. Mr. Big is good person. Thank you, Big Brother." Moy expressed her gratitude to the kind young soldier.

"I come meet Little Sister in one hour. Go home now." He said. He and Moy smiled at each other.

The two young soldiers gave the old woman a hard stare and said, "This old grandma has no shame; lie to small child. I hate it. Disgusting, very unlucky!" They spat on the ground in front of her and walked away.

Moy and Pon's wife went to Small's house. She told her daughter everything. If Small refused to give the ring back to Moy, the whole family would go to jail. Small smiled and lost her sarong in front of Moy. Small took the 24-karat ring with a light, oval-shaped jade from inside her sarong, then threw it on the ground. She called Moy a whore, an alligator, a dog, Chinese rag, and every other dirty name she could think of.

Moy cried to see her beloved Ma's ring thrown on Mother Earth. She picked it up quickly and shouted, "I'm not a whore! I too young; I no whore. If I a whore, you eat my money and that make you a whore, too!"

As always, Small had that cold, dead-fish smile. She held her hand up and ran at Moy, but Pon grabbed her hand to stop her from slapping Moy. But then he also called Moy every dirty name he could think of.

Moy cried at all the insults Pon's family threw at her. She put her ma's ring in a small money bag Keem had made for her in Pailin. Then she looked Pon in the eyes. He had a long, wrinkled face and gray hair, but he was still good-looking. He was very angry, like everyone in his family. Moy was sure that, by now, everyone in Rock Cow knew Pon's family had a kilo of gold belonging to her. Who wouldn't want some of it?

Moy picked up her small clothes bag; then she looked around for the twenty to thirty cans of rice she had made selling candy. They were nowhere to be found. She knew Small had taken them. Moy asked for five cans of rice. Small gave her only *one* can.

"My heart is good; same like Buddha," she told Moy with her cold, dead-fish smile.

Moy just stared at her. Then she walked out of Small's house.

Carrying her little clothes bag over her shoulder, she walked to the governor's office. There were soldiers in front of the office, some sitting on the long wooden swing, but most of them were standing around talking. All the conversations slowly eased to silence as the soldiers watched her walk into the office. The governor was sitting behind his desk, and two large men sat on either side. The three men stopped talking as she walked up to the governor's desk. Everyone looked at her with interest.

"I come to thank Mr. Big and tell Mr. Big I go to Thailand now. I pray to Buddha to give Mr. Big good and long life. Good-bye, Mr. Big." Moy lifted her hands, palms and fingers pressed together under her chin, and lowered her head, paying respect to him.

"Yes, thank you. Little Sister go now?" the governor asked.

"Yes, Mr. Big."

Keem

"Good-bye." He smiled.

"Good-bye, Mr. Big." Her throat was tight, and tears kept coming to her eyes. She looked at this young, handsome, kindhearted governor from Rock Cow. He helped get her ma's ring back for her. She wanted to remember him. All ten of her fingers again went straight up, pressed together under her chin, and she bowed low to the governor one final time.

"No cry. Buddha go with Little Sister." He got up, his hands and fingers pressed together in front of his chest, and smiled handsomely.

"Have a long life, Mr. Big. Good-bye." With that last farewell to the governor, she turned around and walked from the office. She could hear the men whisper to each other, "That Chinese child afraid of nothing!"

The soldiers were wall-to-wall in front of the entrance of the office, watching and listening to the whole thing. They parted in the middle, making room for her, and now Moy was on her way to the train station behind Pon's house and the Rock Cow Market.

Keem Lai's Ring
Book III
A Guiding Light

Keem Lai's Ring: A Guiding Light

Moy had never seen a real train. This train behind the Rock Cow Market was on the old railroad track. It was about twenty or thirty feet long. The old wooden platform had been replaced by a new one with no walls or roof. Some people on that train had come all the way from Phnom Penh. A few people got on or off at Rock Cow's station.

Moy tried to get on the train, but a man stopped her and asked for payment. She took a tiny earning from her ear and gave it to him. He looked at her strangely but said nothing. She watched him put the earring away quickly; then he helped her board the train. There was hardly any empty space on the train filled with women, men, children, and babies sitting on their parents' laps. Each family sat with their belongings of clothes and food.

Moy felt hollow because Keem and Wong weren't on the train with her, and she had no family to sit with. She sat at the edge of the train, holding tightly to her clothes bag on her lap. She looked around the long train. There were about twenty drivers, each with a long, large, round wooden pole in his hands. Ten drivers stood on each side of the train.

"Push! Push!" one man at the front and another at the back shouted. All the drivers pushed and shoved the train to roll it forward. The train went fast, rolling on that old railroad track! Sweat rolled down the drivers' heads, faces, arms, and bodies. The veins in the men's necks popped against their skin as they pushed and shoved the train to go uphill. The drivers got to rest some when the train was rolling downhill.

Moy never took her eyes off Cambodia. The trees, tall green or brown grass, and land flew by as the train took her to the Thai border. This was the land where Moy drew her first breath, learned to say Ma and Grandpa, and learned to play games with her ma. She listened to Grandpa's laughter when she learned to do a lion dance, wearing a toy lion head Grandpa had bought for her. This was the land where she found joy and love, and was loved and filled with laughter in return. And this was also the land where Mother Earth drank many drops of her tears from pain, sorrow, and heartache. This was the land where some people were her friends and some were her worst enemies. This was also her borrowed land.

But she had Keem Lai and Wong Lai's love to carry on. A short ten years of joy, love, and laughter was all she had to hold onto, and she would always cherish that time. The endless tears and sorrows made her a fighter! She was not a troublemaker but an innocent girl, and she was robbed of everything by many people she had trusted.

Chan and her stepmother took some of her gold and clothes. The evil stepmother took her ma's earrings, rings, and clothes. But she gave back a tiny pair of baby's earrings, even as she lied through her greedy and evil teeth to say, "I lost them." And Pon's greedy and evil family robbed her of everything that Keem and Wong had saved for Moy.

This was the land where I took my first breath and drew the first mouthful of milk from my ma's breast. This was the land where I learned to take my first step, first smiled, and first laughed. And I ate my first mouthful of food when my ma and grandpa chewed it,

Keem

then fed it to me. This was the land where I felt my ma's warm arms wrap around me, keeping me warm at night. Ma and Grandpa hugged and kissed me. They smiled and laughed with me. This was the land where I had so much laughter and happiness, full of love from Ma and Grandpa. This was also the land where I shed many teardrops as I watched Grandpa and Ma die in front of me. This was the land where some people forced many storming teardrops out of me, until heaven wept along with me.

And now I'm on a roofless and wall-less train, heading to an unknown land called America, far away from this hateful land and all that I knew and loved, and I'll never look back. My teardrops that stained this land are all it will have of me. I have nothing else left to give! My ma, my grandpa, and my big brother were all taken from me. Now all I have are memories, and this hateful land can't take them from me. I won't say good-bye. I'll simply leave this hateful land—Cambodia—behind.

* * *

At about two or three in the afternoon, the train reached its stop and everyone got off. Moy looked around. This was not what she had hoped for. As far as she could see were just trees and bushes, with small and large mud puddles everywhere. She looked at a small footpath, about four feet wide, in the middle of the thick, dark jungle. No one else seemed to care and started making cooking fires for their lunch. Moy dipped a small oval can (the same can in which she had roasted the grasshoppers) in a tiny mud puddle to get some of the water that sat above the black mud. She cooked her one can of rice, ate half, and saved the other half for the next day.

Moy watched as some traders returning from the Thai border arrived with bags full of things, while others arrived empty-handed.

Other people were on their way to the border along the same footpath. She wasn't sure what to do, but she remembered Keem and Wong always said, "If you want to go somewhere, go! Sitting here not take you anywhere. But look good, good, and listen good, good, and watch what people do and say. Not just follow this one or that one. You must think good, good; then do it."

After lunch it was late, and most people just rested under the trees. Moy didn't think it was a good idea to take off now. She didn't know where the Thai border was. She had thought the train would take her there, instead of just leaving them in this jungle. That night, she slept alone under a tree on the wet, cold earth and was nearly eaten alive by mosquitos. She was mindful to get up when everyone else did, before sunrise, as she didn't want to be left behind. She followed some traders and three families.

Moy walked barefoot, in the middle of the small group on that footpath in the jungle. She did well keeping up with the group on dry land when the footpath was all sand and small rocks. But when the path led into black muddy water up to her knees, she fell way behind the group. No one waited for anyone else. She fell in the mud and water countless times. If it was not the slippery mud, then it was the sharp little rocks cutting her feet. She would just get up, wipe the mud and water off her face, and go on. She tried very hard to keep up with the group, but she got left behind a few times, all alone in the dark and muddy jungle.

"Ma, help me! You must bring good people to help me and chase bad people away!" she cried in her fright.

She walked faster when the mud was not deep or slippery. But at one point she couldn't see anyone in front of her, just the dark jungle. She cried and walked as fast as she could and finally caught up with the group. But every time there was mud, she would fall, get up, and walk on, trying to catch up from behind the group again. She was very happy when the mud field was finally behind her and ran until she caught up with the others. Moy always wiped away her tears of fright when she was a couple of feet behind the group.

Then the small group of people in front of her divided into two. She didn't know which group to go with. Most of the group turned left. Only a Cambodian family chose to go straight. Moy didn't have time to think. She listened.

"We go the long way, it safer. Then we must go across a river," the man told his wife. Each of them had a small child on a hip, their free hands holding their small bags of belongings.

Moy followed them in silence. She didn't have to run to keep up with them. The family paid no attention to her. They walked for a very long time. Then they came to a river, where a middle-aged man was waiting for passengers in a small canoe. He charged two cans of rice per passenger, but Moy had nothing. His stare made her break out in a cold sweat. The family got in the canoe while Moy was frozen at the edge of the river, by the evil stare from that middle-aged man.

The husband looked at Moy, then stared at the middle-aged man. "I pay for her. Little Sister, come down," he said and nodded for Moy to get in the canoe with them.

"Thank you, Uncle. Thank you!" Moy couldn't get in the canoe fast enough. After a few minutes crossing the river, everyone got out of the canoe. The middle-aged man looked disappointed when Moy got off. She offered to carry the kind family's belongings for them, but they said no.

Walking behind them, she heard the husband and wife whispering to each other, "That old grandpa want to torture her. Pity her, all alone." They meant he had wanted to rape her.

Moy welcomed the hot sand under her bare feet. It burned away the pain in her heart. She also welcomed the hot sun above her head that numbed her brain. She welcomed the sweat rolling from her head, washing away the nightmares she had lived through for the last four and a half years. She welcomed the new sunlight shining into her eyes, lending new beauty to nature. Each step she took was one step of Cambodian land she welcomed leaving behind. Her eyes were on the small blinking of candlelight waiting for her on the other side of the dungeon that she was about to walk into.

Moy and the Cambodian family walked past a sand field. Later, they reached a large group of people hanging around in front of a minefield. Moy saw everyone looking scared and confused. People kept whispering, "What we do? Minefield."

"If we walk straight, straight on that footpath, we no get kill by mine. If everyone walk here and there, everywhere, all of us will die! We walk one straight line, no touch anything. Agree?" a man on the other side of Moy said.

"Agree!" everyone shouted.

Trees and bushes were much smaller and shorter here, so it was all blue sky and bright sun above their heads. The minefield was large, surrounded by larger trees farther out and a few small bushes or dry, brown grass clumps here and there in the brown, red, and black soil. Small pieces of clothing, cans of food, and human body parts were *everywhere*.

Moy walked past an arm and hand lying on top of a bush. It was the size of a baby, a sickening gray color, and was being pecked at by something. Like everyone else, she covered her nose and mouth as they walked by. No one made a sound. Even infants were quiet in their parents' arms as they walked through that minefield. Moy saw a perfect white bra on the side of a short bush. But it had nothing to do with land mines, and no woman would take her bra off out in the middle of the jungle and toss it there.

"Never walk in front or back. If anything happens, the ones in the middle will be safe," Wong always said.

Keem

Moy stayed in the middle, or at least made sure other people were behind her. As she walked across the field, sometimes she saw pieces of torn clothing on the side of the footpath. Other times she saw blood on rocks or trees. About twenty minutes later, they walked out of the minefield, and families put down their belongings to cry, laugh, and hug each other.

Moy had no one to hug or laugh with.

"Child, in future I give you good day," she remembered her beloved Ma and Grandpa wishing her success. Those eight words were Keem Lai's gift of love to her beloved daughter before she went to her new kingdom in heaven.

Moy continued walking with the group until they reached a pond in an open field, with a few trees close to the water. The sun had nearly set by then. About thirty families already rested near the pond. The newcomers joined them, and people started making fires to cook dinner. Then they ate, talked, and laughed. Moy had nothing to cook. She went around and offered to carry people's babies in exchange for some rice to eat. That night, she lay under a big tree alone. Before she fell asleep, she heard a Cambodian man say, "We no stay here long. Thief will come out and rob people."

"Vietnamese come here, too. They wait until everyone sleep; then they come out like wolf," another man spoke up.

"Vietnamese no torture us, no?" a woman sounded worried.

"Gold, food, woman—pretty, pretty woman. They take woman to sleep with them."

"Stop talk, Old Grandpa! You talk like crazy!" an old woman yelled at her husband, making the others laugh.

Moy kept her eyes closed. Her right hand reached to get her ma's ring from her underwear pocket, and she put it in her mouth, then went to sleep. Children's laughter woke her. She sat up quickly and looked around. To her relief everyone was still there. She looked at the blue sky. The sun shone brightly. Without a thought, she got up, tossed her clothes bag over her shoulder, and started walking again.

It was like had someone told her, "You must go now and not wait another minute longer." Perhaps it was Keem's spirit urging Moy to get out of that area. Maybe Keem's powerful spirit was there all the time, protecting Moy from harm and guiding her to safety.

A small four- or five-foot-wide footpath cut through the jungle, with a few small bushes, brown and green grass, and rocks lining both sides of the path. As she walked, Moy talked to her ma's spirit in Teochew/Chinese, asking for help. She begged her ma's spirit to guide her all the way to the Thai border. She asked her ma's spirit to chase bad people away and bring good people closer to help her.

She walked all day nonstop, with nothing to eat or drink. But she didn't care. She just wanted to get out of Cambodia. When the sun behind her got lower and lower, and no one was in sight, she began to worry. The sun had almost set when she met a group of men, the first people she'd seen all day. They carried large bags on their shoulders, some also walking old bikes with no tires. She could see sarongs and candies through small holes in the bags on the bikes. The men walked past her quickly. Moy shouted to them, "Uncle, is people at the front?"

"Yes," one of the men shouted back.

"How far?" she asked, standing still for the first time all day.

"Very far!" he shouted back.

"How far?" She ran after them.

"Three hour!" he shouted.

Three hours? She froze, staring at the men's backs. Then she looked behind her at the orange sun sinking behind the mountains. She heard the wolves crying from far away. She wasn't sure if she should follow the men back or go forward by herself. Tears started dripping from her eyes. She turned around and ran away from the men, crying and begging her ma's spirit for help. She fell a few

Keem

times but picked herself up and ran until she couldn't run anymore. Then she walked as fast as she could, crying harder. "Ma, Grandpa, Great-Grandpa, and Great-Grandma, come help me! Ma, help me. Bring good people closer to help me, and chase bad people away. Ma, you must come and guide me to Thailand. I have no one to help me. Help me, Ma. Pity me!" Moy sobbed aloud, running and praying as tears streamed from her frightened eyes. She didn't want to get eaten alive by wolves. The sun was nearly gone, and more wolves called for one another, this time closer to Moy. She never stopped walking or running.

"*Ma, help me!*" she screamed aloud, glancing back.

The sound of wolves calling for each other got closer to her with each passing second. Every now and then, she glanced at the sun behind her, and each time she looked, it was lower and lower. Then the footpath in the open field ran into thick, dark jungle, where only a narrow path remained. One side of the sky was already dark. The wolves cried more intensely and much closer to her. The tiny footpath kept turning left and right.

"*Ma, help me!*" Moy kept calling for her ma's spirit. She could hardly see the footpath in front of her as she ran through the sharp turns. Then she heard something and ran faster.

"Ma, I hear people's voices!" she told Keem's spirit excitedly. Moy felt less frightened.

She saw the small tip of a roof and ran even faster. She saw smoke from far away and could barely make out the shape of a house. She laughed and cried at the same time when she saw shadows of people moving around ahead, near the smoke. She kept running until the house was in clear sight; then she slowed to a walk and looked at the house. There was a man and woman inside selling cooked rice, water, and other food. Moy walked past and kept going. There were more people on the other side, and campfires lit up the jungle. Many small plastic tents had been set up down from the shop. People sat in groups of two, three, or more around small cooking fires, eating, talking, and laughing.

At the smell of food, Moy's stomach protested. She went to a large tree and put her little bag down for the first time all day, then leaned back on the tree, resting for a minute. Then she got up and walked toward a cooking fire where a couple of women were eating. It would break Keem's heart if she looked down from heaven and watched her only child standing in front of someone and begging for food. Moy lifted her hands up, pressed her palms and fingers together under her chin, and lowered her head.

"Aunt, I beg for some rice to eat. I hungry." For the first time in her life, she begged for food, because she wanted to go to America.

"*Child, in future I give you good day.*" Keem had wanted her to live, so Moy begged.

The kind woman gave Moy a big bowl of rice with salt and fresh garlic mashed in, and a can of water to drink. Moy thanked the nice woman, then went to sit under the big tree. She ate with her fingers slowly. She saved some water and washed the bowl for the kindhearted woman, thanking her again.

"Pity her; have nothing to eat all day," the kind woman whispered to her friends.

Moy slept under that big tree until something cold dripped on her face. She turned on her side, but something wet and cold woke her up. She heard thunder and lightning from far away, and rain kept dripping on her face. She was wet and cold, but she went back to sleep. Then a loud rumble of thunder made her sit up straight. She looked around, but no one else was up. Most people were inside their tiny plastic tents. She rubbed the water off her face. Though it was raining very hard, not much water actually came down to the ground, because the trees in the area were large, with thick leaves to block the rain. But the sound of thunder was so loud it could wake the dead, and lightning flashed across the black sky.

The fury of nature that night was almost the same as the night Keem/Sue Chae Lai went to heaven and left Moy alone, at the mercy of the Khmer Rouge and strangers. She and Wong had worked so hard, saving all their money and jewelry for their Moy. If they did look down from heaven, it must have hurt and infuriated them, especially Keem, when she saw her little girl stand in front of a woman begging for food.

Moy looked around. Some people sat under other trees, like her. Then thunder exploded so close, she screamed and fell on her side, covering her head with her arms and hands. She didn't know what time it was, but the sky was still dark. She got up and went across the small footpath and behind a large rock to take her bath as the holy rainwater of Keem's tears rained down on her from heaven.

She looked around carefully. No one else was outside, so she took her shirt off, pulled her sarong up to her chest, and tied a knot. Moy smiled as she washed her hair and rubbed her arms, legs, and face with the heavy rain pouring over her. She washed off the dirt, the smell, the injustice, the suffering, the tears, the nightmares, and the pain that she had lived through on that land.

Just as Moy finished her bath, the rain stopped. Just like magic! Then the sleepy sun peeked up from behind the mountains. She was purified.

She took her wet clothes and went to sit on a big rock to wait for other people to get up. She was ready to face a new life in a new country. Would she survive? Only time would tell.

Suddenly, a group of people came running into the camp, pale faced. Women and babies were crying. Moy remembered them; most of these people had rested at the pond, and she walked across the minefield with some of them.

"What happen?" a sleepy woman asked, coming out of her tent.

"Vietnamese, Khmer Red disguise as Vietnamese! They come and rob everyone," a woman cried.

"They take my clothes, food, and gold. They take everything," an elderly woman cried.

"When it happen?" a man asked.

"Yesterday, when the sun go down, they come out like wolves," a young mother cried, her baby sucking on her breast.

Moy felt sorry for them and was glad she had left early in the morning the day before.

* * *

Moy picked up her clothes bag and again walked on that small footpath. She had no idea where she was going; she just followed that footpath with trees, grass, and rocks caging her in from both sides. She kept walking and never looked back. She walked all morning, and she kept going. Then she heard voices, Khmer. She turned left toward the voices and let the footpath lead her. She walked over a fallen tree and turned right into more muddy land. There was not a soul or sound anywhere, so she kept going.

Then she came to dry land and stood still, staring at the giant wall of trees, bushes, rocks, and grass in front of her. The footpath ended there. She felt like a sheet of ice wrapped slowly around her from the inside out, and small sounds escaped from her throat. There were no people—nothing—just the jungle staring cheerfully at her. She couldn't even cry.

"You cheat!" a man shouted.

Moy woke up from her fear. She blinked and looked to the right, where she saw a wooden house.

"I no cheat! Give me back my money!" This voice sounded like a young man.

Keem

She turned around and walked back toward that house. When she happened to look to her left, she saw the footpath on the other side of a gigantic fallen tree. She had to lay flat and wrap her arms and legs around the tree to climb over it and onto the footpath next to that house. This footpath was new, and grass still grew on it. She was happy to have a path again and walked for a while, in mud and water, sometimes up to her ankles, cooling her bare feet. She walked until the sun was straight up in the sky. *Voices!* The longer she walked, the closer the voices got. Then she heard more voices.

Each step forward took her one step closer to the voices. She couldn't hear what they said, but she kept walking on that black, muddy footpath to the future Keem wished for her to have. She was excited! She turned right one more time, toward where the voices came from. Moy would enter the Thai border. Then she might…vanish.

Camp 007
Cambodian and Thai border
1979

23

"Too expensive," a woman shouted.

"How much you want to pay?" another woman asked.

Moy heard the argument but couldn't see anything because of the trees in front of her. She kept walking toward the sounds of people arguing, laughing, and talking and children demanding food while their mothers yelled.

She made two more turns into a large, open field with more black mud and ankle-deep water. People moved around everywhere. The tall trees, grass, and bushes on both sides were like an open doorway, with an entrance no more than four feet wide. She walked through the black, muddy entrance and left the jungle behind. She smiled and kept walking forward, looking only at what was in front of her. She looked left and right, but she never looked back.

The black, muddy market was crowded. Young and old women sat on small beds selling cooked rice, meat fried with vegetables, sweet banana soup, and many more homemade foods. Men sold pork noodle soup off two-wheeled wooden wagons. The Cambodians hung new sarongs, shirts, and pants to sell off the wagons. The whole store was filled with laughter, talking, and arguing among the sellers and buyers.

Moy couldn't stop smiling after arriving at the border. She walked and watched buyers and sellers exchange paper money from hand to hand. She walked until she left the muddy store behind. Then she came upon a hill of dry and sandy land. The first thing she saw on that hill was the soldiers' long wooden house. The house had only one wooden wall, with the rest covered by brown grass. The soldiers wore green or blue uniforms and had long guns hanging from gun belts on their shoulders. Some soldiers were talking and laughing in front of their house. Hammocks were tied to three or four long lines of wooden poles. These soldiers were Cambodian, but they called themselves Thai soldiers. On this hill, there were countless shelters made from grass, tree branches, or blue plastic.

This hill was for big business, with table after table piled high with all kinds of cigarettes in long packets, candies that were twelve bags in a pack, canned food twelve to a pack, and sarongs twelve to a pack. People sold pork noodle soup inside a one-walled shelter with long wooden tables and benches where people could sit and eat. The roofs of the shops were made of grass, coconut leaves, or plastic. Women, men, and children wore clean sarongs, pants, and shirts. The businessmen and women sitting behind homemade tables all looked clean.

Moy walked farther up this wonderful hill. *I can sleep on dry land and not in the smelly black mud!* she thought, giggling. She saw some women selling cooked duck and chicken eggs out of large, hot pots. A variety of foods were sold inside these family shelters. Looking around, Moy bumped into someone.

"I beg forgiveness." She turned toward the unlucky person.

"Little Sister Candy?" a man asked.

"Uncle Noodle!" she shouted, excited to know someone there. She had eaten his pork noodle soup almost every day when she lived near the Buddhist temple in Cambodia.

"Little Sister Candy, it you," the round-faced, half-Chinese and half-Cambodian man repeated.

"Yes, it me. I not know Uncle Noodle come to live here."

Keem

"I come three month ago. I still sell noodle, and people still call me 'Uncle Noodle'!" He laughed good-naturedly. Looking around, he asked, "Where your mother and father?"

"I come by myself," she told him.

"Your mother and father let you come? You say play?" He meant she must be joking.

"Grandpa and Grandma Pon not my birth mother or father. I live with them because my ma tell me to."

"Where your ma?" he wanted to know.

"My ma died during Khmer Red."

"Why I see you carry water for Grandpa Pon and his wife's bath every day. You look after Small's cow and help her cook. If they not your family why you do that?" He frowned.

"I live with them, and I help them. And they take all my ma's gold. They no give them back to me." Moy lowered her chin.

"Where you go to live now?" The man seemed worried.

"I not know. I not know anyone. I just get here."

"You want to live with my family?" he asked.

"Yes, Uncle!" she smiled.

She liked him. Uncle Noodle was a large, dark-skinned gentleman and seemed nice. He had black hair, black eyes, a sort of round face, and round, thick lips, like her big brother Ming. Uncle Noodle was between five ten and six feet tall, and neither fat nor thin. Like most men, he didn't smile much.

"Then come with me. My house is small. We sleep on the ground. My house have no wall, but a roof over our head," he told her.

Moy followed him as they walked a couple of minutes up the hill. It was crowded up there. They turned left toward his house, where a long wooden bench and table and a brick stove next to it took up half the shelter. The one-walled house was eight to nine feet wide and about seventeen feet long, and coconut leaves covered the roof.

Their belongings were shoved against that single wall covered with dry grass. Uncle Noodle's mother sat on a grass mat at the other side of the shelter, where everyone slept.

"Mother, this child come to live with us. She no has anyone here," he shouted loudly for her to hear.

The bald-headed elderly woman made no response. She just looked at Moy then looked away. She was locked up inside herself somewhere, in her own world. Uncle Noodle had carried his mother from Cambodia to get there, because she couldn't walk.

"Grandma," Moy bowed.

"No talk to her. She no talk to anyone or listen to anyone. She old." He sounded sad. Then he changed to a fatherly tone. "Now, what you do?"

Moy took a tiny earring from her ear and put it in his large hand. She asked if he knew where she could sell it. He weighed it in his hand and looked at it.

"Gold like this very expensive; you can sell it more than fifty baht." (Baht is Thai money.) "Don't sell for less. Go near the soldier's house; people buy and sell gold over there," he told her.

"Thank you, Uncle. Tonight I come and sleep here," she told him. She was very happy this good man helped her. Uncle Noodle wanted to know what she was going to do that afternoon, and she said she would go look around.

"Then go," he encouraged her, like Keem and Wong used to.

Of all the people in Camp 007, Moy ran into Uncle Noodle upon her arrival. At that time, she didn't really think about it. Much later, she came to believe that Keem's powerful spirit must have chased him out of his house that day so he could give Moy shelter.

* * *

Keem

Moy walked toward the soldiers' house. She went up to a man leaning on a two-wheeled wagon under a big tree. She couldn't tell if he was sleeping, and she couldn't see his eyes. She stared at his large tummy. It was as big as a nine-months-pregnant woman's. Then she looked at a small gold scale inside the wagon.

"Uncle want to buy my gold?" she asked.

"A small child like you have gold to sell?" He didn't move or look at her, but he must have seen her coming.

She smiled at his large cheek, then waved a baby's earring in front of his nose. His whole body turned sharply toward her, and he nearly fell off his small wooden chair. His head turned left and right, following the little earring between her fingers as Moy waved it around.

"Let Uncle see," he shouted, his eyes getting larger. He leaned forward to reach for the earring.

"How much per gram?" Moy asked.

"Let me see; let me see!" His eyes followed the earring like a cat after a fish. His large hands reached left and right trying to grab it. Moy tossed the earring in her mouth, and he gasped and stared at her.

"How much for one gram?" she asked again.

"You eat that, you die." He shook a large finger at her.

"If Uncle not want to buy my gold, I go to that aunt over there." She pointed at a woman nearby, standing next to her two-wheeled wagon. The woman kept making signals for Moy to come over to her.

"Old witch! Let me buy and sell. No bother my business!" he shouted angrily, trying to get out of his chair as he shook a finger at his neighbor.

"Fat pig! Niece, come here." The middle-aged woman waved Moy over.

"You stay here!" he said to Moy. He still struggled getting to his feet. "Let me see; let me see." He held his hand up.

MOY

Moy took the earring from her mouth and dropped it in his palm. He gave her a dirty look, wiping his hand and the earring on his white shirt. He looked carefully, then weighed it on the scale.

"Forty baht," he told her.

Moy reached to take the earring off the scale.

"Forty baht." He caught her hand quickly.

"How many gram?"

"Two."

"Uncle lie."

"I no lie," he shouted.

"Uncle no yell at me."

"I no yell." But he had been yelling ever since he met her.

"One hundred fifty," she told him.

"One hundred fifty? You crazy?" he said.

"Let Aunt see it. If Aunt like it, Aunt buy it for one hundred fifty," the middle-aged woman shouted over.

"Old witch! No bother my business," he shouted angrily at his neighbor, his face red.

"Fat pig!" she yelled back.

"One hundred fifty or give my earring back." Moy held her hand out, palm up.

"Sixty," he offered.

"One hundred fifty."

"Seventy!" he shouted.

Moy kept silent.

"Seventy-five...Ninety!"

Moy smiled and looked in the middle-aged woman's direction. The woman smiled back.

"Old witch!" the man shouted over Moy's head.

"Fat pig!" she shouted back.

"Ninety-five." His nose was almost touching Moy's.

Keem

"That aunt over there wait for me." Moy pointed in the middle-aged woman's direction.

"Where you learn do business like this?" he asked, dropping the earring in his undershirt pocket and pulling out some bills. "Here!" He handed her some Thai money.

She smiled and counted the bills and, without looking up, told him, "Uncle owe me ten baht."

"Take it! Go, go!" He chased her away after handing her the ten baht.

"Thank you, Uncle," she giggled.

"Go, go!" He fanned her off with both hands.

Moy danced away, tucking the money into her shirt pocket.

Keem and Wong had taught her that if there were more sellers than buyers, you should pay as little as you can to the seller, and not be afraid to argue and make a deal. If one person won't sell it, another might. It worked the same way for buyers—you want the highest offer you can get it. If one won't pay the price that you want, another might.

"That's how you make a living," Keem and Wong had trained Moy when she was still a child.

* * *

With 150 baht, she could start a business. She didn't go to the muddy main market. Instead, she walked around the hill, looking left and right and listening carefully. Everywhere she looked, people were buying and selling. Then she came to a dead end where women, men, and children formed a long line in front of a building. Just then, a man came out of the building, and Moy rooted to the spot, her chin dropping. She tried many times to snap her mouth closed, but her jaw kept dropping, and there wasn't a thing she could do about it.

To Moy's eyes, the man was as tall as an oak tree and as wide as the Mekong River. Everyone has hair on his head, but this man had hair all over his face, too! She could see his two eyes, but he had no lips! Just the tip of his nose peeked out of the hair on his face. Each of his arms was a mile long, and the black hair on them was longer than the hair on her head. Then a Cambodian man came out after the big monkey man. The Cambodian man was only as tall as the monkey man's hip. Both men wore white short-sleeved shirts and long, dark pants. They stood side by side and talked to an elderly woman who had a small baby in her arms. Then they moved to the next person in line. Suddenly, the monkey man pointed at Moy.

The spell was broken. Moy snapped her lips together. The Cambodian man walked over and asked, "Little Sister sick?"

Moy kept her eyes on the monkey man not far away. The monkey man's eyes smiled as he walked slowly toward her. As he came closer, he looked three times bigger and taller than before! When he stopped a few feet away from her, she almost broke her neck trying to look up at his face. He said something to the Cambodian man that sounded like "ceechewa."

"Little Sister afraid of him?" the Cambodian man asked, smiling.

"He big." She couldn't take her gaze off the monkey man's smiling eyes.

The monkey man laughed loudly when the Cambodian man translated for him. Then the monkey man knelt in front of her.

Moy stepped away and took off like the wind. She hid behind a big tree and peeked to see if he had followed her. To her relief, he was still sitting on his heels laughing. His shoulders shook. Most people waiting in the long line also laughed and pointed in her direction.

Her chin up and shoulders pulled back, Moy marched out of her hiding place. She went farther up on the other side of the hill. Next to

Keem

the hospital was a wall-less building with a grass roof and big wooden poles. A lot of young girls and boys lived there, some playing, others arguing over a piece of meat or a small fish. They were the orphans. Their parents had been killed by the Khmer Rouge, or they had been separated. The children were all ages, from three years old to teenaged. They slept on a large piece of blue plastic on the ground. Moy didn't want to live with these orphans.

Fighting over a small fish? No, Moy thought as she walked away. She went higher up the hill and came upon some men, women, and children waiting in a long line, metal or plastic buckets next to their feet.

The line was for several large water tanks sitting on top of short wooden stands under the trees. Some people talked and laughed; others argued over something. Mostly, they waited impatiently under the hot sun. Just then the water trucks arrived, and everyone cheered loudly. The trucks stopped behind the water tanks, and the drivers climbed on top of them.

Moy watched from afar. She couldn't see what the drivers were doing on the water tanks, but people pushed their buckets under the middle of each tank. Children carried two smaller metal or plastic buckets of water each, while each adult carried a larger bucket, one at the front and one at the back of a carrying stick perched on his or her shoulders. Some of the adults carried water buckets on the carrying sticks on one sides of their shoulders and carried young children on their other hips.

Something on the opposite side of the water tanks smelled very bad. Moy looked left. *Oooh, the smell!* She saw kids and adults sitting on their feet in an open field doing their human business. Flies were everywhere! Small flies, big flies, and green-headed flies the size of a baby's fingers. *I hate Aunt Wipe House!* she thought. Moy couldn't walk away from the open-field outhouse fast enough.

Some old men sitting in front of the open field outside, wearing old sarongs and no shirts, shouted, "Well water, well water, two baht a bucket!"

Some women, men, and children were bathing near the outhouse field. Each woman tied a small knot on her sarong, above her chest, or held her sarong with her teeth, while her hands disappeared inside to rub and clean her body.

The men wore no shirts, just pants, shorts, or sarongs. They scrubbed and rubbed all over for everyone to see. It didn't matter where they rubbed or scrubbed; they were men!

"Very ugly to look at, scrub yourself like that. I hate it!" a few women screamed, picking up their water buckets and moving away from the men. Some of the mothers also grabbed their children and water buckets to go somewhere else.

"Help! I can no clean myself without woman, woman yell at me," the men laughed.

Children giggled or laughed aloud until their mothers slapped their heads and yelled, "This unlucky one! Why you laugh? No do what those short life do. It embarrassing!"

Moy looked away from the open-field outhouse and bathing area. Later she learned the open-field bathhouse was also a field of comedy. Every evening, when she came to buy water for a bath, she would listen and laugh. Few men acted like gentlemen while they bathed. Some of the men loved to tease the women. Other men were simply *dirty*. And a few men got yelled at by their wives for nothing.

"Why you scrub yourself like that, because you see pretty, pretty girl?" some wives yelled at the unlucky husbands.

"Scrub like what?" angry husbands yelled back.

"I'm dead! If I no scrub, you say I smell bad. You not let me make baby with you. When I scrub myself clean for you, you yell I scrub. Buddha help me!" other husbands complained, making people laugh.

Keem

"No scrub yourself in front of young girl," wives shouted.

"Yes, Madam Wife. Help! Why I can no look at pretty, pretty girl like those man, man?" husbands would ask, pointing at the single men.

"I your wife; you look at and scrub in front of me. Not to those girl, girl!" Some of the wives got mad and threw water on their husbands.

"Yes, Madam Wife. Buddha, why you give me mean wife?" The husbands laughed while protecting their faces with their hands and arms from the water their wives threw.

Even some single men got yelled at by women and mothers.

"Help, I come to bathe in this shit and pee water and still get yell by woman, woman and mother, mother. Mother, help your child. Mother, pity me! I can no clean myself. I not know where to go to scrub myself clean!" the men laughed in good humor.

2 4

Every night, Moy slept next to Grandma on the plastic and grass mat, like Uncle Noodle's family. Ten people slept together in one long line. The first morning after she came to the Thai border, she bought a bowl of pork noodle soup from Uncle Noodle to eat. It cost about seven baht. Then she went around figuring out how to make a living. She hadn't gone far on the hill when she heard, "I can no buy a pack!" One man was shouting at another man standing behind a small table full of cigarettes.

Moy stood there, watching and listening.

"I no have money for a pack," the man yelled.

"Then no smoke! I no sell one or two cigarette. I sell pack." The men were nose to nose.

I can help! Moy thought, remembering how Keem and Wong had taught her to do business, even before she could speak properly. They would say, "If you want to do business, no afraid. Be brave. Go and do it! You might lose some and make some money; that how you make a living."

"Uncle, what kind of cigarette you want to smoke?" Moy asked as she walked toward the angry men. Both men frowned at her. She waited.

"That!" the thin man pointed at a pack of cigarettes.

His pocket is empty but he wants to smoke good cigarette, she thought, smiling. "How much a pack?" she asked.

Keem

"Ten baht," the seller told her.

"I go sell it. Uncle must let me make some money."

"You have money buy my cigarette?"

"I no ask if I no have money."

"I sell it to you for nine baht."

"Five." She waited.

His eyebrows knit together, and he straightened up. "Eight."

He and Moy went back and forth. "Eight. I no sell cheaper than that. You can go anywhere; no one sell it for eight baht."

"Six, or I go buy it from someone else," Moy pointed at other tables.

"Seven fifty! Give me the money; give it!" His fingers fanned under her nose.

"Seven, or I go buy it from someone else." Moy stuck to her offer.

"Seven fifty!" he yelled.

She turned her back on him.

"Give me the money!" he shouted.

Moy pulled a small, colorful money bag out of her underpants pocket. The money bag was yellow with red, green, orange, blue, and white polka dots of different sizes, and large blue or orange circles. Keem had made an outfit for Moy one Chinese New Year in Phnom Penh and made that little bag for Moy with the leftover material. Moy gave the seller a hundred baht, then put the change he gave her back in the money bag.

She opened the pack and sold the thin man three cigarettes for a baht. He couldn't have been happier.

When he turned to go, Moy ran after him. "Uncle, wait!"

He stopped.

"I give Uncle one cigarette for free. Today is my first day selling and exchanging. Uncle let me make a lot of money?" she handed him another cigarette.

"Yes! Uncle pray to Buddha let Niece make a lot of money! Thank you, Niece." He smiled happily about his extra cigarette.

"Thank you, Uncle." *My first day of business at the Thai border, I needed someone to wish me luck!* she thought.

There were twenty-four cigarettes in a pack. Moy knew it in her sleep. Her family sold cigarettes in Pailin for more than two years. Keem and Wong sold opened packs of cigarettes to the bus drivers and poor people who couldn't afford to buy whole packs.

Moy knew where to sell her cigarettes—the soldiers' house! She went around asking the soldiers if they wanted to buy her cigarettes.

"Niece, Uncle have no money to buy and smoke cigarette; they too expensive," some soldiers told her.

"I sell three cigarettes for one baht," she told them.

"You joking. No nice; it a sin!" some of the soldiers yelled, looking angry.

She showed them an open pack of the expensive brand, pulled three cigarettes out, and waved them back and forth in front of the men.

The soldiers' jaws dropped slowly. Their eyes shifted left and right as they stared at the cigarettes waving in her fingertips.

"Three cigarette for one baht." Moy held them up.

The soldiers stared at her with big eyes, then snapped their lips together, jumped to their feet, and reached for money from their pants pockets.

"Sell it to me!" The soldiers piled on top of each other, reaching for the cigarettes from her hand. Many of them looked like they were about to cry. Her first pack of cigarettes was gone in less than a minute, but Moy told them not to worry, that she would be back with more. Some soldiers followed her and watched from afar, wanting to make sure she came back with cigarettes to sell to them.

She only made one baht per pack, not enough for her to make a living. So a few days later, she sold only two cigarettes per baht. The soldiers and men complained, but she reminded her customers that she had to eat. She had no one buying food for her. None of her customers said anything, and after that Moy didn't have to look for customers. Word went out fast that a Chinese child was selling two cigarettes per baht, and the men came looking for her.

"Little Sister Cigarette, I hear you sell two cigarette for one baht. Is it truth?" a man came running toward her, asking hopefully.

She told him yes, and that large Cambodian man's smile and the glow in his eyes made her happy! She made a great deal of money from her little business. Later, she sold two more kinds of cigarettes in addition to the very expensive brand. The soldiers and most of the men in the camp were poor and didn't have the money to buy whole packs of cigarettes. By selling them a few cigarettes of an expensive brand, Moy made them feel richer and happier.

She liked watching her customers. It made her smile when they showed off the golden print on the butt of the cigarette to their friends or neighbors to prove they could afford to smoke this expensive brand. Moy made life in the camp more pleasurable for the soldiers and men who smoked. In return, they made her richer and happier. She ate whatever she wanted for breakfast, lunch, and dinner. No one told her what to do or what to eat.

Her life went on smoothly for the first two months.

Then one morning, everything turned upside down on her. Moy didn't know that she was very sick when she escaped from Cambodia. While she was living near the Buddhist temple, she would eat salt like candy every night. She ate three or four pieces of salt, each the size of a chopstick or the tip of a little finger. One day, she had a fight with Seron, Small's son. He stood there and stared at her face as he told her, "You think you that strong? You near death and still not know it."

MOY

* * *

One morning, Moy woke up and found her feet and arms swollen. She was weak and sleepy, but she didn't stay home. She went out doing her business like she did every day. All the big businessmen and women liked her. She bought their cigarettes every day to sell. Nearly everyone in the camp called her Little Sister Cigarette. A few of the big businesswomen and men would bring her noodle soup or give her some candies to eat. That day, she was selling cigarettes when Uncle Noodle told her to go see a doctor about her swollen body. The soldiers told her the same thing. But she didn't listen.

"I all right. I no sick," she told Uncle Noodle and her concerned customers.

She continued doing business until she could hardly see anything. Her whole body, face, and eyes were badly swollen. Only then did she go see a doctor, and she didn't have to wait in the long line. A large yellow-haired woman saw Moy and took her into the building right away. The yellow-haired woman took her to a small bed and said something, but all Moy heard was "ceechewa."

The yellow-haired woman pointed at a bed she wanted Moy to sit on. Then a monkey man with blue eyes came to check on Moy. He looked at her eyes, mouth, and ears. Then he tapped his large fingers here and there on her body. A Cambodian woman translated for Moy. The doctor wanted to know how long her body had been swollen like that. She told them two weeks and that she waited that long because she had to sell cigarettes for a living. If she didn't go out and sell cigarettes, she had nothing to eat. The doctor wanted to send her to a hospital in Khao'I'Dang because she was too sick for him to help her there. The doctor had the interpreter tell Moy to bring her family and go to Khao'I'Dang together. Moy told them she didn't have a family, but the doctor didn't care. He just wanted her in the hospital *that afternoon.*

Before she left the doctor's office, he gave her some small black pills. Moy went home and told Uncle Noodle that the doctor wanted her go to a hospital in Khao'I'Dang. Then she went around and told her customers and the businesswomen and men where she was going. Everyone was happy, and sad, to see her go. They wished her well and told her, "No work too hard. Look after yourself."

"Thank you, Uncle. Thank you, Aunt. I pray you have long life."

"Thank you, Niece. Have long life."

Moy got her clothes bag from Uncle Noodle's house, said goodbye, and thanked him and his family once more. Then she went back to the doctor's office and waited. Soon, a roofless army truck stopped in front of the doctor's office. The large doctor lifted her up onto the truck full of sick women, men, and children going to Khao'I'Dang. She had no idea where the camp was, but she knew the good doctor wanted to help her. The truck was on a small, dusty dirt road for many hours. Then it came to a stop.

Camp Khao'I'Dang

**This picture was taken in 1979,
in Khao'I'Dang. I was fifteen.**

It was a couple of weeks after I left Camp 007.
The navy-colored shirt I had on belonged to Ma.
I took it off Ma after her bath
the morning of June 18, 1977, the day Ma went to heaven.
Ma had the same shirt on but blue.
And the hairclip I wore was the one Ma bought for me in Pailin.

2 5

The dirt roads and streets were light brown and pink soil, with small bushes and grass here and there. People were everywhere, walking, standing, talking, and laughing. A lot of people had come hoping to find loved ones at the truck stop. Moy looked around. About ten large, green plastic tents stood on one side of the dirt road. On the other side were small, blue plastic tents, all the way to the side of a mountain. Some small houses covered with cardboard and a few grass houses were mixed in among the long lines of plastic tents.

Everyone got off the truck as Moy continued looking around Khao'I'Dang. Then a large monkey man and a Cambodian woman came and helped her off the truck. A yellow-haired woman came from behind the monkey man, and the three of them took Moy to a big green tent. Inside, there were numerous small metal beds on each side. There was pink dirt and some grass under the beds and in the hallway.

A few people sat on empty beds, talking to the sick people who lay on the other beds. The Cambodian woman told Moy to sit on an empty bed. The monkey man and yellow-haired woman wanted to know where Moy's family was. Tears from painful memories fell from Moy's eyes as she told them what had happened to her beloved Ma and Grandpa and how she had gotten there. They listened; then the monkey man took Moy to the orphan's center. He carried her clothes bag for her. She didn't want to go, but she had nowhere else to stay.

They walked on a new dirt road for a long time then came to an area surrounded with white wooden fences. Moy looked at the three enormous brown tents inside the fences. Some girls and boys ran in and out of the tents, with monkey men chasing after the giggling children. The monkey man walked Moy through the gate and into a small brown tent.

Another yellow-haired woman was inside. The monkey man said something to her, and she looked at Moy, then had her sit on a tiny bed. The monkey man went out and came back with a Cambodian man, and the three of them sat on chairs facing Moy. The monkey man had some papers in his hands and asked Moy some questions as the Cambodian man translated and the yellow-haired woman took notes.

"What is your name?"

Who am I? Is my name Moy? She wasn't sure if she knew who she was, and tears fell from her eyes. The monkey man and the yellow-haired woman seemed to understand and waited patiently.

Moy was a child who was born in a land called Cambodia. She was a child who saw so much death and blood. She was a brave little tiger who fought with her teeth and claws to live, one second at a time. That little tiger also fought with every tooth and claw to escape from her cage. Her four strong legs had carried her to the border. Moy was a child who was born to fight battle after battle. Moy lost when Keem and Wong went to heaven. But after that, she won the wars. Cambodia, the jungle, the river, the sand and mud fields, and the minefield were all behind her. The wars were over! There were no more battles for Moy-the-brave-little-tiger to fight.

"Luong. My name is Luong," she sobbed aloud, brokenhearted. She didn't hear the next question.

The yellow-haired woman moved to sit next to her and pushed Luong's hair away from her face, drying her tears.

"What is your last name?"

She told them. Whether by coincidence or faith, or perhaps as a result of Keem's powerful spirit's doings, they spelled it Eng instead of Ung.

"Your last name is Eng?"

Eng is eagle, she thought in Teochew. She didn't know if the spelling was correct, but it didn't sound right. She remembered she had seen a picture of an eagle when she was a child. It had big, strong wings. And that's what she wanted—strong wings to fly. Fly up high into the sky and far away from Cambodia. *Yes, Eagle is my last name.*

"Yes, my last name is Eng." Moy said this good name as she wiped the tears from her eyes. Eng Luong was born and took over.

The monkey man moved to sit next to her and patted her hand. He said something to the interpreter and showed her his sad face. The interpreter told her this American doctor and nurse felt bad about Moy's parents' deaths. They wanted to be her friend. Would she like them to be her friends? She looked at the American doctor and nurse's kind faces. They understood her loneliness and heartache, and they offered to be her friends. Eng Luong nodded. The doctor and nurse hugged her. Eng Luong sobbed aloud. Her new friends whispered softy and comforted her. She didn't know why she cried so hard. Perhaps Moy had said good-bye. Eng Luong didn't know if Moy would come back again. Only Moy had that answer.

She cried until there were no more tears left. The nurse cried with her. The doctor's eyes were misty. The three of them looked at each other, then suddenly burst out laughing together. The nurse and doctor shook their fingers at her. The interpreter told Eng Luong the nurse and doctor cried for her pain. She looked at their friendly faces, then pulled a small pack of pictures out of her bag to show them.

Moy never went anywhere without that small pack of pictures. She learned that from watching her ma. Keem had kept the pictures inside a plastic bag that she tied on the roof, between the grass. Moy hid those pictures on the roof from the Khmer Rouge, the same way her ma had. Every time the Khmer Rouge sent her from town to town, Moy made sure she had that small pack of pictures with her. She had saved her ma and grandpa's pictures. The doctor and nurse were impressed, and they gave her kisses.

Then the doctor examined Eng Luong while the nurse took notes. The doctor looked into Eng Luong's mouth, ears, and eyes, then tapped his fingers on her swollen body. The interpreter kept asking, "Hurt here? Is it hurt when the doctor touch here?" She answered yes or no, and after the doctor finished examining her, the nurse gave Eng Luong a cup of water and some small black pills to take. Then the doctor, nurse, and interpreter took her to a large brown tent.

Inside the tent, pink dirt and grass grew under the small metal beds and in the hallway. Each of the hundred or so beds stood a foot away from the next. Girls and boys slept on both sides and in the same tent. Some kids were sleeping, some were sitting on their beds, and some were playing. A Cambodian woman wearing a black shirt and red sarong came from the other end of the tent and welcomed Eng Luong into her care. She talked to the doctor for a while, took the small clothes bag from him, then grasped Eng Luong's hand and said, "Little Sister, come with Big Sister."

Eng Luong looked at her new friends. The doctor and nurse said something to the interpreter.

"No afraid. They not leave Little Sister. They the children's doctor and nurse. Little Sister will see them every day," the Cambodian man told her.

The friendly Cambodian woman took Eng Luong to the middle of the tent and put her bag on an empty bed. She wanted Eng Luong close to her, and it was the only empty bed. Then the woman went outside, leaving Eng Luong alone with the children. The children stared at her strangely. They whispered to each other and giggled.

"She ugly!"

"She swollen like pig and very ugly!"

Eng Luong heard their whispers but said nothing. She looked at a white pillow and blanket on the bed and sat down. The bed was soft. She lay down and closed her eyes.

Eng Luong slept on a soft, clean bed, with a clean blanket and white pillow. Moy had slept in the mud, in the rain, and with no blanket. Wherever Moy turned there was hatred and people who stole from her. Moy had very few people help her. Wherever Eng Luong turned, people were there to help. When Moy looked up, there was the ceiling. When Moy looked left or right, there were the walls. When Moy looked down, she saw the earth. Eng Luong saw a road on the right, people on the left, and a floor under her feet. A blue sky was above her head, and the sunlight shone into her eyes. However, Eng Luong had just been born and didn't know a thing about this world.

The Cambodian woman returned with two clean towels, a new pair of flip-flops, and a small bar of soap for Eng Luong. Eng Luong thanked the woman and went out to take her bath. There were ten large, white, square water tanks inside the fences for the children, and girls and boys all bathed in the same place. When they saw Eng Luong coming, they moved out of her way, whispering and giggling about her swollen face and body.

"She ugly, swollen like that."

Eng Luong found a plastic bucket. She put it under the faucet and turned the handle. *Clean* water poured out of faucet into her bucket. She carried the bucket away from the water tanks, like the children did, unbuttoned her shirt, and pulled her sarong up to her chest. She took her shirt off and dropped it on the concrete platform in the bath area. She tied her sarong in a knot on one side on her chest, then used a small plastic bowl to dip water from the bucket and pour it over her head. She washed her hair, arms, legs, and body with that small soap.

After her bath, she changed to a dry towel and washed her clothes, then put on dry pants and a short-sleeved shirt. She returned to her tent and went to sleep.

Later, the doctor, nurse, and Cambodian woman woke her up. They gave her medicine with a cup of clean water.

"The doctor say he no want to wake you up when he see you sleep. Little Sister hungry?" the Cambodian woman asked.

She told them yes. All three people smiled. The doctor said something to the woman, and she left, returning soon with a large bowl of white rice and big pieces of brown meat for Eng Luong. The three people talked while she emptied the bowl. They asked if she wanted more rice, and she shook her head. The doctor said if she took two more pills, he'd give her something. She took the pills, and he handed her a small toothbrush and toothpaste—things she hadn't seen for five years. She grinned from ear to ear. The doctor and nurse laughed and patted her head gently then told her she should go back to sleep.

The yellow-haired nurse came a couple of times during the night to give Eng Luong medicine. Then the nurse would put her back in bed and pull the blanket up under Eng Luong's chin. The kind nurse mumbled something softly and kissed Eng Luong's forehead. She closed her eyes and went to sleep with a smile. Throughout the first two or three weeks, the doctor and yellow-haired nurse gave Eng Luong the small black and yellow pills a couple of times each day. She didn't go out much. She always felt sleepy and tired. Breakfast, lunch, and dinner were brought to bed for her. Sometimes she heard the ladies inside her tent whisper to each other, "Doctor say she no live long. Pity her, so young!"

The children in that center called Eng Luong Swollen, and one day the Cambodian woman yelled at the children, telling them to stop calling Eng Luong Swollen because it was mean, and she was getting better. The swelling had gone down every day. Eng Luong was still Moy inside, and she pulled through her sickness. One day she went outside, sat in front of her tent, and stared out into space. An American woman came over and told her to stand up next to a boy who lived in the same tent with her. The American took their picture together.

In the picture, Eng Luong wore Keem Lai's V-necked, navy-colored, short-sleeved shirt. Keem had worn that navy shirt the morning of the day she went to heaven. Eng Luong's hair was too short, and some escaped from her ponytail at the back and the white hairclip on the right side of her head. Eng Luong stood sideways and looked straight ahead. The boy didn't want her picture with him, so he cut it in half and left it on her pillow.

Moy wore her beloved Ma's shirt almost every day. It was torn in many places, but Moy sewed the torn shirt with white thread. She wore it so much that the navy color faded. She also had worn Keem's black silk pants and shirts, just before the Vietnamese overthrew the Khmer Rouge.

That day was the first time Eng Luong had walked out of the gate since going to live in the children's tent. She looked around. People were buying and selling homemade treats, Thai food, and clothes on the sidewalks, like in Camp 007. In Khao'I'Dang, there was no store yet, but trucks full of people arrived every day from Camp 007 or other places.

The first thing she bought was a bag of one hundred pieces of candy. She ate as she walked, making her way back to the children's tent. When the kids saw the bag of candy in Eng Luong's hands, they were like ants all over her. Every one of them asked for a piece, and Eng Luong gave one to each child. The bag was empty in no time, and the children left her alone.

"You have no shame of yourself? When Eng Luong sick, all of you mean to her. You call her Swollen. Now you beg her for candy to eat. You no embarrass?" the Cambodian woman criticized the children, but none of them said anything.

As the days went by, the children whispered to each other, "Swollen is pretty!"

"Look at her face red, red!"

"She has good heart; she share her candy with us."

"She very quiet!"

The older boys looked at Eng Luong differently. But an eagle doesn't make a lot of noise, and Eng Luong never said anything to anyone in the tent, though she would answer briefly if someone asked her a question. She was like a wild eagle just freed from captivity. This eagle couldn't just take off and fly up in the sky. This eagle needed to exercise her wings and build her strength. Then she could fly from the treetops up into the sky and head to her dreamland, America.

The children at the tent center had their own doctors and nurses and better food to eat. None of the children worked. They ate, slept, and played all day. Every morning some American, English, and French women sang songs with the children while the men made funny faces at the children. Everyone laughed or giggled, and the young children and men would run and chase each other. Eng Luong watched and laughed like everyone else, but she didn't sing or play any games. She liked to just watch and laugh. She felt she was too old to play games.

Moy's new identity and life at the orphan center in the camp was unreal, like a dream. Eng Luong was like a fictional character Moy had hidden inside. Moy would always remember her life as Eng Luong.

A few months later, all the children at the tent center were sent to live with the orphans in different blocks. They all cried and hugged their American doctors, nurses, and friends, saying good-bye. Before the children went to their block centers, they stood in three long lines in front of their tents to get their picture taken.

Keem

* * *

Eng Luong went to Block One Orphan Center, which was large. It had four long houses with grass roofs and walls. The four houses formed a square facing each other, one house for the girls, and three houses for the boys. At the center of the four houses was a small, wall-less sitting room with long bamboo benches around it. Next to the sitting room was a small house where the three women managers of that center lived with their daughters. A small kitchen faced the managers' house, close to the gated entrance for the center.

When she lived at the tent center, she had had large pieces of pork, beef, and chicken stir fried with different green vegetables and rice to eat. Eng Luong understood why the children from her previous center weren't happy to come here. The food was poor, and the children had only rice with tuna fish every day for lunch and dinner. The tuna was really just the heads and a lot of juice. However, the managers ate chicken, pork, beef, and vegetables at every meal. And they sold most of the children's cookies, keeping the money for themselves. Besides the food being poor, the children weren't allowed to leave the center. If anyone wanted to go out of the gate, they had to ask the lady (group manager) for permission. If their lady said no, the kids couldn't leave.

Inside the girls' house, there was one long wooden bed against a wall. Eng Luong's group was between ten and twelve girls, as were the other three groups of girls. All the girls ate and slept on that one long bed. Nowadays, though, there was nothing bothering Eng Luong. What was were there to bother her? All she did was eat and sleep.

Months later, the center got a three-month-old baby boy, and the head manager sing-songed, "Eng Luong, Eng Luong, I know we can depend on you. Go see the baby." The manager pushed her toward the baby's house.

She didn't know a thing about babies, but she learned how to hold, feed, bathe, and sleep with him like a mother. The baby had been left on a rock near the side of a mountain at Camp Khao'I'Dang. Some IRC (International Red Cross) personnel driving by saw the little baby and took him to the orphan center. Eng Luong was free to go in and out of the center with the baby, without having to get permission from her lady. She took care of him for a long time, until the center had an older woman come to take care of the baby.

By then, more long wooden buildings had been built for doctors, the IRC offices, and hospitals in Khao'I'Dang. The open field market also got larger. People bought and sold everything from homemade treats to Thai candies, cookies, and more.

* * *

The doctors' new office was a couple of minutes from her center. One day, she wanted to see what the office looked like. She walked to the office and looked through the windows. There were men sitting behind their desks doing something. Then she heard someone shout her old name, "Moy, Moy!"

She turned around and smiled at Pon's grandson.

"Seron, how you do? Where Mother and Father?" she asked.

"In Cambodia." He smiled and stared at her face.

Strange, she felt nothing for Pon. She had just asked out of respect. She and Seron stood there talking for a while, and she told him she lived at the Orphan Center.

"You lose a tooth, but you prettier than before," he told her.

Moy had broken a front tooth in Cambodia when she lived near the Buddhist temple.

He told her he had come to live in the camp with Pon's friend. Then they said good-byes. A few weeks later, she ran into Pon's friend. She was just walking, looking around and the elderly woman saw her. She invited Moy to sit down in her blue plastic tent. She told Moy Pon's family was very poor, and that they couldn't find a can of rice to eat. After Moy left Cambodia, the people in the town of Rock Cow hated Pon's family, and no one wanted to do any business with them. Everyone knew Pon, his wife, and his daughter had stolen all of Moy's gold while Moy had to feed herself.

"You not know?" the elderly bald-headed woman asked.

"No, Grandma." Moy shook her head.

"What you think happen? It sinful! Very sinful, lie and steal from small child. You no see? People take their cow after cow from the field. People take all their rice out from under their head when they sleep at night. Then no one wants to buy their beef. People take their dry beef when they not look. People take their cooked beef in the pot from their house." The elderly woman went on saying it was sinful and that Buddha didn't like old people who did ugly things like Pon, his wife, and daughter Small had done to Moy. It was sinful and very ugly what Pon's family had done to Moy. And Buddha let Moy see their sin. Moy's ma and grandpa's spirit didn't like the ugly things Pon did to her, either.

"Grandpa Pon not my friend anymore. I no like old people do ugly thing like that to small child. I feel bad for Seron, and I take him here with me. He steal all my money and some gold and go back to Cambodia. The whole family is thieves!" the elderly woman screamed angrily.

Moy felt bad for her. She and Pon's wife had been friends since they were little girls.

* * *

Months later, the IRC personnel came and interviewed all the children. The interview with Eng Luong included:

"Where were you born?"

"Cambodia," she answered.

"Where are your mother and father? How many brothers and sisters you have?" A Cambodian man translated for the IRC officer.

"I have no brother or sister. My father die when I three years old. My ma and Grandpa die when I between twelve and thirteen," Eng Luong answered in tears.

The first interview about Eng Luong's history went on for hours. During the interview, Eng Luong sort of disappeared and Moy took over. She told the interviewers how she got across the Thai border. The interviewers asked the same questions in different ways to see if she was lying. Every few weeks, different personnel came to do interviews, but they didn't seem to be interested in the other children. They were focused on Eng Luong. Every time they came, they asked painful questions about her past and made her cry. Then one day, the questions were different.

"If you have a choice of Canada, France, or America, which country do you want to go?"

"America."

"Why America?" The IRC officer looked and listened carefully as an interpreter asked the questions.

"I want go to school. I want to live in a free country. I want my freedom."

"You want to go to America and study?"

"Yes."

"If you get to America, what will you do?"

"I study hard and be a good student."

"What do you want to learn in school?"

"I want to learn to read and write."

"Why you want to go to the United States of America?"

"The United States of America is a free country, and I want to be free."

"Where did you hear the United States is a free country?"

"I hear people talk."

"You heard people talk, and you want to go to America?"

"Yes."

"What do you do if you don't have money?"

"I go work and save money, then go to school."

"Will you join Khmer Red if your country calls for your help?"

"*No!*"

"You like communism?"

"*No!*"

"If you go to America, do you want to become an American citizen?"

"*YES!*"

"You like to go to America?"

"*YES!!*"

Both the officer and the interpreter laughed at her answer. The officer said something to the interpreter.

"See you next month."

"Thank you, Mister. Thank you, Uncle."

"This American says he hopes he no make you cry next time."

"No problem. I get use to him make me cry," she smiled.

The American and the interpreter laughed harder.

* * *

A few weeks after the interview with the Americans, 1979 was gone and 1980 just beginning. One dark evening, a flower bloomed to its full force. Moy—Eng Luong—was that blooming rose, a woman at last, and she became more concerned with her appearance. She sold Keem's pants and shirts and bought new sarongs and shirts to wear. She did keep Keem's black silk pants and wore them but threw

Keem's old shirts away, the shirts her inner-self-Moy couldn't live without. Eng Luong didn't like wearing old clothes. She threw all Moy's old clothes away. The eagle liked her beauty. However, there was still enough Moy inside Eng Luong to keep her from selling everything Moy had brought from Cambodia that belonged to Keem.

Nowadays, more and more Khmer Rouge were coming into Khao'I'Dang, where they lived with everyone else. The first time Eng Luong saw the trucks full of Khmer Rouge in Khao'I'Dang, she was shocked, like everyone else. The Khmer Rouge still dressed in black. They looked around with interest as they stood in the trucks. Everyone wondered why the Khmer Rouge had come there and why the IRC brought these human-heart eaters across the Thai border.

A couple of weeks later, the orphan center had a meeting. The head manager told the children they were to move to the next camp, Sa Khao II. No one wanted to go there, where the Khmer Rouge lived. Some children ran away from the center, but Eng Luong didn't know where to go. So when the army trucks came, they took her with the children to Sa Khao II.

The tent center in Khao'I'Dang, 1979

There were more or less a hundred
children living in each of these tents.
Some of the children aren't in these pictures.
I am sixth from the front, on the first line, on the right.

Camp
Sa Khao II
Thai Border

Sa Khao II

Block 188

The girls and I lived in this house.

His house was on the right.

(I respect people's privacy and removed them from this picture.)

26

Eng Luong was surprised. All the houses in Sa Khao II were alike and much better than in Khao'I'Dang. They stood three feet off the ground, with three gray walls and white, standard metal roofs. The spaces between the back walls and roofs were about a foot wide. Each house, about fourteen feet long and six feet wide, was divided in half, so two families lived in each house. If a family was unusually large, they could have the whole house. Four houses formed a square block with a little free land in the middle, and each block had a number. People grew whatever they wanted. Each block also had two connected concrete water tubs about four feet high and five feet long.

The children who came from Eng Luong's center lived in Block 187 and Block 188. The two blocks were back to back. Eng Luong's group had only eight girls and lived in a house with four girls in each room. Dry bamboo trees were sliced in half and left at each block, so the boys helped the girls nail the bamboo slices to make a three-foot-tall fourth wall and a door. The bamboo slices had already been cut into the three-foot-long slats, and nails had been left for people to use. So each family, as well as the orphans, added six-foot-wide beds. The extra space was used as a cooking area, sitting room, and napping area. When night came, the orphans draped long, brown plastic from wooden poles to cover the whole cooking and sitting area.

ENG LUONG

Eng Luong liked the houses in Sa Khao II. And they had electric lights at night! People dropped off the II and called the camp just Sa Khao. Every day at five, some blocks had water came in for the tubs, but others didn't, and those people had to go around looking for water. Eng Luong's Block, 188, had no water. The food in Sa Khao II was in short supply, and the girls didn't have enough rice to eat. Mostly, the orphans got only rice and salt, and had fish, beef, or pork and vegetables with their rice only once a week.

There was a large school in Sa Khao II made of brown wood, with a white metal roof. The orphans had to go to school. If they didn't want to go, they had to go to work for the Thai people. The girls sewed shirts and pants that Thai women picked up from the sewing house. They were paid ten to fifteen baht a week for their sewing.

Later, there was also a small Buddhist temple, an English school, and a French school. People who were already educated in foreign languages went to those schools. And a beautiful library had a second floor next to the English school. People went to read or borrow books from the library. The English school was on the opposite side of the street from where the Thai soldiers lived, and two blocks away and opposite from Eng Luong's block. Two or three months later, a store was opened in a block in front of the Thai soldiers' house. The Thai people came in trucks and cars with clothing, shoes, and food to sell to the Cambodians, and the Cambodians made homemade food like rice cakes, sweet banana soup, pork noodle soup, and more. The store was open from eight to six.

Eng Luong went to school with her roommates. Although she enjoyed life in Sa Khao II, she was tired of being interviewed by the Americans and the Thai people. They interviewed her two or three times after she went to live there. The questions didn't bother her as much as they had before. She lived through each day with prayer and hopes to get out of Thailand. It never occurred to her she might have to make a sacrifice in order to go to America.

* * *

It all started on a day that she had to cook for her group. The girls took turns cooking and filling the water tanks. Eng Luong must have missed one of her turns, and that day was also her turn to fill the two water tanks for her house. Eng Luong and her teammate agreed that one partner would stay home to cook while the other went out for water.

Eng Luong didn't want to go eight blocks away to get water. "Old Grandma," the girls' nickname for their period, was visiting, and she had stomach pain every time! At that time, the girls couldn't eat or sleep right, and they couldn't bathe! With boys everywhere, the girls were afraid to leave the house. They were afraid the cloths they made from torn sarongs or shirts to use inside their underpants might drop out if they walked around or bent over, or that blood would stain their sarongs. They even had to wait until midnight, when no one else was up, to bathe and wash their bloody cloths. So they stayed at home like an *old grandma*.

I hate Old Grandma! Eng Luong thought. She just wanted to lie down and sleep, praying the pain would go away. But the water tanks were empty. However, she was lucky. The new boys from Sa Khao I had dug a water well behind their house, next to hers. With two buckets in her hands, she walked to the front of the boys' house.

"Anyone home?" she shouted.

No answer. The house looked empty, so she went to back, stood at the edge of the well, and used a long rope to lower a bucket into the well. She had filled one bucket, and just put the other bucket into the well when a sleepy voice came from the house above her.

"Thief steal my water."

She startled and the rope dropped from her hand into the well. She looked up and saw a sleepy face peeking out between the roof and back wall of his house.

"I ask, but no one home," she told the boy.

"Who you ask if no one home?" He smiled handsomely, rubbing his sleepy eyes.

"I…" She couldn't think of what to say, and just smiled. "I drop my bucket in the well. You scare me, and I drop the rope," she complained, peering into the well.

"You steal my water," he accused her.

"I…" she snapped her lips closed as he disappeared back inside the house. *Bad boy! He frightened me, and I dropped the bucket into well, and now he walked away just like that!*

"It sinful to steal water," he spoke up behind her.

"You scare me!" she shouted.

"Why you scare so easy?" he laughed and peeked into the well. Then he stared at her with interest, leaned closer, and sniffed.

"No do that!" She stepped backward, away from him.

"Sorry, Big Sister, I smell…"

If he says it, I'll die from embarrassment! she thought. But he just stood there and stared at her, then finally said, "Face white, white. You sick? No worry! I will get the bucket for you!" He shouted over his shoulder as he walked away quickly.

Her face was on fire. *Boy! He has a nose like a broomstick! The boys could sniff it out if a girl didn't have her underwear on!* she thought.

He came back quickly, bringing a long rope with a hook tied to one end. In less than a minute, he had her rope in his hook. She grabbed the rope and pulled the bucket up. Halfway out, he grabbed it from her. "Let me take it," he said.

Keem

"Thank you."

"How much water you want?"

"Two tank."

"That all?" he asked, smiling.

"That a lot!" She returned his smile.

He looked at her sideways, showing her all his even, white teeth. She had a missing front tooth. He got the water from the well, carried it to her house, and filled up the tanks.

That was the first time Eng Luong talked to him. He walked past her house to school, work, or to the other boys' house every day. She had never talked to him, but she knew his name. She was shy with all boys, not just him, but she was grateful for his help. She thought he was a nice boy, even if he did have a nose like a broomstick, smelling everything! Then again, every boy has a nose like a broomstick. They always seem to know when a girl had her period, and it was embarrassing! She thanked him when the water tanks were full.

"No problem," he told her.

Eng Luong told her teammate he had helped her with the water. The two girls agreed he was a nice boy. After lunch, Eng Luong and her partner brought him a bowl of soup, but he was not home, and the other boys who lived in the house kept the soup for him. That evening, he brought the bowl back for Eng Luong, and they sat in front of her house making small talk. After that day, they were friendly toward each other. She thought he was nice to let her use his well. Sometimes, he filled the water tanks for her. She thought, *That's how friends should be, helping each other out.* She knew the boys didn't know how to cook, so when it was her turn to cook, she sometimes brought some food for him. Whenever he saw her he would mumble, "Big Sister Luong."

She would smile and go on with whatever she was doing. His house and hers were only a couple of feet apart. Every evening, one of

Eng Luong's older roommates would read romantic stories. He, and most of the boys and girls, would come to Eng Luong's sitting bed, where they sat in a big circle listening to the stories. The girls would cry if the story was sad, and the boys would laugh at the girls' silliness.

The girls criticized the boys, "Boy, boy not know about love! Boy, boy and man, man never care for girl, girl. They go love this girl and that girl and forget their wife and girlfriend when they see pretty girl."

"Why you yell at us? It just story! Girl, girl can no tell from book to real life!" the boys shouted with laughter.

Eng Luong kept silent but smiled or laughed at the disagreements. Every now and then she caught him staring at her. She would smile, and he would smile back. He was quiet, like her. Whenever he was not busy, he liked to spend time on her sitting bed. Then one day, everything changed. She was cooking and listening to her roommate read a story. He sat at the other side of the bamboo bed and listened, like her. Eng Luong heard a loud thud. Everyone gasped then laughed. When she looked, she saw he was rubbing his head, and looking about to cry. Someone had done something that caused a large stick to fall on his head.

"Here is Big Sister Eng Luong," one girl spoke through her laughter.

"Help him!" another girl shouted at Eng Luong.

"Let Big Sister Luong 'luong' you, Little Brother," the story reader said, meaning let Luong bribe him. In Khmer, the word "bribe" sounds like "luong."

Eng Luong watched him rub his head furiously with both hands. He turned his face sideways and smiled at her. She didn't say anything and went on with her cooking, but all the girls and boys started teasing.

"Luong come over here and bribe him, or he'll cry!" they shouted.

"She embarrass," some of the girls and boys laughed.

Keem

"Little Brother no cry. You have your own Luong to luong you!" the girls and boys shouted with laughter.

From that day on, everyone called her Big Sister Luong or just Luong, dropping Eng. She was embarrassed by the teasing and stopped talking to him. But he was not shy; he wanted to talk with her. She ran away whenever he went near her. If he was on her sitting bed, she went to the baby's house. Later, when he saw her coming, he left. He would sit in front of his house and listen to the story from afar. Then one day Eng Luong's housemother asked her, "Luong, you how old?"

"Eighteen." At the time, she was actually sixteen, but when she was living in Khao'I'Dang, she didn't know how old she was. She had told the doctor she was eighteen, so she remained eighteen.

"He nineteen; he a good person. It hard to find someone good like him. He want you to marry him. Take him?" the housemother asked.

"No." She had been of half a mind to say *yes*. She very liked him but was too shy to say so.

"Think on it. Then tell me, yes?" the housemother asked.

"Yes."

He bore a resemblance to someone very special to her, but she couldn't remember who it was. His face was sort of round, with high cheekbones, thick lips, black eyes, black hair, and a deep voice. When he laughed, it sounded beautiful to her ears. She was a couple of inches shorter than he.

One day in school, she happened to looked toward the window, and he was there watching her. Another evening, she went to spend a night with her friend outside the orphan center. She was talking to her friend and happened to look under the house, where she saw his bare legs. He always wore short pants. He had hidden behind her friend's house, listening to the girls talk. Ever since the Thai and Cambodian dentist installed a new front tooth for her, he had been following her around.

ENG LUONG

Eng Luong went to school for a couple of months, then stopped. She could read and write very little in Khmer. Instead, she went to the sewing school and learned to sew. Each time she went, she had to tell her housemother where she was going. The title had changed from lady to housemother. The mothers of her house and his were former Khmer Rouge. Eng Luong wondered why the IRC and the Thai let the Khmer Rouge live at the Thai border and work at the orphan centers.

Eng Luong understood some people were good and some were bad. She liked her housemother and the housemother liked her. The two housemothers asked her every other week if she wanted to marry him, and each time, her answer was *yes*, but the word that came out was *no*. Perhaps she was afraid he might leave her, the way everyone had left Moy. Did he truly care for her? Only he knew.

One late night, when Eng Luong thought everyone was asleep, she tiptoed out of her house to go to the water tank for a bucket of water. She took it to the back of her house to bathe. Old Grandma was again visiting. It was hot, and she had been dying for a bath all week! She was very happy when her period came to an end and hoped a nice, cold bath would help her sleep better. First she washed the bloody cloths so she could use them again next month. She had almost finished her bath when his deep voice came from the darkness behind her back.

"Why a lady come out and bathe in the dark like this?"

She screamed and threw the water cup over her head. It landed on the roof of the elderly people's house next to hers.

"You scare me to death!" She was half bent over, turning around and around, both arms wrapped tightly around herself.

"You not know it danger for a lady, come out and bathe in the middle of the night like this?"

"No one ask you; go away!" she shouted.

"*Luong*," he stressed her name, sounding frustrated.

"It Big Sister Luong, not Luong!" she snapped.

"I one year older; you must address me as Big Brother!" he shouted back.

"Short life." She turned her back on him. *I will never call him Big Brother! He means honey/sweetheart. Never!* she thought.

"What? If you want to say something to me, speak up!" He sounded angry.

She grabbed her bucket and marched away from him. *I hate him!* She didn't have the courage to say it to his face. She had never been intimidated by anyone before, but with him it was different. She heard the soft laughter and giggles of the boys, girls, and the elderly couple who lived behind her.

"Children, romance children," they whispered to each other.

"You need?" a boy shouted through his laughter.

"Who can help me?" he asked, coming around the other side of the house. He watched her march up the steps and into her house.

"Pray to Buddha, pray!" some of the girls and boys shouted through their giggles.

"You two yell very loud and wake everyone up!" a girl who slept next to Eng Luong giggled.

"Worry your own problem," she whispered to her roommate. She was grateful no one could see her red face. *Bad boy! I will not talk to him again.* She changed into her dry sarong then went to sleep.

She didn't talk to him for months, and he gave up and started following another girl, but his eyes were on Eng Luong whenever he saw her. He would give her a hard look if she happened to meet his eyes. That didn't bother her. He could follow any girl he wanted. And she could talk to any boy she liked. He was not her husband. *If he doesn't like what I do, then he can go and hang his neck.* Since she had gotten her new front tooth installed, she laughed and smiled more. She thought he had lost interest in her, until a boy pointed him out to her one day.

"He not like to see you talk to me," the boy laughed.

She looked behind her. He was in front of the other girls' house across from hers, leaning on a wooden pole, arms folded across his chest. He was staring hard at them. She turned around and told her male friend, "I no care."

Her friend laughed. The boys looked at her differently, now that she had a new front tooth. One of her roommates belonged to a dance group and had makeup, so during a Cambodian holiday, she put some black eyeliner and lipstick on Eng Luong. They were going to the Buddhist temple, where all the fun was. When Eng Luong stepped out of the house, the boys got silent. Then they went crazy whistling and cheering her on.

"Luong, you very pretty!" the boys told her.

"Boy, boy crazy!" she laughed. But she quit laughing when she saw him.

He sat with other boys, smiling slightly, his eyes roving up and down her new sarong and shirt. Then he stared at her face.

"Big Sister Luong, come. We late!" Her roommate dragged her away.

Eng Luong had no idea what she did at the temple. Maybe she went to see the Khmer Rouge try to sing and perform opera, laughing along with the other few people who were there watching. Or she was jammed together with everyone else in front of the civilian play on a stage a few blocks away from the Khmer Rouge, where there were free shows every Saturday and Sunday.

27

One day, Eng Luong and her roommate were talking and agreed that the boys had to shout for the world to hear just to fill up the two water tubs. Some boys heard them and said their job was not easy, that they sweated over their work and the girls had big mouths. So they would let the two big mouths do the work; then they'd know how hard the boys' work was. The boys' mothers agreed with them, but Eng Luong's housemother told Eng Luong and her roommate to go to the boys' house and apologize. Both girls said no, so the four housemothers told the two girls to fill up the tubs as their punishment.

The girls at the center weren't happy with Eng Luong and her roommate because they got yelled at by the boys. The boys sat in front of their houses talking, laughing, and waiting to point their fingers at the two girls. And most of the girls sat in front of their houses waiting to see what Eng Luong and her shorter, dark-skinned and cross-eyed friend would do.

It was not easy to find a water holster. The two girls refused to borrow it from the boys, so they borrowed one from a family who lived behind their house. It was long and heavy for the two girls to carry to the water tubs, but they did it! With Eng Luong pulling on one end and her friend pulling on the other, they took it to the water pipe three blocks away. Eng Luong pulled and yanked the water holster, finally throwing it headlong into the tubs, out of breath.

She looked up. There he was, standing at the side of her house, leaning on the wall, his ankles crossed over each other and arms folded in front of his chest. They stared at each other. He looked somber. She looked away from him, but he kept on watching her struggle with the water holster. She tossed more of it in the tub, then ran past him. She was tempted to run *on* his feet but didn't have the courage to do it.

She ran to help her younger friend put the water holster on the water pipe. The two girls took turns running back and forth, checking on the water tubs. Many people felt sorry for them because the two girls were nice. They took the holster out of the water pipe so other people wouldn't have to wait to get their water. The boys would hold up the line while the two large tubs filled. People from other blocks liked the two girls since they didn't have to fight with the girls to get their water.

When the first tub was half full, he went to the water pipe. "Work hard?" he asked cheerfully, standing in front of the two girls.

"If Mr. Boy afraid no have water to bathe tonight, no worry. We will have water for Mr. Boy this morning," the younger girl snapped angrily. She and Eng Luong had been looking for someone to take their anger out on all morning.

Here comes the good boy; now he got it! Eng Luong thought, trying not to laugh.

"What wrong with girl, girl? Why girl, girl so mean? All I ask if you work hard?" He lost his smile.

Eng Luong stood back and watched the two of them go into battle. She wanted to take her anger out on him like her friend was doing, but if she yelled at him, he might yell louder and harder than. *It was nice to see someone else have the last word for a change!* she thought. He stared at her twice, but she kept her smile and ducked her head. *It's very nice listening to my friend tell him what she thinks of him!*

"We mean because Mr. Boy, Boy think girl, girl can no do the thing that Mr. Boy, Boy does, all Mr. Boy, Boy does is order girl, girl around like servant!" the girl shouted.

"Right, right," Eng Luong agreed aloud.

"What?" he turned toward her.

She stepped away and pointed at her friend. "You argue with her, not me, but she right." Eng Luong couldn't help laughing.

"Say it again. Let me hear it." He took a couple of steps toward her.

She walked backward, toward her friend, and the two girls stood shoulder to shoulder, squaring off with him.

"Go argue with boy, boy" the girls told him. Then they laughed.

"Girl, girl!" he shouted, staring them down.

The girls watched him storm off, taking long strides.

"You mean!" Eng Luong hugged her friend, and they giggled.

"I afraid you might take his side," the girl told her.

"Never!" Eng Luong told her.

"Why on earth must have girl, girl to break man, man's heart. Or have man, man worry about them to death?" he complained loudly.

"If there no girl, girl, then where you come from, rock?" the girl shouted at him.

Eng Luong saw his back stiffen and stopped laughing. He turned around and walked back to them, looking angry enough to slap the younger girl senseless. And there wouldn't be a thing she could do about it. If he did slap her, and she told her housemother, the housemother might say, "If you didn't yell at him, he wouldn't slap you. You shouldn't talk to him like that; he is a boy. Don't you respect boy? It is right that he slapped you, because you didn't respect him."

"You want to know where I come from?" He stood nose to nose with the girl, his face like steel.

"Let me hear Mister tell it," she said smugly.

"You want to know where baby come from?" he asked.

"I want to know where you come from, not where baby come from." She was stubborn, but so was he. They stood eyeball to eyeball.

They could have had a standoff all day, and Eng Luong didn't want to do all the work by herself. Her friend was angry, and he smiled smugly.

"Enough." Eng Luong tried to pull her friend away.

"I want to hear this mister tell it," she shouted and yanked her arm free.

"I want to tell her where baby come from," he said.

The two of them shouted over each other.

"And I say it enough!" Eng Luong told them.

"Short life; go to hell!" her friend shouted over her.

When he took a step toward her friend, Eng Luong stepped in between. "She younger you; no hit her!"

"If you ever yell at me like that again, I'll slap you senseless!" he pointed at Eng Luong.

"You very good at slapping people! Mr. Boy like to slap girl, girl when you no want to hear what we say is true. Mr. Boy like slap girl, girl and someone smaller and weaker than you! You no embarrass with yourself?" Now Eng Luong was angry.

"If you dare talk to me like this again, I will slap you. I no joking," he warned, pointing at her.

"If you dare slap me, I go to the IRC and tell the American on you!" She was furious. Time went by slowly and silently. They were breathing fire at each other, having a staring war.

"What you think the American do to me?" he asked.

"They no take you to their country!"

She saw the palm of his hand coming toward her cheek and couldn't find her tongue. She just stood there and blinked.

Keem

"What your American do to me now little sister girl?" he asked, smiling handsomely and brushing his knuckles under her chin gently. Then he turned around and whistled all the way home. He was very bold in words and actions.

It took Eng Luong a while to get her tongue back, but when she did she shouted at his back, "I hate you!"

He turned around. All his even, white teeth were out. He walked backward, shaking a finger at her. "You love me, then you can hate me," he laughed, before continuing to whistle all the way home.

She just stood and stared at his back.

"I afraid he slap you. But he pat your cheek instead!" her roommate giggled.

"If you dare tell anyone, I kill you!" Eng Luong told her friend.

"He must love you very much!"

"I kill you!" Eng Luong chased after her friend, who ran and screamed with laughter.

After the fight with him, Eng Luong and her friend returned to their work. The tubs were filled up in less time than when the boys did it. Plus, the two girls filled up every pot, bucket, and jar in their houses, and they also filled up the two water tubs for the family they borrowed the water holster from. The family couldn't thank the girls enough. And there was no water or mud on the footpath in front of the elderly families' houses on the way to the water pipe.

The two girls whispered to each other and laughed while they bathed near the tubs. They shared a private joke, saying the only thing girls couldn't do by themselves was make babies. After that day, the girls in Eng Luong's block walked around with their noses pointed skyward.

"We girl, girl, strong like boy, boy," the girls sang proudly.

Before, the girls cleaned the outhouses, and the boys got water for the two tubs and went to get the rice, meats, and vegetables for their block. They always took extra rice, meat, and vegetables saying they needed it because they did the harder work. After Eng Luong and her friend got water for tubs, the girls wanted change. And the families living behind the orphan center and in front of the footpath to the water pipe, they came to talk to the head woman at the orphan center. They said she should let the girls get the water instead of the boys. The boys made too much noise and left water and mud on the footpath in front of their houses. The families told their housemother how quiet the girls had been while they worked.

"You have two good daughter," they told the girls' happy housemothers.

Then the four housemothers had a meeting, and afterward, they said the boys would clean the outhouses, the girls would get the water, and the girls and boys would take turns going to get the food for their block. The boys got yelled at by their housemothers and walked around with their chins to their chests. After that, the boys learned some respect for the girls and looked at them differently.

The girls laughed at the boys cleaning the outhouses, and sang out, "Boy, boy say 'Girl, girl can no do this. Girl, girl can no do that!' If boy, boy can, girl, girl can, too! Boy, boy say, 'Big Sister Luong and her friend can no fill the water tub.' Just two girl, and they fill them up! No eight or ten boy. We girl, girl stronger than boy, boy."

The news of what Eng Luong and her friend did reached the girls and boys from other orphan centers, and they came to Block 188 to see Eng Luong and her friend. Eng Luong didn't even know that, though she had noticed a lot of strange girls and boys coming to her block. Almost immediately, the girls from the other orphan centers also wanted change, so all the housemothers and fathers met. Afterward, the girls and boys had an equal share of work and food.

Eng Luong looked at the situation around her like any other day. She hated it when people said, "You can't do it." If she was being challenged, she wouldn't walk away. She'd take it as well as she would give it. However, she was no fool. She wouldn't arm herself to fight a war that she couldn't win.

* * *

The teasing of Eng Luong and him got worse after her friend told everyone he had patted Eng Luong's cheek. If someone couldn't find him, they came to ask her where he was and what time he would be back. One day she got angry, and shouted at a boy, "I not his mother; no ask me!"

"You not his mother but his future wife." The boy smiled and walked away.

After the fight, he smiled mysteriously at her every time they saw each other. Every day, he went to make soap for the Thai, and he gave some of the cheap soap to all the girls except Eng Luong. The girls couldn't say enough good things about him.

Eng Luong didn't care for his cheap soap. It smelled awful! One day, she went to the market and saw a green soap that Keem loved to use occasionally. Eng Luong paid ten baht for that one bar of soap. She washed her hair and body with it. Coming home from her bath, she walked past him in front of his house and he stared after her.

"Luong, Luong smell like flower," the boys sang and laughed, making way for her to walk up to her house.

"Crazy!" she whispered.

Then the boys turned to him, saying, "What *you* do? Luong smell like flower, some man might steal her from you."

Her dark brown hair reached past the middle of her back. She always kept it in a ponytail high on the back of her head and only let it down after her bath. One evening, she sat outside on the bamboo bed in the sitting area rocking left and right while combing her fingers through her wet, long, and tangled hair. She sniffed at her hair and laughed softy. She loved the smell of perfume from the soap on her long hair.

Suddenly, he was standing in front of his house staring at her. She didn't know why every time she saw him she didn't have the will to look away immediately. He looked troubled as he stared at her that night. She lost her smile, ducked her head, got up, and went inside the house.

"Buddha pity me!" he moaned loudly.

Why he had to call Buddha to pity him? All she did was sit out there and comb her fingers through her hair!

28

1980 was over, and 1981 passed day by day, then month by month. One day, Eng Luong sat outside in the sitting area, thinking. *If his housemother asks me to marry him again, I'll say yes.* Just then, like magic, or as if Keem's powerful spirit was at work again, one of the boys from her block who worked at the IRC office shouted from his house, "You Eng Luong?"

"Yes."

"Your name on the blackboard. You will go to Chonburi next month," he said.

She froze on the sitting bed. Then, just to make sure she heard him correctly, she asked, "What you just say?"

"I say, you will go to Chonburi next month!" he shouted again.

She jumped down and ran the ten blocks to the IRC office. There it was! Her name was printed on the blackboard in English. She stood outside the IRC office's gates staring at her own name, written in a language she didn't know how to read. She had seen her name written in this strange language so many times that she had memorized it. She ran home and told everyone the good news! Later that same day, a Cambodian man came to the center and asked the housemother to see Eng Luong. They sat on the sitting bed, and the man told her he worked for the IRC office and had been following her around for three months.

"Wherever you go, I go. I ask your mother to see if you tell the truth."

"Uncle follow me? Why?" she asked.

"The Americans want people who tell the truth. They no want bad people go to their country," he told her. He was like a plainclothes policeman from the IRC office.

"I go to the United States of America?" she wanted to know.

"You go to Chonburi and wait. You have a final interview with the American judge. If you pass, you go to America. If not, they send you back to Cambodia."

"I no want to go back to Cambodia," she told him.

"If you do what you do now, you will pass. No lie; do what people tell you. I know you will pass the interview. You a good girl." The officer smiled reassuringly.

"Thank you, Uncle." She returned his smile.

They were friendly to each other after that, and the officer came to see her now and then. They made small talk about nothing important. Now that she knew people were trailing behind her, it made her nervous. One wrong step and she'd say good-bye, Thailand, and hello, Cambodia! *Wouldn't it be a good laugh for that two-eyes-in-one girl if I got sent back to Cambodia? Too bad One Eye already left,* Eng Luong thought about a girl who had such crossed eyes that they looked like one. Everyone called her One Eye behind her back. Eng Luong hadn't gotten along with the girl. One Eye had family in the United States, but Eng Luong had no one. One Eye and everyone at the center always laughed at Eng Luong for wanting to go to the United States. One day, she and One Eye argued over something, and One Eye yelled for all to hear, "I have family in America; still I wait. You will wait until your hair is white! And you still wait and wait until you old, old grandma, cripple and ugly! And you still wait here!"

Keem

One Eye must have thought she was the queen of Aunt Wipe House, being a high and mighty pain in the you know where, who thought she didn't have to wait for anything.

Eng Luong was furious when everyone laughed at her. Even *he* laughed at her. She said nothing, just turned around to stare him down. If Keem, Wong, and Ming had been there, they might have told him, "When Moy looks at you like that, if you smart, you run!"

But Eng Luong was not Moy. Lucky him! She just stared until he got quiet and looked away. If looks could speak, this was what she told him, "You may laugh all you want. But watch me. I *am* going to America. I will be there!" She had come this far and wasn't about to go back to Cambodia. Everyone at the center could bet his or her last underwear on that!

The month of waiting was a nightmare. She dreamed every night that the IRC sent her back to Cambodia, crying in her sleep and waking up with a wet face. She went to look at her name on the blackboard in the IRC office a few times each day, always fearing her name might not be there. Sometime during the last week before going to Chonburi, Eng Luong went to see her former housemother, who now lived in another block. She had to leave the orphan center when either the IRC found out she was a former Khmer Rouge and did a lot bad things or they wanted a younger Khmer Rouge woman to work at the center. Eng Luong wasn't sure which.

Eng Luong and her former housemother were outside on the sitting bed, talking.

"Eng Luong, you leaving?" the older woman asked

"Yes."

"What will you do with him?" She sounded like a mother.

"He want someone else."

"He want only you." The housemother looked sad.

"He no want me."

"He tell me. He want you."

"I not know what to do," Eng Luong was confused.

"You want him?"

"Yes, but I want to go to America." She played with her hands.

"If you want him, you must stay. Someone else will have him if you go."

"I not know what to do!" Eng Luong felt like crying.

"You love him?" she asked.

Eng Luong just stared as the housemother kept smiling. "I not know, but I like him." She looked down at her hands.

"Let me see your hand."

"What?" Eng Luong looked up and stared at the housemother sitting in front of her.

"Let me see your hand." She reached out, waiting.

Eng Luong lowered her chin and held up her right hand out. The housemother took it, then something warm, large, and firm wrapped around Eng Luong's small hand. She looked up sharply. He was standing next to her, smiling like a proud peacock, holding her hand in his. She froze for a second, then yanked her hand free, jumped to her feet, and took off like the wind. She didn't know where he had come from or how long he had been there. How much of her confession did he hear? *He not only has a nose like a broomstick, he also has ears as large as an elephant's!* she thought, embarrassed. She didn't see him again after that.

The day she was to leave Sa Khao II, nightmares from Cambodia came back to remind her of who she really was.

On September 7, 1981, Eng Luong wore a sweet-cream-colored long-sleeved shirt with small black eagles printed on the material. A few months earlier, the Thai people had given the material to the orphan centers, and all the girls and boys had gotten a shirt made from it. She was deep in thought while walking home from the IRC office, where she had gone to take another look at her name to be certain she hadn't misread someone else's name on that blackboard. She was heavy hearted when she first walked away from the IRC office. But now she knew what she wanted—him. She felt carefree, and her smile widened. She was much happier.

But immediately, her past shattered everything.

She didn't know what to do—run, cry, or scream for help, and did none of them as her legs robotically kept moving her forward, one step after another.

Coming from the opposite direction was Vulture, the Khmer Rouge who had tried to rape Moy in the jungle when she was thirteen years old, when they lived in Head Tiger in Cambodia. He was the monster who threatened to cut her big brother Ming in half and take Ming's heart out, chop it to little pieces, fry them in pig oil, and eat them with rice. Vulture was the evil one who threatened to rape Moy and Ming's wife in front of Ming before taking Ming's heart out. Vulture still dressed in black. When he saw her, he quickly looked straight ahead.

When she saw him, Eng Luong, the fictional character, immediately disappeared, and Moy resurfaced. Moy said nothing. She kept walking, but Moy and Vulture both looked from the corners of their eyes when they walked past each other. Inside Moy's mind, her past replayed like a movie in slow motion.

※ ※ ※

Moy heard her own screams when Vulture grabbed her upper arm and threw her toward that bed in the jungle. Then he ran like a wild animal. She saw her younger self lying on the ground, her knees bent, head up, and hand rising toward heaven. Black dirt fell in Ming's mouth and eyes.

Moy saw her beautiful Ma laying on three pieces of wooden boards. Keem's eyes and mouth were open. She had no blanket to cover her beautiful body, or even a small towel to cover her beloved face. Moy saw her sweet and gentle grandpa die with a beautiful smile on his face. He ate that cooked baby mouse, the size of a small finger. The next morning, he died with that breathtaking smile on his handsome face.

She saw her younger self crying and holding a small picture of her ma. Moy cried and held her hands up toward heaven while her ma's remains lay in front of her. She saw her ma cover Grandpa's body and face with a blanket.

She saw her younger self crying when she fell in the mud, then took a bath in the rain. She cried…and she laughed. Ma and Grandpa were laughing, but Moy was crying. Eng Luong was crying, too. Ma was smiling at her, then turned around and walked away, leaving Moy to stare at her ma's back.

* * *

"Luong! What wrong with you?" someone shouted at her.

"What?" She didn't know where she was. She stared at a woman in front of her.

"You white like a ghost. You sick?"

"Sick?" Moy echoed her.

"Come here," the woman pulled Moy toward her, then shouted, "Buddha! You cold like ice all over! You shaking very hard." Whoever the woman was, she pulled and yanked Moy toward the house. "If you sick, you can no go."

"If you sick, you can no go," the words ricocheted in Moy's head. It was like icy water had been thrown on her face, waking her from a horrible nightmare!

Keem

"I no sick." Moy yanked her arm free from her housemother and ran up into the house, where she sat in a corner hugging her knees under her chin while she wept. "Buddha, help me!" She covered her mouth, sobbing hard into her hands.

No matter what names she hid under, Moy couldn't run away from her past and memories, nor could she run away from the pain. She had tried to be someone else, living as Eng Luong, someone like a fancy character out of a book, a girl of seventeen in love. But Eng Luong wasn't real, and he couldn't have her.

On September 7, 1981, Moy would fight another battle, and Eng Luong would make a sacrifice, or else both would die there at the Thai border. Eng—Eagle—Luong had been waiting for two years. Now, the eagle's wings were strong. The eagle must walk out of her cage slowly, then spread her wings, ready to take her first flight up into the treetops.

The brave little tiger Moy was not willing to be left behind. Moy had fought hard to get across the Thai border. There, she found herself a new friend in Eng Luong, a fancy character to heal Moy's wounded heart. But this eagle was ready to take off, and the little tiger must go along. Eng Luong must take Moy with her, or they would die together there. Eng Luong must carry the little tiger inside her eagle's talons, flying up into the treetops, where she would wait. When the right time came, the eagle would take off into the sky, headed to Moy's dreamland, America. Moy's past was what made her strong. Moy's memories made her who she was. Eng Luong, the eagle, would carry that past and memories wherever Moy went. That's how Moy existed.

That day, the day of her departure, before two o'clock, Eng Luong came out of the house to wash her face. Then she ate some lunch and went back inside the house to get her clothes bag. She smiled and said good-bye to all of her housemates before she walked down the staircase like a queen walking the red carpet to her throne, one step at a time. When both her feet had landed on the last step on the staircase, she looked to the left, and their eyes met.

He was standing in front of his house. His arms were folded across his chest, and she looked at the color of his skin, darker than hers. She watched his eyes drop to the small bag in her hand. He stared at it for the longest time! Then he looked up slowly and their eyes met again. He seemed much older that day and taller; also his black hair longer. He was somber. Every inch of him tight as steel—his face, his eyes, his lips. He stared hard at her clothes bag but never said a word.

These two, fancy characters from a fairytale life, had started with an omen neither youth knew about. Eng Luong was a thief who got caught stealing water from his well. He had caused her to drop her rope and bucket in fright. Then he sniffed out her weakness and gave his water thief a smile before turning around to become a knight in shining armor, armed with a long rope and hook to get her rope and bucket. He had filled up the empty water tanks for her, and along the way, the water thief stole his heart with her missing-front-tooth smile. So he offered his heart to her in the most respectful way of their customs. He had his housemother ask her housemother for Eng Luong's hand.

Now—at this moment—if she took three steps backward, he would have her hand. But if she took one step down, she would go to America. Eng Luong waited and looked at him, but neither the water thief nor the knight in shining armor moved their lips. He was real, but he was in love with a fictional character, Eng Luong. After staring at each other a very long time, he turned his face sideways, away from her.

Good-bye. Have a long life and be safe from all harm, she thought but didn't have the courage to say to him aloud.

Eng Luong didn't cry.

She kept her eyes on him as she stepped off the staircase. First one foot landed heavily on Mother Earth; then the second foot followed. Eng-Eagle Luong's feet were on Mother Earth, and the eagle edged its way slowly out of the freedom…cage. She stood in front of the staircase, staring at him, but he kept his face sideways, turned away from her. So she followed his example and turned from him.

She walked through her block, away from her house.

Finally, the eagle spread her wings out fully, outside the cage. She tested the power of her wings, and then she was ready to take off for her first freedom. Eng Luong headed toward the IRC office.

"Good-bye, brothers and sisters! Good-bye to you all!" she smiled and shouted to everyone in her block.

"Good-bye, Eng Luong. Safe journey!" some of the girls and boys shouted back and waved as she walked by.

She never looked back. At two o'clock, she was at the IRC office, waiting with one of her housemates.

Eng Luong's good friend hadn't gone to see her off. "I can't," her good friend had said.

The girls hugged and cried until there were no tears left. As Eng Luong waited, she occasionally looked left and right for him but didn't see him anywhere.

At three o'clock, a small van came. Eng Luong hugged her housemate good-bye, then climbed into the van. She was on her way to the final camp.

* * *

There were five girls and five boys inside the van.

"Eng Luong? You very thin! You sick?" A girl who knew her from Khao'I'Dang at Block One Orphan Center was also in the van.

"No," Eng Luong responded.

The van stopped at a gate just three feet from Sa Khao II. Eng Luong looked out the van's window while two Thai soldiers looked into the van and counted the people, then studied everyone's ID with care. It took the soldiers about half an hour to check all the paperwork. Then the soldiers opened the gate and let the van go through. She watched the sun set slowly from the small van window. Suddenly, she broke down and cried her heart out, though she didn't know what she was crying for.

Perhaps it was because she had had to leave Keem and Wong behind. *No.* Keem and Wong would go with her. Not in person, but in spirit. They would always be with their little Moy. Maybe because she knew the boy was lost to her. But Eng Luong believed that if they were meant to be together, then by some miracle, they'd meet again and have a happy family. If not, he'd always have a special place in her heart. Eng Luong would always be his water thief, and he would always be her knight, arming himself with a long rope and hook to get her.

Finally, the eagle sniffed the cool, free air for the first time after eight long years of captivity.

The van made three or four more stops as it pushed closer to Chonburi. At each stop, the Thai soldiers looked inside the van and counted people, then checked and rechecked all the paperwork. Eventually, the gates were opened for the van to go through. The sun had almost completely set when the van pulled up in front of the final camp.

**Camp
Chonburi
Thai Border
September 7, 1981**

Eng Luong/Moy

This picture was taken on September 7, 1981, in Chonburi.
It served as ID and passport for me to come to America.

29

There were about thirty Thai soldiers standing in front of a large gate. Some had guns hanging down from gun belts on their shoulders. Other soldier held their guns aimed, ready to shoot. The van stopped in front of the camp, but this time, the soldiers asked everyone to get out. Two Americans stood next to the orphans. Eng Luong watched.

Some soldiers went inside the van, while two soldiers checked everyone's paperwork. They looked at everyone's small picture and paperwork carefully, then looked at the person in front of them. When they were satisfied, a third soldier took all the paperwork and spent a few minutes also looking at the paperwork and picture of each person. He asked the Americans some questions, and the Americans looked angry, arguing with him. Finally, he stood in front of Eng Luong. He looked at her paperwork and her picture in his hands. Then he looked at her and made a funny face. He sniffed his nose and rubbed his eyes, then smiled at her. She smiled back. He said something and waved her back to the van. When everyone was back in the van, the soldiers opened the gate, and they rolled into Chonburi.

The van stopped in front of a long wooden building, the IRC office, and everyone went inside to wait some more. The officer gave each person five numbers written on a small blackboard. Eng Luong held the small blackboard with five numbers in front of her while her picture ID was taken. Her number was CB 12345 (CB=Chonburi). In the picture she was wearing the sweet-cream-colored eagle shirt.

An officer told the orphans not to lose their picture IDs. Wherever they went, they must have them with them at all times. If Thai soldiers asked to see the ID, "You must show it to them." And if anyone lost their ID, "You must notify your lady or Uncle right away and hurry back for another picture. If you lose it again, you go back to Cambodia. If you want to go to the United States of America, no lose it!"

The Thai allowed orphans to replace their IDs and numbers only once. But for elderly people and families, there were no second chances. If they lost their IDs, they would go back to Camp 007. Going back there was like going back to Cambodia. The Thai wanted the Cambodians off their border, and there was fighting between the Khmer Rouge and Thai soldiers at the border. For the last month, Eng Luong had heard bombs dropping and gunfights from far away every night. And those Khmer Rouge crawling around all over Sa Khao II and Khao'I'Dang with the civilians—*pity the civilians!*

In Chonburi, people couldn't buy anything from the Thai if they didn't have their picture IDs. Sellers had to log the ID numbers in their books, noting what they sold to each individual.

Farther up from the IRC offices, on the opposite side of the main street, was the orphans' center. The walls of the four long houses were wooden boards and bamboo trees, with white metal roofs and concrete floors. There were three houses for the boys, formed around the girls' house, and a small sewing house. Every girl and boy slept on his or her mat on the floor, and each person had a small mosquito net tied to the walls.

The left of the entrance to the orphan center, there were two wall-less common kitchens, one for the Vietnamese and one for the Cambodians; each had long wooden benches and tables inside. The Vietnamese Orphan Center was back to back with the Cambodian

Keem

one. Within the center, there were two concrete outhouses where users threw in a bucket of water after each use.

All the girls and boys who arrived with Eng Luong each got a new pair of pants. The older girls also got some pads to use for their period that they could throw away afterward.

Chonburi was not like the other camps. There were Chinese, Vietnamese, Thai, and Cambodians on the main street. Everyone spoke his or her own language! Eng Luong couldn't remember ever seeing so many Thai soldiers on the street. There were a few soldiers in Sa Khao II, but none in Khao'I'Dang or Camp 007. The Thai soldiers never bothered anyone; they just patrolled the streets or the blocks, as it was their duty. They came often in groups of twelve to the Cambodian and Vietnamese children's centers. The Vietnamese and the Cambodians fought like cats and dogs over this or that, every day, especially the elder cooks. The Thai soldiers would always get angry and shout at everyone to stop fighting.

Eng Luong didn't understand what the Vietnamese and Cambodians fought about. Her main goal was waiting there to go to the United States. When she arrived in Chonburi, she went to work at the sewing house, making pants and shirts for the Thai. She worked from nine to eleven-thirty, and then from one to five, and got paid fifty baht a week. She came home for lunch, then went back to work. Then she went home, ate dinner, took her bath, made some small talk with the girls, and went to bed.

During her stay in Chonburi, sometimes she wrote letters to her friends in Sa Khao II. Her reading and writing was poor; she had only gone to school for seven or eight months at the most. Each time she sat down to write a letter, she thought of him. She remembered one event. There was a boy with the same name as him at her center, and that boy and he were almost the same size and height, except her boy was built like a fighter. She couldn't remember what the boy with the same name said to make her mad, but she slapped him so hard it left fingerprints on his cheek. The boys and girls were all shocked.

That boy was angry and looked like he was going to slap her back.

"*No!* If you dare hit Luong, he will come over and kill you. He watch us from over there," the other boys and girls warned him.

Eng Luong looked around in time to see him refolding his arms across his chest. He leaded back on the other girls' sitting bed, his face hard as he stared at that boy. But his eyes softened when they landed on her face.

"I keep this slap like a love memory from you," the poor boy spoke loudly while he laughed nervously.

Later, Eng Luong apologized to the boy for slapping him. He accepted the apology, and they became friends. But that made *him* mad! He would give her and that other boy dirty looks when he saw them talking.

She also remembered another event when her housemate was reading a story to a group of girls and boys on their sitting bed. He came in late, and the only empty spot left was next to her feet. She was sitting on the doorway of her room, her feet resting on the sitting bed. He stared at her, then at the empty space. After a second of hesitation, he climbed on the sitting bed, then crawled over and sat next to her feet. Her roommate quit reading. Everyone stared at her with big eyes. But she didn't get up and leave like she had every other time he came near her.

"What you look at?" She was tired of running away from her own house because of him.

No one answered, and her roommate went back to reading out loud. Then something happened in the story, the girls and boys disagreed, and they argued. The girls got mad and kicked the boys out.

"Let us listen. We no argue with you anymore," the boys whined.

"Go home! We no want you here!" The girls waved the boys off.

Keem

He remained sitting where he was, his arms wrapped around his legs, his chin on top of his knees.

"Go home! Why you still here? We no want boy, boy here anymore!" the girls yelled.

"I no say anything; let me stay and listen," he complained.

"No! Go home!" The girls waved him off.

"Please let me stay?" He edged off the sitting bed.

"He say nothing," Eng Luong spoke up.

Everyone was quiet, staring at her like she had four heads on her shoulders.

His mouth hung open, and he stared with big eyes.

"Why everyone look at me like that?" Eng Luong asked, remaining where she was.

"Nothing," they all answered. He stayed, and they tightened the circle to listen to the rest of the story.

"Why he still sit there and you no kick him out like you kick us boy, boy out?" one of the boys shouted from his house.

"You no have Big Sister Eng Luong hold your feet," a housemate said, defending them.

"I no hold anyone feet. I just say what I see and hear," she had defended.

No one uttered a sound, and her roommate went back to reading the story.

A few days before she left Sa Khao II, she stood in front of her house. Without thinking, she had begun singing. Like always, he appeared in front of his house. He sang her the boy's part in the song's tale of a man and woman's parting. Now all Eng Luong had were memories. She didn't have the courage to ask her friends how he was doing, and her friends and housemother gave her no hints about him. Hopefully, she'd eventually forget him. For now, she kept working for the Thai.

She was going to be paid eighty baht when she finished a cross-stitch for her boss. She worked on it during the evenings and on Sunday, when the sewing house closed. One morning when she was working on it, the orphan's manager walked into the girls' house, and his shadow fell over Eng Luong. She didn't look up. She just wanted to finish the cross-stitch for her boss. Near her, two Cambodian girls were fighting.

"One sit there like Buddha; the other fight and argue until the mountain fall down on my head!" he shouted angrily.

Eng Luong was tired of people fighting. She just wanted to do the job right, earn some money, then go buy some candies, cake, or a bowl of noodle soup to eat—or maybe a new sarong or a shirt to wear.

"Luong! Why you no tell these two to act like you?" He pointed at the two girls arguing over something.

She looked at the angry girls, then lowered her eyes and went back to working on the cross-stitch.

"They older than me, Uncle," she told him.

"Not just sit there like Buddha! Go to your lady in my office, now!" he said, taking his anger out on her.

"Yes, Uncle." She got up, taking the work with her.

"Why take that thing with you? The American come to see you; leave it here!" he yelled.

"Yes, Uncle." She put the cross-stitch on top of her clothes bag and followed behind him. He stopped so suddenly in front of the entrance that she walked into his back. "I beg forgiveness, Uncle!" She lowered her head.

"Learn some good manner from this one," he shouted over his shoulder to the girls in the house. His office was in the small sewing house and two Americans, a man and a woman, were waiting inside.

Keem

"Eng Luong. Come sit here." The manager's wife patted an empty chair next to hers.

The Americans had Eng Luong sit between them in a circle.

"How are you today?" the lady translated for her.

"Good, thank you."

"We come to tell you something."

Eng Luong felt hopeful looking at the Americans, then at her lady. They all smiled, and the lady translated to her, "We found a family for you in America. The family has a ten-year-old daughter, an eight-year-old son, and two dogs. You like dogs?"

Eng Luong couldn't speak. She nodded.

"Are you happy?"

"Yes! I happy. I very, very happy!"

The Americans and the lady laughed aloud. "But—" the American man said and held a finger up.

Eng Luong held her breath. *I don't like this but!* she thought.

"You will be interviewed by Grandma Beth, twice. She is very difficult, Luong. Be careful with what you say to her. Blue-eyed witch! She mean like witch, very, very mean!" the lady told her.

Eng Luong's jaw dropped slowly.

"This American no understand what I say. No worry." The lady smiled.

I hope not! she thought. Then asked, "What kind of people are my new family?"

"They are Americans."

"American!"

"You don't like to live with the Americans?"

"No! Yes! I like very much go live with American."

The two Americans watched her closely. Then the woman took notes while the man talked. The Americans said something to each other, and the lady nodded occasionally. Then the lady talked while the Americans listened.

The lady told Eng Luong to stay in the office. She said the Americans had something else to tell her, and the interpreter who came with the Americans would help Eng Luong.

After the lady left, a Cambodian man came into the office. He took the empty seat facing Eng Luong. He talked and listened to the Americans. Then he told Eng Luong the lady gave good reports on her. The report said that Eng Luong worked six days a week in the sewing center. She never argued with anyone and did what she was told. The manager also gave good reports, saying Eng Luong never lied. She went where she said she would and always told her lady before she went.

The interpreter said if she failed the first interview with Grandma Beth, then she'd wait two to three months before a second interview. If she passed both interviews, then she would be interviewed by an American higher officer. If she passed that one, she would go to America. The interpreter stopped to clear his throat, like he couldn't bring himself to say the last word.

"If you no pass the interview, you will stay here until they send you back. Understand?"

"Yes, Uncle." She was scared.

He told her that a boy from the IRC office would come the next morning to take her to Grandma Beth's office. He reminded her to say what she'd told the Americans in Khao'I'Dang and Sa Kho II. If she said anything different from those reports, Grandma Beth would be hard on her.

"No talk. If she asks question, answer. You have very good report," he told her.

"Thank you, Uncle." She also thanked the Americans.

Keem

That night she dreamed she climbed up to the Buddhist temple in Pailin, the highest temple in Cambodia, at the top of a mountain. When she lived in Pailin, she and Keem had gone up to that temple once. They climbed up the beautiful stone steps and under the roof of red tiles. It took them half day to get up there. Keem had had a bad dream about her daughter and took Moy there so the head monk could pray and bathe the bad luck off Moy.

In her dream, Eng Luong saw herself climbing all the way up to the top of the temple. A few people made it to the top with her, but most people didn't. When she got up there she was smiling, and she woke up still smiling. Now she knew she'd be going to America. That day, she didn't go to work. Her lady went to the sewing center and told Eng Luong's boss about the interview.

Chonburi

The Orphan Center

The girls and I lived in this house.

(In this picture, I removed people from both sides of me.)

30

Grandma Beth sat behind a large desk, and Eng Luong sat facing her. A Cambodian woman sat next to Grandma Beth. Grandma Beth's face and hands were wrinkled. She had red cheeks, wore red lipstick, and had something on her eyelids to make them blue. Grandma Beth's face was like steel, and her large, red-and-blue flowered dress did nothing to soften her appearance.

The first question from Grandma Beth was, "How old are you?"

"Eighteen."

Where were you born? Where are your parents? Were they killed? How did you get here? Do you have any brothers or sisters? The questions went on and on. After the interview, Grandma Beth took Eng Luong's hands and examined them like a doctor. She checked from her shoulders all the way down to her fingertips and palms. She turned Eng Luong's hands and arms back and forth.

The Cambodian woman translated as Grandma Beth told her, "Go home. I'll see you later."

Two days later, Eng Luong was back in Grandma Beth's office. This time, she suffered Grandma Beth's interrogations for only an hour. The first interview had been two hours.

Two weeks later, about ten in the morning, the manager's wife rode her bike to the sewing center to get Eng Luong because a Cambodian boy from the IRC office was waiting for her at home. He took her to the office of the highest American officer, in some beautiful brown wooden buildings. Each building was fifty or seventy feet long, and the four offices formed a square around banana trees, flowers, and other plants in the middle. The Americans workers also lived in one of the four long buildings.

If Eng Luong thought that first American she saw in Camp 007 was a monkey, then this one must be King Kong. Perhaps she was too scared. Everything and everyone looked larger than they were. His arms seemed to be a mile long and a mile wide, and they were covered in long black hair. All men have two eyebrows, but this man had just one thick, long, black eyebrow. Sitting at his desk, he looked like a large mountain towering over the small town of his desk. He was not old. When he opened his mouth, the floor shook under her nervous feet where she stood, about ten to fifteen feet from the desk.

"Are you afraid of me?" a Cambodian woman translated. She stood next to him and, with him seated, they were the same height.

"No." Eng Luong actually didn't know which she was more afraid of, his size or the interview. Maybe both!

The King Kong smiled and said something. He gestured at her with a finger that looked like an elephant's trunk. Eng Luong understood he wanted her to come closer. She eyed his smiling face and took a small step forward. He had a good suntan and was young, maybe in his thirties. He kept mumbling something, his chin resting on top of his folded arms, while he kept cocking that finger, telling her to come closer. King Kong and the tiny interpreter laughed. Finally, he straightened up, mumbled something, and shook his head. He smiled, revealing his white, strong teeth. He had the interpreter tell Eng Luong, "Raise your right hand and swear to tell the truth?"

"Yes."

"Where were you born?"

"Cambodia."

"Where are your mother and father?"

"My father died when I three year old. My ma died when I thirteen year old."

"How many brothers and sisters do you have?"

"I the only child."

"Which countries do you want to go?"

"America."

She watched him shut the folder, and then he folded his arms on top of the desk and gave her his King Kong smile. He said something to the interpreter, who translated, "Congratulations! I hope to see you in America some day." The interpreter paused, then added, "He says by then you won't be afraid of him anymore," and both the interpreter and King Kong laughed aloud.

Eng Luong lowered her eyes and smiled.

"You are free to go!" He waved her off with both hands.

"Thank you, mister. Thank you very much." Her fingers straightened up and pressed together under her chin. She bowed and walked backward. "I pray for mister to have long life. Thank you, mister."

"Thank you." The King Kong smiled, imitating her with his large hands and fingers pressed together awkwardly.

Later she was told he had only passed her and two or three families. After that he failed everyone.

*   *   *

Eng Luong ran all the way home and shouted, "Lady, lady, I pass!"

"Good, very good!" Her lady walked toward her with a big smile.

"What question he ask?" all the girls asked as they surrounded her, and she told them the whole story.

That evening, the manager came to the girls' house and told Eng Luong she would have to go the next day for an X ray of her chest and a physical examination. If the tests showed she had any illness, she would have to stay in Chonburi to see the doctor until such time the doctor says she is all right. Then she would have another X ray. If that test said she is healthy, then she'd go to America. If not—you know what would happen.

The next morning, Eng Luong walked with some Cambodian and Vietnamese girls and boys to the X ray building. It took them half an hour to get there, and hundreds of people were waiting in line to get in. The girls and boys hadn't brought any lunch, and they had arrived in the morning but didn't get inside until late in the afternoon. After their X rays, they went to the next building for their physical exams. Babies in mothers' or fathers' arms, women and men—everyone waited in one long line.

Inside the small office, there was an interpreter, a Thai woman, and an old Thai man. The girls were told to take their shirts and underclothes off and pull their sarongs up to their chests. When Eng Luong got in there, the woman snapped at her sharply, "Take off your clothes!"

"What?"

"Undress, undress!" the woman shouted impatiently.

She looked around but didn't see anywhere she could undress.

"Undress now!" the Thai woman yelled again.

"Here?" she looked at the old Thai man staring at her.

"Here and now."

"And him?"

"He is the doctor. Undress!" The Thai woman was very impatient.

Eng Luong looked at the doctor. His face was wrinkled, and he was giving her a hard stare that reminded her of long ago, when someone had looked at her just like that. She heard people say they had to take their clothes off in front of a Thai doctor. But she wasn't prepared to undress under this man's ugly stare.

She stood naked in front of the old man, covering herself with her hands and arms. The Thai woman yelled at Eng Luong to remove her hands and arms, and the old doctor told her to bend over, then turn around and raise her hands and arms over her head.

Eng Luong fought back tears. *You can look, but I'm going to America!* The old man's eyes moved slowly up and down her body. He told her to turn slowly around and around. She had no idea how long he enjoyed looking at her young, naked body. She couldn't do anything to stop it. She was chilled inside, feeling dirty under his evil eyes running up and down on her. *I want to go to America. I want to go to America,* she kept reminding herself.

The men stared and smiled when she walked out of that dirty old Thai doctor's office, and she stared back until the men looked away. *It's not just me! Everyone here will be stared at, too. Just like he did to me,* she thought. Lifting her chin up, she walked out of the building.

A flower is the beauty of its nature, and its beauty is like all young innocent girls who haven't been touched and remained unseen by evil men such as him. If such men were nearby, beauty would be marred by the ugliness of the human world.

Three days later, the manager told Eng Luong to pack up her clothes. The next morning, she must go to the IRC office, then leave Chonburi.

About twenty Cambodian and Vietnamese girls and boys waited in the IRC office for hours before a small bus came, and a Cambodian man had the children get in. He told the orphans to stay together as a group when they reached the new camp.

"If anyone run around and get lost, no one go look for you. You will stay there, then go back to Cambodia," he warned them.

It took the bus many hours on a dirt road to reach the new camp.

Across a White Gate to Heaven
Or
Live in Hell

Eng Luong looked at the camp from the bus's window. It was like a nest of ants and flies in an open-field outhouse. There were a few blue plastic tents here and there, but no houses. The land was mostly black mud and water. Piles of fresh and old yellow, brown, and black colored shit were everywhere! People were all jammed together on the dry land, with some spilling over onto the muddy land. They walked over or on the shits, and some were cooking near them. Small flies, large flies, and green-headed flies were everywhere. Some of the green-headed flies were the size of fingers. And mosquitos landed on anything that didn't move.

Eng Luong pointed her nose skyward when she got off the bus, but it didn't help with the stench. This place was like sitting inside a filthy outhouse with no window. The flies welcomed her face and nose right away, and she lost count of the flies she pulled from her nose. Like everyone else around her, her hands never stopped whacking at mosquitos on her cheeks, ears, head, neck, and arms. She had on a long-sleeved shirt, but it didn't do any good. She had to cover her mouth when she spoke to keep the flies from getting in her mouth. She had no idea how they were expected to live in this outhouse camp!

The Cambodian man left the orphans under a loudspeaker on dry land. He told them he had some paperwork to do before he left. The orphans looked at each other in disbelief. Then, in between crying bouts, they giggled.

Later, Eng Luong asked a woman why there were no houses there. The woman told her no one dared go anywhere or do anything, because they didn't know when they would be called. If they missed their names being called they would be sent back. She said, "We live here forever! They call our name only once—no more!"

I will die if I have to live here! Eng Luong thought.

Some people were sleeping on blue plastic with black mud beneath it. Most people walked around. Suddenly, the loudspeaker came to life, and men, women, and children ran toward it to listen for their names. Few names were called out of the hundreds of people waiting there. Eng Luong listened hard, but she couldn't understand what the speaker said. After the speaker finished calling the names, people ran back and forth.

They asked, "What the name he call?"

"What he say?"

"What you hear he say?"

Everyone looked worried. Now and then they would curse, "Short life; go to hell!"

Eng Luong's group looked petrified. Hours had gone by without their names being called. They hadn't eaten all day. They just stood there doing battle against flies and mosquitos. When the sun was down and the sky almost dark, Eng Luong saw a number of buses rolling into the camp. Many happy families grabbed their children and belongings then headed for the buses. One by one, the buses drove away from the dark camp.

"Why they no call our name?" the orphans whispered to each other.

"Don't know. Buddha, I no want to live here!" Some of the girls looked and sounded like they would cry.

Keem

Eng Luong's heart dropped to the bottoms of her feet. There was only one bus left, and more families were heading to it. She almost cried aloud when she heard, "Orphan, where the orphan?" A man's voice was shouting from somewhere.

"Here, over here! Let go, let go!" They all shouted and ran toward the voice.

"This is the orphan group?" a Thai man walking toward them asked.

"Yes!" the whole group answered in unison.

The Thai man mumbled something, then spoke in Khmer, "We forget all about the orphan, sorry! Come, come!" He waved the orphans to follow him, and he couldn't walk away from the outhouse camp fast enough.

Eng Luong's group had to run through the crowd to keep up with him. Armed Thai soldiers stood on both sides of the gate in front of that bus. The Thai man said something to the soldiers, and they nodded. One of the soldiers went up to the bus, and then everyone got out and came back to the other side of the gate.

"Orphan, line up," a Cambodian man standing next to the Thai man shouted.

The Thai man had some papers in one hand and a pen in the other. He called each orphan's name, looked at each ID, then checked the name off and nodded or mumbled something. Two soldiers would check the ID again, then open a metal gate and let the person pass. Four soldiers from another gate stepped aside to allow the chosen through. Eng Luong was the third-to-last person called. The guardian angel glanced at her picture ID then stared at her.

"You?" The Thai man pointed at her.

"Yes, mister." She lowered her eyes.

He looked at her ID then stared at her some more.

He's not going to let me go! she thought fearfully, as she went cold inside.

He pushed his bottom lip out. A hand went up to his face and came down below his eyes.

"Sad?" he asked in Khmer, nodding. Then he turned around and showed the picture ID to the soldiers behind him.

They mumbled among themselves and looked at her picture ID while she watched. Each soldier took her picture and studied it with great interest.

He's going to send me back! she thought.

The Thai man hadn't shown any interest in anyone else's IDs. He said something to the Cambodian man.

"No sad, be happy! Little sister goes to America, now!" the Cambodian man translated.

"Thank you, mister! Thank you, Uncle!" She bowed to the Thai man.

A young soldier returned her ID with a smile.

"Thank you, mister." She took her ID with both hands and bowed. "Thank you very much, mister!" She bowed to the Thai man again.

"Safe journey, Niece," the Thai man spoke in broken Khmer, his head lowered.

She walked slowly, like she was in a dream. She couldn't hold back her tears and turned around once more to look at her Thai guardian angel. He had a round face; smooth, red cheeks; a smooth pink chin; black eyes; and very short hair. He wore a white, short-sleeved shirt and long black pants.

"Good-bye. I pray for mister to have long life. Thank you very much." She waved to her guardian angel as tears dripped from her eyes.

"Good-bye!" he smiled and waved back.

Eng Luong looked at each soldier's face that she walked by. The soldiers wore dark green uniforms and ankle-high black boots. Each

Keem

soldier had a long gun on his shoulder or in his hands, ready to shoot. None of the soldiers were older than their late twenties.

"Thank you, mister. I pray you have long life and safe from harm," she told them.

A soldier smiled and nodded.

Now she faced four more soldiers on the other gate. They looked meaner and bigger than the ones before. A soldier behind her said a few words, and a giant, the meanest-looking soldier who held his gun in his hand, nodded once. With his free hand, he pulled the white, painted-metal gate open to allow her to walk through.

In a way, this white gate had kept her in hell for more than five years. **Finally, it lifted up and opened.** *At the order of a Thai man and a Thai soldier, they allowed her to walk out of that hell on earth. Eng Luong, the wild eagle, finally broke through the cage, and was now standing in the treetops, her wings spread wide, ready to take off for her dreamland.*

From the other side of the gate, she turned around and shouted, "Thank you, mister. Thank you, everyone! I pray you safe from all harm and have long life!" Then she bowed. She saw the Cambodian man say something to the others, and the Thai soldiers lowered their heads or nodded. She turned around and stepped up and into the bus.

Inside it was very clean and cool! The red seats were large. That Thai man had called this last bus the Orphan Bus, as it was meant for the orphans only. But they weren't taking up all the seats, so the Thai allowed some families to get back in until all the seats were filled. Then the Orphan Bus moved slowly away from that outhouse camp. They traveled on a dirt road for a long time, and finally the bus emerged from the jungle and onto the highway.

**Thailand
Bangkok's
Airport
November 1981**

Eng Luong sat next to the window, looking out at the flowers growing in the center of the big highway. Buses and cars flew by back and forth. Her chin dropped slowly when she saw a highway above her bus! When the bus entered the city, she saw all the shops and people all over the sidewalks and streets. Women wore sarongs; men were in long or short pants and white shirts. Men, women, and children hurried along everywhere she looked! The streets, tall buildings, and shops were lit with beautiful, sparkling colored lights.

"This is Bangkok!" she heard people saying.

Thailand! Eng Luong thought. This was real, not a dream or movie. She had seen a few American movies at the orphan center. In them, the cities were beautiful, lit up in different colored lights at night. When there were movies of snow falling from the sky, the kids would laugh and say it was teeny-weeny pieces of white paper, make believe snow.

"Ice comes down big, big piece, not little like that," some kids said. If it were real snow, people would run and hide inside their houses.

Shortly after the bus passed Bangkok City—she saw them. Beautiful! Powerful! Those giant wings were absolutely powerful and beautiful! Now and then, Eng Luong had heard them flying over her head, and their thunderous roar was the sound of freedom to her. The airport was right in front of them, and her heart beat madly in her chest. But before the bus could enter the airport, it stopped at one final gate. Thai soldiers came on the bus asking to see picture IDs. Finally, the soldiers got out of the bus, opened the gate, and waved them through. The bus stopped in front of the airport's entrance, and everyone got out and went inside the building. The airport was large, with all-glass walls Eng Luong could see through to look around the airport.

When Moy's family lived in Siem Reap, Cambodia, she had traveled on airplanes with Wong to Phnom Penh or Battambang many times. She remembered those airports as tiny dirt fields with one runway and no glass walls. People walked to and from the airplanes and climbed stairs to get in or out of them. Those airports were nothing like this!

She looked through the glass walls at the big and small airplanes everywhere. The roars of their engines were beautiful music to her ears. *Soon, very soon, I will be inside one of them*, she thought. Then she heard a boy talking to someone, not far from her. He warned his friend not to get too excited, because some people got sent back to Chonburi even after they were inside the airplane. He said the Thai soldiers sometimes went inside the airplane and told people to get out before the plane took off, because their reports weren't good.

"When plane fly up high, high in the sky, then you can be happy," the boy said.

If they asked me to get out after I'm already on the airplane, they can just shoot me there! Eng Luong thought.

Much later, the Thai brought rice and tuna fish for people to eat. She was not hungry and ate nothing. That night she didn't sleep. Not many people did. She paced back and forth near her group and looked

Keem

at the beautiful airplanes. She was happy, scared, and worried all at the same time. Sometimes she stood in front of the glass walls, looking at the blinking red and blue lights on the airplanes in midair. Some of the planes' noses pointed down for landing; some pointed up when leaving Bangkok.

Very early in the morning, the Thai came to wake everyone up. They told them to stay in one long line as they walked through lines of Thai soldiers on both sides, then stopped at a group of long tables. Everything got pulled out of their bags and dumped on the tables. The Thai women and men checked everything, shaking out every piece of clothing. Then they shoved everything back into the bags. Eng Luong picked up her bag like everyone else, then walked out of the building and past another line of soldiers. She got on a roofless and wall-less bus with everyone else. In less than a minute, they were at a large airplane's stairway, where a beautiful American woman stood. She smiled and mumbled something as each person walked off the bus and up the stairs to the plane.

Eng Luong climbed each step slowly. Inside, she looked at three rows of big, red chairs. A row of three seats on the left and right sides, against the walls, and seven to ten seats in a middle row. Some people went up to the second floor. But she walked all the way to the back of the airplane and settled in an empty seat next to two Vietnamese boys. Later she found out she was sitting near the wing. People kept coming in. It felt like they waited forever before the aircraft moved. Some people talked and laughed. She did neither. She sat still as a stone in her seat. She held her breath when people at the front said Thai soldiers had come on board.

I'll die here. I won't go back, she thought.

But she never saw any soldiers. She felt the airplane move. *It moved!* But then—it stopped. Waiting and waiting. *I will not go back!* she kept thinking, her stomach feeling hollow.

Finally, the airplane's engines roared louder and louder, and she felt the airplane move faster and faster! Then she felt herself leaning steadily backward for a while before the plane returned to a flat horizontal.

At last! The eagle has finally taken off from the treetops and flown away from the cage! It looked skyward, thrusting its beak up and soaring through the air. The eagle's wings were spread wide, every now and then flapping up and down a little. The eagle went higher and higher into the sky, heading for America—and freedom, just like that airplane taking Moy/Eng Luong to her dreamland. Would the eagle make it over the ocean and survive?

A week earlier, Eng Luong had dreamed she was swimming in the middle of the ocean, in the middle of the night. There was nothing and no one around. She couldn't swim, but she nonetheless swam hard until she saw a tiny, blinking candlelight at the other side of the ocean. She saw nothing else but water and darkness surrounding her. She kept her eyes on that toothpick-sized blinking candlelight and swam as hard as she could toward it. Then she woke up. And now she was inside an airplane flying to America.

31

An American woman came and asked her something. Whatever she said, it sounded like "cocoa" and "ee." Eng Luong kept smiling. The yellow-haired woman pointed at her own mouth. Eng Luong nodded that, yes, she wanted to eat. The woman said something else. Eng Luong kept smiling. She nodded if the woman nodded, and shook her head if the woman shook hers. They both laughed. The woman gave up and walked away smiling. Then she returned with rice and chicken on a tray for Eng Luong. Everyone had the same food.

The two Vietnamese boys sitting next to her were not happy. Eng Luong got sick, throwing up every once in a while. It seemed the American rice and chicken didn't agree with her stomach. She got so sick, the Americans took pity on her, coming by every now and then with a warm towel for her forehead or to cover her with a blanket.

Many hours later, the plane landed in Hong Kong. The doors opened, and icy air woke her. She looked out of the emergency exit door where she was sitting. It was foggy, but she could see houses everywhere on the mountainsides. She watched the Chinese men working below. Some men pushed carts down away from the plane, and other men pushed carts up to it. After a long time, the doors were closed, and the airplane took off from Hong Kong.

* * *

Moy's memories played back for her. Wong Lai took her on airplanes to see the parades in Phnom Penh on Chinese New Year, or to visit his friends in Battambang. Keem and Wong had told her that the first time Wong took Moy on the airplane she was only two years old. Most frequently, he took her to Phnom Penh with him on business. They always stayed in the large hotel, in a big room with a large, soft bed, and big bathtub. Cold and hot water came out of that thing like rain, and there was a white, tall toilet in the bathroom. The hotel was right in front of the New Store.

Moy loved to play under the rain shower. Whatever made her happy made Wong happy. She always begged him to bring her to that hotel where she could play in the rain, and Wong always replied, "If you act good, Grandpa take puppy there again."

Moy also remembered that when she went on an airplane with Wong, she would either sit on Grandpa's lap, or in her own seat next to him. She was full of questions. She would peek out the window and ask, "Grandpa, what that? Grandpa, what this? Where we go, Grandpa? We go to that hotel again?" Little Moy moved up and down in her seat. Sometimes, she tried to climb over Grandpa's head to see what was hidden behind his seat.

"Yes, we go to that hotel. Puppy no move around like little worm; no ask many question. Grandpa bored! Now sit down." He tried to peel her choppy little hands off his white, short-sleeved shirt. "Puppy no pull and play with Grandpa's eyeglass. You have many hands and very busy. I can no keep them all away!" he complained, peeling her fingers off his eyeglass, then putting them back on again.

Moy smiled sweetly. She hopped around in her seat, then leaned over and slapped Grandpa's large tummy. She gave him her angelic smile while she abused him.

"Puppy, no hit Grandpa's stomach. It hurt!" He brushed her hand away gently.

Keem

"Grandpa give me a little brother?" she asked. To the world, she was a little boy with apple cheeks. Wong had her hair cut short and kept it that way, like a little boy.

"No."

"Why?" she was busy pulling on Grandpa's hair.

"I a man." He fought a big battle for his head's freedom from her busy hands.

"Why?"

"Woman have baby."

"Why woman have baby?"

"They have big stomach! Quit it!"

"Grandpa's stomach big, big, too. See?" She tapped his tummy.

"I just fat!" He pushed her hand gently away again.

"Woman fat, and woman have baby. Grandpa fat; Grandpa give me a little sister and a little brother?"

"I a man; I can no have baby. Puppy, quit it!"

"Tickle, tickle, tickle," she teased, her hands all over him.

"Sit down and quiet," he laughed, trying to grab her hands.

"Tickle, tickle, tickle," she giggled.

He laughed and wiggled around in his seat, trying to get away from his active little granddaughter's clever hands.

"You want to come with Grandpa again?" He picked her up from his lap and put her back in her own seat.

But she continued to tease and giggle, and he laughed and tickled her back. She screamed in delight and wriggled around.

"Yes—tickle, tickle…" Her small hands were touching Grandpa's face, and she stared into his laughing black eyes. Then Grandpa's face faded away little by little. His eyes were blue, not black, and his black hair had turned yellow and long.

"Grandpa?" she asked in Teochew.

The face hanging above her was not Grandpa's. It was a stranger—a woman who said something Moy couldn't understand, then turned away from her.

"Grandpa, I want Grandpa," little Moy cried, looking around for him. Grandpa was not next to her. Moy cried harder, but he didn't come back for her.

* * *

Someone shook her shoulder gently. Moy opened her eyes and saw rice and meat on a tray in front of her. She looked away from the food, wondering where Grandpa was. Then a yellow-haired woman woke her up and took the tray away. Moy closed her eyes again. She heard a woman's voice from a speaker, saying in Khmer, "Welcome to America."

America...America! Eng Luong sat up straight in her seat. Now she was fully awake. She looked around, and to her relief, everyone was still inside the airplane. But she felt something missing and got scared.

She was afraid the airplane might turn around and go back to Thailand, that they lied about being in America. *When I get out of this airplane and see my feet on American soil, then I'll say this is America, but not now. Not yet*, she thought. She sat on the third seat from the window. She had no idea what it looked like down there. Outside, the sky was dark. Everyone talked and laughed, but not her. They sat for a while before Eng Luong felt the hard touchdown of the airplane landing. She prayed this was America, not Thailand. Then the airplane stopped, and she rose from her seat and stood in line like everyone else. She walked slowly toward the main door to get off the airplane.

America, here I come!

**America,
November
1981**

Eng Luong came off the airplane and just stood in front of the doorway, welcomed by the cool November wind whipping her long hair around. She pulled her hair away from her face, and the November wind hitting her hands felt like a cold knife, but she didn't hide her hands. Her nose and face welcomed the friendly winter wind. It was cold and sweet, and it meant freedom. *But how long would she live to enjoy it?*

The stars were twinkling in the black sky. The silver moon was nowhere in sight. Eng Luong stood at the bottom of the staircase and drank her fill of the sights she had been hungering for. As far as her eyes could see, small, orange-colored lights stood in lines up and down runways. She looked at airplanes of all sizes, and they were everywhere. Their wings were large and powerful looking. She loved them all!

"Step over!" someone spoke in Khmer and pushed her shoulder.

Eng Luong didn't say anything. She turned around and looked at a Cambodian girl about her age who was giving Eng Luong an unfriendly stare because she couldn't get by.

"You no push people," she told the girl. Then she stepped off the staircase, and first one foot, then both, were in America. Moy had finally reached her dreamland.

Moy/Eng Luong first stood on the land of freedom in November of 1981.

"Walk faster!" the Cambodian girl hissed from behind.

She turned around, blocking the Cambodian girl and many others behind her. Everyone except that Cambodian girl looked left and right with great interest in this new country.

"We in America now. If you walk fast, fast, you walk back to Cambodia. I no go back, miss." Eng Luong stepped aside to let the girl pass.

The girl's lips were tight as she raced off, hips swaying left and right!

Eng Luong looked around as she walked behind the impatient girl. American men were all over the airport. Some men walked, while others drove funny-looking cars filled with bags and with no walls or roofs. Her feet felt cool in her flip-flops. She got on a wall-less bus with the others, and it took them to a door where everyone rushed into the building. American women and men wearing white uniforms were checking people's bags behind a line of long tables.

Eng Luong's bag had only two changes of clothes, a set of embroidered pillowcases, and "mosquito-net-eyebrow" handmade by Keem when Moy was a baby, Keem's gold-framed and green-lensed sunglasses from Hong Kong, and her black winter jacket from China. In Cambodia, during the Khmer Rouge and in the camps on winter nights, Moy wore the jacket to keep warm. She threw Wong's old mosquito net away at the airport in Bangkok. She had felt unsettled, embarrassed, and something else…she couldn't say what. After she threw it away, she felt much lighter. Keem's ring was on Eng Luong's finger. When they were all inside the warm building, the Americans gave each of them a winter jacket and a bag with the names of their sponsors written on it. Then they got on a large bus.

"A woman drive bus!" the Cambodians whispered to each other. In Cambodia, no woman drives a bus!

Eng Luong had a window seat and looked out the window, counting the four lanes of cars on the highway. She had never seen so many cars, buses, and trucks on a highway in her life! Highways zigzagged left, right, around, above, and below her bus! Then the bus entered the city, with large and small buildings everywhere, some of the buildings reaching into the sky! Moy and Wong, and sometimes Keem, too, often stayed at the tallest hotel in Phnom Penh—a ten-story building. The buildings she looked at now were so much bigger.

A few people were out walking around on the sidewalks, and some shops were still open. *Food stores!* Eng Luong thought. Her itchy hands couldn't wait to grab the American food, and her mouth watered as she stared at the food store. Her feet itched to get off the bus and walk into her first American shop to see what was inside.

The bus stopped in front of a tall, long building where she stayed for a few days. The room had two small beds, one on each side of the room, a tiny dresser, and two tiny chairs. She shared it with another girl. Her first American meal was white rice, two chicken legs with some sweet, red stuff on them, and a can of sweet drink.

Yesterday was over, and it was history. Whatever may come tomorrow remained a mystery. When the sun king rose tomorrow morning, she'd let the mystery or mysteries unveil. She hoped she had the courage and strength to face them all. Seeing today's sunrise was a gift.

Today, the sun heralded the birth of Eng Luong's new life in the United States of America. But she was not out of the dungeon yet. She knew there would be challenges, and she would accept them, like in her dream. She didn't know how to swim, but she nonetheless swam hard toward that tiny, blinking candlelight on the other side of the ocean. Now that she was in America, she was like a newborn kitten in a wild jungle.

The eagle had flown across the ocean and finally landed in the wild jungle. This eagle had been kept captive in its cage for too long. It had been fed and cared for. This jungle might be too wild and free for her. Would the eagle be able to care for herself, remaining on its feet and not giving up by just lying down?

Moy was a fifteen-year-old girl who had borrowed someone else's name. She lived under that fancy name at the Thai border. Eng Luong didn't have to worry about food or anything else. She just waited to come to America. She had a handsome boy ask for her hand in marriage, something most girls dreamed of and hoped for. She and her young man had a few beautiful love fights. And they sang a farewell song together. That kind of thing only existed in fairytales. But the fairytale had come to an end. Could Eng Luong become a true character in real life, or would she vanish?

* * *

A few days later, she flew from California to Boston, Massachusetts. This airplane was much smaller than the one coming from Thailand. A lot of Americans were onboard with the handful of Cambodians. Eng Luong couldn't wait to meet her American family.

At lunchtime, an American woman gave her a tray of food. On it was a white plastic knife and fork, a large piece of beef that could feed a whole family if it was cut to small pieces and fried with vegetables, and a small brown cake with black spots here and there—a chocolate-chip cupcake. There was also a small bowl of uncooked, mixed vegetables, a white potato, and a cup of coffee. And something small, soft, and yellow between two pieces of white paper, as well as yellow water in a small plastic cup.

Keem

Eng Luong looked at the strange food and had no idea how to eat it. She couldn't ask for help, because she didn't speak English. She looked around and listened to the Cambodians mumbling, "I'm dead! How I eat this American food, no rice? American give me half a cow on my plate but no rice!" Some people just finally laughed and ate with their hands.

Eng Luong turned around and peeked in the space between seats at two elderly American women sitting behind her. They talked and talked while their hands were busy working. One of the women picked up a small white paper bag, shook it, opened it, then poured something white in her coffee.

Eng Luong turned around, looked at her tray, and found two white paper bags. She picked them up and studied them. They were the same size, but the letters on them were different. She didn't see anything else different, and opened one of the bags quickly, shaking the white contents into her coffee. She turned around, and peeked in the space to watch some more.

The same woman picked up the next white paper bag, opened it, and shook the white stuff on her meat.

Eng Luong smiled. There was only one bag left. She picked it up with her fingertips, like the American had, and shook the white stuff on the beef. She turned around to peer through the space again.

The same woman picked up a small plastic bag, opened it, and squeezed liquid on the uncooked vegetables.

Eng Luong turned around and giggled in her hands. She picked up the plastic bag in a child-like way, opened it and squeezed the liquid on the uncooked vegetables. Then she peeked at the women one last time.

They were still talking and hadn't noticed her spying on them. She watched one woman pickups the coffee cup and drink it.

Eng Luong sat up straight in her seat, puck up her cup of coffee, and drank. She put the cup down quickly, and groaned. She didn't know what to do with the coffee in her mouth. She looked around but couldn't find anywhere to spit it out, so finally just swallowed it. She turned around to stare hard at the elderly lady.

Her hands were wrinkled, her cheeks hung down beside her chin, and she wore a big red flowered dress.

Some Americans show their age because they drink coffee with salt, not sugar, Eng Luong thought, then turned back around in her seat. She picked up the knife and fork, and tried to cut a piece of meat, but it kept slipping away from the knife. She finally held the meat down with two fingers, cut off a small piece, and popped it in her mouth. Her eyebrows went upward as she enjoyed the sweet taste. She turned toward her left at a Cambodian boy next to her, and he looked away quickly. Then they laughed together. He was imitating her, and spying, too.

"Good food." He couldn't stop laughing.

"Yes!" *I hope he didn't put sugar on his meat*, she thought. She turned around to peek at the elderly lady again. *I guess it has nothing to do with aging. The fault is with the person who couldn't read—me!* Then she turned around to enjoy her first American meal.

The Cambodian boy got off at the stop before hers.

**Boston,
Massachusetts
November 13, 1981**

It was early in the morning, and stars twinkled in the sky. Eng Luong got off the airplane and walked down a long hallway. When she got to the end, a tall man called out to her in Khmer, "Little Sister, you Eng Luong?" He walked toward her.

"Yes, Uncle." She walked to meet him.

"Welcome to America."

"Thank you, Uncle."

"These people are your American mother Mary and father Ed," he told her.

Eng Luong looked at the tall, beautiful woman, with a sort of round face and short, sandy-colored hair. Ed was tall and thin, with a long face. A little girl and a boy hid behind Mary. Mary and Ed mumbled something as they hugged her, and Eng Luong smiled and turned away shyly. Then they went to sit on the long chairs, where the interpreter told her a few things. But she was so tired she didn't hear much. After a few pictures were taken, the new family took her to their car.

They drove on the highway for a long time. Eng Luong never tired of looking at the city filled with colorful lights. Buildings and cars were everywhere, just like the movies she saw in Chonburi. Then they came to a small road where now and then a car went past them. She saw small, round blue lights on tree trunks! The road was dark and in the middle of the jungle! It reminded her of when she got off that wall-less and roofless train in Cambodia and walked through that jungle to the Thai border.

The family's car pulled into a driveway, and they went into the big, clean house. Mary took her to a bedroom where a small bed was pushed against a wall. Mom said something and left her. Eng Luong felt very lonely as she lay on bed. She was in the United States of America, her dreamland, yet she was not happy.

In the morning, Mom's smiling face hung above hers. Mary said something and pulled the blankets away. Eng Luong got up and went to the bathroom with her. Mary showed her how to turn the water in the sink and shower on and off, and how to use the toilet. There were two different bottles of soap to wash her hair with, and a bar of soap for her body. She also had three different sizes of towels. The largest towel was to dry her body, the medium sized one for her hair, and the tiny one was for her face.

Then Mary gave Eng Luong the breakfast she'd made—two pieces of thin, brown toast and one fried egg. She put the plate of food and a glass of yellow water on the table in front of her new daughter.

Eng Luong looked at the strange food in front her. *Where is the rice?* She looked at the white thin bread sitting on the table in a plastic bag. Mary used her hands and fingers, telling Eng Luong to eat. Eng Luong liked the yellow-water orange juice; it was sweet! But she hoped Mom would give her more bread and eggs to eat. Mary didn't.

What a cheap woman! She gave me only two pieces of bread and one egg. I can eat hundreds of those little breads and I'm still hungry! No rice? she thought. Not knowing the language, she was embarrassed to ask for more food. After the tiny meal, Mary took her outside.

I came to America to live in a jungle, she thought, shocked.

There was a house next to hers and a house across the street, but everywhere else, behind her house and across the street was jungle. She was very disappointed. If she had wanted to live in the woods, she could have stayed in Cambodia or at the Thai border. *Where is the city? What do these people do for a living? Why did the American government bring me here to live with someone so poor they have to live in the countryside in the woods?* she thought. In Cambodia, the middle class and rich people lived in cities, and the poor lived in the countryside.

But later she finally realized, *I have a good Mom.*

* * *

About a week later, an American woman came to test Eng Luong's education level. But what was their test? She didn't know how to read or write. Two days later, Mary and the American woman took her to Concord Carlisle High School, where she met a handful of Chinese and Vietnamese students who offered to help when she came to class.

I'll take whatever classes you want me to. I want to learn to read and write, like Ma and Grandpa always wished, she thought.

For the first time in her life, she took an interest in education. She wanted to speak and read English like all the Chinese and Vietnamese students in class. *I want to read a book like that!* She watched American students reading their books from the other side of her ESL classroom and pictured herself reading large books like that. She remembered she said to the Americans in Thailand, "I want go to school to learn to read and write."

A couple of days later, the social worker who had met her at the airport came to her new home. He told her he spoke Teochew and Vietnamese.

"You have good name. Eng/Eagle is the American symbol for freedom," he told her.

"My last name is *Yellow* not *Eagle*," she told him in Teochew.

"What?" He looked at his paperwork.

"My last name is Yellow, not Eagle."

"In here, it says Eagle." He showed her the paperwork.

"I tell them Yellow, but that how they write it."

"If it is *Yellow* then it *Ung,* not Eng," he said.

She did hear the difference, but as for writing she wouldn't know if *Ung* was the moon and *Eng* the sun! The social worker said something to Ed and Mary and they shook their heads or nodded. Then he told her he had to fix the mistake and change the *E* to a *U.*

And just like that—so simply—Eng Luong, the fairytale character, came to an end. Or did she?

Moy had gotten very sick and nearly died, but the IRC doctors and nurses saved her, and Eng Luong was born. Now, with the simple switch of a letter, she would disappear and Ung Hong Luong would take over. This new Luong didn't have the experience of Moy's hardship or Eng Luong's love life. Would she be as strong as them? Moy's dreamland of America was not as tame or welcoming as she had hoped. Some of its people were just as cruel as some of the Cambodians. To survive in this new country, she would need her most powerful friends, Moy and Eng Luong.

32

No doubt, that day in January of 1982, Keem and Wong were smiling, if they were watching from heaven, as Mary waited in front of the house with Luong for the bus taking Luong to her first day at school.

On the bus, American kids would giggle or laugh when they saw her. She knew she was different but felt disappointed by their treatment of her. It seemed that no matter who she sat next to, that person would get up and go sit with someone else. This went on for weeks until she learned to look for an empty seat where she could sit by herself.

At school, she took ESL (English as a Second Language) and math. Whatever her teachers said, she would smile, nod, or shake her head. Her math teacher was not tall or short, had a round tummy, and wore eyeglasses. His hair was a mix of silver and black, and his face bore a few wrinkles. He used his hands and fingers to communicate with her.

"Luong, look." He pointed at his eyes, then toward the blackboard.

She focused on his hands and fingers. *Mr. Teacher wants me to look at the numbers he wrote on the blackboard!* She was very happy she understood him.

"Luong, listen." He spoke slowly, pointing at his ears. "Luong, look." He turned his fingers toward the blackboard.

Mr. Teacher wants me to listen and look at the numbers on the blackboard! She was proud for understanding.

That was how this one understanding and thoughtful man taught her math every day. Her English teacher taught her how to say:

Hello.

Hi.

Good-bye.

Good morning, how are you doing?

Hello, my name is Luong Ung.

As each day went by, speaking and understanding English got a little easier. But writing, spelling, and reading were very difficult for her. These words could be written in so many ways! She liked to write in capital letters because the characters didn't go left and right, or up and down like snakes rolling around in the grass.

I hate the past and present tense! she thought.

In this land, a person would say, "I went yesterday," or, "I will go tomorrow."

"I'm going right now."

One *chair* but two *spoons*. The *s* and *ed* made her crazy!

And the words *bear* and *beard*! She didn't know whether the *beard* had four legs, or if a *bear* hung down from a man's chin.

Whoever created the English language should be hanged by the toes!

Ahh! Unlike the easy Teochew language, where one says simply, "I go tomorrow," or, "I go yesterday." One woman. Ten woman. One car. Hundred car. See how simple that is? She thought.

Then again, how would she know? Well-educated Teochew people might speak differently than her. She had never gone to Chinese school. Who was she to make fun of other people's language? If the Americans were to learn the Teochew language, they might think it as difficult as English was for her.

Keem

Moreover, the American school shocked her. She saw girls and boys kissing in the hallway on her first day. In Cambodia, boys and girls, husbands and wives, didn't hold hands walking around in public places. Even the flower girls, who sell their bodies for a living, wouldn't kiss someone in a public place, though some might let a man kiss her in a corner if it was dark enough.

Luong was shocked when Mary took her to Chinatown in Boston. She saw Americans asleep on the sidewalk, and some sitting around looking drunk and dirty. Their clothes were old and torn, and they looked like they hadn't bathed in weeks.

America is like any other country; there are poor people and rich people. But America is a free country where people can say bad things about their president and not get arrested. America has schools where people can learn to read and write, like me, she thought.

In ESL classes, the students who spoke English better than Luong would banter back and forth with their teacher. Luong couldn't, and she felt dumb. In her second math class, a young male teacher said, "Luong is not smart."

She knew she was not smart. How smart could she be? She couldn't read or write. She couldn't speak, but she understood more.

Sometimes, in the hallways, kids would spit in Luong's face when she walked by them. Or they ran by her and spit in her face. One day while she waited for the bus to go home at the bus stop, a boy who lived a couple of houses from hers walked up, spat on her face, and ran off. Some kids saw what he did but said nothing. They just stared at her. She wiped the saliva off her face with the back of her hand, like she always did, then got onto the relative safety of the bus.

At home, Luong wanted to talk to her mom and dad, but she couldn't say what she wanted to and always ended up in tears. Tears were her best friend. They understood her loneliness. There were new tears for Luong and old tears for Moy, when she cried herself sleep most nights. In a free country, she cried for a new freedom—freedom from home and school...her new cages.

I don't know what people said to me. All I did was smile, she thought and cried harder.

Luong remembered her embarrassment on one of the big American holidays a few weeks after she came to America. She helped her mom in the kitchen with this and that, and Mary and Ed's friends came for dinner. On the table were a big turkey, corn, some soft, red thing, uncooked vegetables, a pie, and many other strange-looking foods.

There were about ten people at the table. Mary gave her a turkey leg, and Luong tried to cut it with a knife, but the leg kept moving. Then the turkey's leg shot off her plate and all the way to the other end. As soon as it happened, people laughed. She looked around, feeling her cheeks light on fire in embarrassment. But Ed didn't smile. He said something to Mary, who smiled and took the turkey leg away, then gave Luong some boneless meat.

"Eat!" Mary told her.

Luong just swallowed the strange food.

Then one day, in math class, her wonderful teacher said something. She tried very hard to understand but couldn't. But she understood the word "homework." *Mr. Teacher wants us to do homework tonight and bring it in tomorrow!*

Then he said something else.

"No, that is too hard!" the kids complained.

Yes, it is "hard." She understood that. *It is very hard to learn English, and it is hard to eat American food.*

The teacher said something else, then turned around to her, "It's a piece of cake! Right, Luong?"

"No, thank you. I don't want any piece of cake," she told him and lowered her eyes. She wondered how he knew it had been her birthday the week before. Mary had bought her a cake for her birthday party—her first birthday cake ever. She also wondered why he would offer her a piece of cake in the middle of class.

The classroom exploded in laughter. She looked around; all the kids were laughing. One boy laughed so hard he fell off his seat. She saw that her teacher looked miserable.

"No, Luong. It not—no cake to eat," he pointed at his mouth. "I meant…" he turned to tell the kids to be quiet, but they couldn't stop laughing.

I didn't understand Mr. Teacher. I must have said something wrong, and that's why the kids laugh. She lowered her chin, trying to hide her embarrassment.

"Luong," he touched her shoulder gently. "I'm sorry. I no want make Luong cry." He pointed at his chest, then his eyes. He looked very sad.

No. Mr. Teacher wouldn't want to make me cry. Mr. Teacher is very nice to me, she thought. She would never get mad at him. He used the simplest words that he knew she could understand. Though he was not her English teacher, he taught her English through body language and math at the same time. Every day he spent at least ten minutes after class with her, and he always smiled.

One day, when she could speak English better, she would thank Mr. S. (I can't remember how to spell his name) for his lessons, kindness, and understanding. And they could talk and laugh about a piece of cake!

Ung Hong Luong

(Last name first, in Chinese)

September 7, 1982

My eighteenth birthday and my first birthday cake

Luong didn't like winter. She couldn't go anywhere when it was very cold. She screamed the first time she saw snow. Everything was white, the road, the trees, the house, the driveway. Her little sister, Holly, and brother, Max, took her outside to show her how to play with snow. She had fun playing and laughing with them. But Luong still liked summer best. Mary bought an old bike for her, and she learned to ride it. She rode it into the bushes, getting herself cut and bloody from thorns. Then she went out biking with Ed, Holly, and Max. Sometimes she rode the bike from Carlisle to the shops in Concord.

Later, Mary found a job for her. Luong rode her bike to West Concord and cleaned people's houses. They paid her three dollars an hour, or ten dollars for three hours' work. On the weekends, she cleaned two houses to earn twenty dollars a week. Mary also gave her five dollars a week. Luong spent some of the money and saved the rest. She didn't know anything about banks, so she kept the money under her pillow. She had some good times with the family going to museums in New York and New Jersey, the aquarium in Boston, Cape Cod, and a witch town, somewhere near Boston. She liked to see and try new things. But she didn't like eating peanut butter, and it seemed that every time they went somewhere, Mary made peanut butter for everyone.

Mary and Ed didn't take anything from her, like her adopted Cambodian families had. When Luong was sick, Mary took her to see a doctor. Mary also took her to the malls or stores and bought new clothes for her. Mary took her to one doctor who put ugly, little metal things on each and every one of her teeth. The metal cut her lips and the inside of her mouth. Luong had those awful things on her teeth for five years!

"You will have a beautiful smile when they come off," Mary told her.

Once or twice a week, Mary took Luong to a different building where Mary handed her a thin, long, silver thing called a foil. Mary made her wear a face-mask/helmet and fight with different people. She growled inwardly whenever Mary got out her large blue bag of fencing equipment. Luong had no idea that Mary had signed her up for fencing class after school, and Luong didn't like to fence. But she liked watching Mary fence against the others. Once in a while, Mary taught fencing at universities. Luong also liked watching Mary judge fencing tournaments.

Mary never smiled as her gaze followed a pair of fencers slowly left and right. Mary would occasionally shout something like "point," or "halt!" She would hold her hand between the two fencers and say, "En guard. Fence!"

Ed was different. He got up very early in the morning and rode his bike for more than an hour to work every day, then rode home for an hour. Ed loved his bike. And he liked to play different instruments. He played the piano, viola, trumpet, tuba, and cello. Some nights or weekends he would take Luong with him to watch him play music with friends. She didn't understand what the music was about, but it sounded beautiful. At home, Mary and Ed hired a piano teacher to give lessons to their children. Luong tried very hard to play the piano like her new dad. She had that piano under

Keem

her mercy when she played "Old MacDonald Had a Farm." You can't say she didn't try!

One day at home, Ed was working on something and Luong was fascinated.

"Dad, what you doing?" She was still learning English.

"I'm typing," he told her.

She stood next to him and watched. His eyes were on the papers on his desk while his fingers moved around on the keyboard and letters printed on the paper in the typewriter. He stopped, looked up, and smiled.

"How you do that? Your eyes on paper, your fingers on keyboard, and letters come out over there." She spoke in poor English, pointing at the typewriter.

"Tell me to type something," Ed kept his eyes on her. She did. His eyes stayed on her as his fingers moved around on the keyboard and letters came out on the paper.

"I want do that!"

"Then you will take a typing class."

That evening, he told Mary to sign Luong up for the class.

* * *

Luong's inability to speak English frustrated her every day. Language was a barrier to sharing and expressing her feelings. And she couldn't tell Mary or Ed about the kids spitting on her in school. She also felt guilty that her ma and grandpa didn't survive. *They weren't here living in America with her.* That guilt and being bullied in school created a firestorm of anger in her. And there were a lot of misunderstandings between her and Mary. Because of the language gap, they would wind up arguing over this or that. Still, she liked her American parents and adored her younger sister and brother. As each day went by, her language skills got better, and things were about to change.

One day in school, Luong walked around in the cafeteria, looking for a table to sit down and have her lunch. She had a hamburger and chocolate milk on her tray. The same neighbor boy who always spat on her was coming her way from the opposite direction. He took the pink chewing gum out of his mouth and shoved it on top of her burger. She didn't know what to do at first. Some kids saw what he had done, but no one said or did anything. They just stared at him, then at her. She picked up the pink chewing gum and threw it away; then she went looking for the school police. They wore white-and-navy uniforms. She ran down a crowded hallway after a large woman in that uniform. The food on her tray slid left and right as she ran.

"Excuse me?" Luong touched the woman's large arm.

"Yes?" The woman turned around, surprised.

"My food..." she tried to think of how to explain what had happened.

"What is the problem?" the security woman asked.

"I—this food. I walk, I walk with food. Boy take gum out, put on food my." *There I got it!*

The security guard listened carefully, then spoke slowly to confirm her understanding, "Some boy put gum on your food?"

"Yes! No good gum. Boy take gum out his mouth put on food my," Luong translated the words from Chinese and Khmer to English.

"A boy took his chewing gum out of his mouth and put it on your food?" the security guard asked.

"Yes!" Luong said, happily thinking to herself. *She understands!*

The security guard straightened up, looking angry. "You know him?" she asked Luong, then looked up and down the hallway.

"Yes." Luong nodded.

"You remember him if you see him again?" she asked while she pointed at her own eyes, then around the hallway at the kids.

"Yes." Luong nodded.

"Come on and look. You tell me if you see him." The security guard had Luong walk next to her.

It didn't take Luong long to find him. He was in the hallway with some other kids.

"Him, him!" She pointed at the thin boy.

"Hey, you, over there! Stop!" the security guard shouted loudly for all to hear.

"Me?" A lot of kids froze in the hallway, pointing at his or her own chest.

"No. Him, *him*," Luong pointed again at her neighbor's son.

"*Yes, you!*" The security guard also pointed at him. "She said you took your chewing gum out of your mouth and put it on top of her food."

"She's crazy. I've never seen her before!" he argued.

"Come to the office with me," she said to the boy. She pointed at Luong. "You go eat."

Luong thanked her but didn't move. She stood there and watched as the security guard held onto his upper arm, and the boy yanked it free.

Luong turned around, walked back to the cafeteria, and sat at an empty table. She didn't want to go back to Cambodia by getting him in trouble. But she was angry, hurt, and was fed up with his abuse. She ate her food and drank the milk that mixed with tears dripping from her cheeks.

That evening when she got home, she did something to spark an argument with Mary. Afterward, Luong didn't think. She just walked into the bathroom, locked the door, and opened the cabinet. She grabbed the first bottle of pills she saw. Someone in the mirror stared at her. The girl in the mirror had no expression on her face, and her dark brown eyes were dull. Outside the mirror, Luong looked at the bottle and opened it. She emptied all the pills into her hand and swallowed them all with a cup of water. Then she unlocked the door, walked to her room, and lay down on the floor.

Little by little she felt her body relax. Luong had never felt so relaxed in her entire life. She could feel her body move left and right a little. Then she felt like she was floating up and down a little. Somewhere in a darkness far away, she heard a scream. Then someone opened her eyes and a bright light shone in them. Someone else put something in her mouth. From far away, someone kept calling her name. Then she heard sirens—very far away.

Was this how it would end?

* * *

In the sugarcane fields of Cambodia, the killer Khmer Rouge, human heart eaters, with guns and knives couldn't break her. She stood up to a killer and rapist when she was only thirteen years old. She smiled and stared him down at the end.

She had the commanders eating grasshoppers. "Eat; they taste like peanut!"

Then she took on Pon's wife in the governor's office at Rock Cow, fighting with everything she had to get her ma's ring back.

Finally, she got on a wall-less and roofless train, then walked and ran through thick jungle, mud, sand, river, and a minefield to reach the Thai border because she wanted to go to America.

Now that she was there, she had forgotten her history and who she was. She became defeated and tried to end her life in the freedom… cage with a handful of pills.

No Mercy

The Khmer Rouge are coming!
The Khmer Rouge are coming!
They chase me out of
My home
They can't understand
That I'm not alone

They tear my home and car
Apart
And I walk away
With a broken heart
They burn my shoes
Apart
While my bare feet are falling
Apart

The earth is my bed,
The sky is the roof
Over my head,
Tall grass is my blanket,
And it itches
My pains away

The Khmer Rouge are coming!
They forced me to work and bleed
In the forest and they say
"We have the force to destroy
Your family and security
So many ways
Apart."

The Khmer Rouge are coming!
The Khmer Rouge are coming!
I call them friends
They call me buddy,
They'll torture me
Then they'll kill
Me.

I'm so hungry and thirsty
But they have no mercy
They take my food
away from me

I'm so weak,
Down on my knees
And beg for mercy,
But they give me
Heat and blood,
By kicking me with their black feet

I walk with my two feet
They defeated me down
On my knees,

They rip and tear my clothes
Apart
And they rape me
Apart
As if they don't have a heart
And where is my God?

I scream in pain!
They laugh with joy
I scream in terror!
They laugh with humor

I live with a broken
Heart
Tears and blood
I don't know
If that is me

All these causes are all
The Khmer Rouge's fault!
In a land called…
Cambodia
A name reminding me of the
Nightmares
The Khmer Rouge

by
Luong Ung-Lai

Afterward

"Run!" a stranger shouts.

"I'm running!" she shouts back, not looking at him.

Her feet are running down the stone steps along with hundreds or thousands of people. The sun is high above their heads. Everyone hugs a small bag of food or clothes to his or her chest.

"Run faster!" he shouts.

She keeps silently running down the steps. He is ahead of her and falls down a few steps from the road.

"Help me," he whispers like an old man. His hand reaches out to her.

She stands still. Three steps down in front of them is the big road. She looks at him for the first time. He looks about fifty, with a long, thin face, long chin, black eyes, and short black hair. He looks like a skeleton. His skin is dark. His brown pants have a tear in the front that reaches below his knees. His brown, short-sleeved shirt is also torn.

"You have to pick it up for me. Don't leave it," he pleads.

She looks where he is pointing at his small bag of food one step above where she is standing. Looking at him again, she pities this thin old man. She runs up the steps, grabs his bag, and jumps down. She doesn't care if she breaks a leg. She hands him the bag, then picks him up by the elbow. She and her girls run with him for a while before they lay him down.

"I want some water," he tells her.

She finds his small can of water and hands it to him. "I must go," she tells him. She turns toward her girls.

"Wait! I'm old. I can't move. If you're leaving me then give me more water. I can't move!" He pleads with her, looking terrified.

She gives him a gallon of water and opens the cover. The water inside looks like coffee with milk.

"This is all the water I have. Sorry."

"I'll drink it." He smiles.

Something about him makes her uneasy and frightened.

"Come on!" Her female friend pulls on her arm.

She turns to her friend, and they run together.

"Wait!" She yanks her arm free and pushes her friend behind the boxes in front of them.

"What?" her friend asks, leaning toward her.

"Something about him—I don't know what it is, and I want to find out," she tells her friend.

"What is it?" the friend asks as she follows her.

She peeks from behind the boxes and is surprised to see the old man gets up to his feet when he thought everyone has gone.

"Oh my!" her friend whispers.

"I told you! Something about him bothers me." She doesn't look at her friend, just watches the old man.

The old man takes out a machine gun and a long belt of bullets that he attaches to the gun. Then he starts shooting around the area, though she doesn't see anyone around. The old man walks around the house and disappears from her sight.

Then she sees a young man in black clothes walking toward them, a gun in hand. She makes a hissing sound to get his attention, and he looks toward her hiding place. He comes to her and bends over.

"It was the old man! He did all the shooting!" she tells him.

"Where did he go?" the young man whispers back. But she refuses to tell him, fearing he might get hurt. "Where?, I asked," he demands.

"Please don't go," she pleads.

"Tell me!"

"Please don't go. He'll hurt you," she cries. He turns away from her. "Please come back," she whispers to his back as she watches.

He walks around the house and shows up at the other side. There, the old man's back is to the young man, and the old man is doing something. He doesn't know anyone has come up behind him. The young man aims his gun.

"Drop your gun, and put your hands up!" he shouts when he is a couple of feet away from the old man.

The old man calmly keeps everything in his hands as he turns slowly around to face the young man.

"Dro—!" The young man's word is cut short when unseen hands wrap a thin wire around his neck. The young man drops his gun and grabs at his neck. The unseen person yanks him backward.

"No!" she whispers, watching in horror. She can't run or scream. She just stands and watches.

"'Drop your gun,' you said," the old man laughs.

The unseen person's hands pull the wire again, and the young man steps backward. Hands push the young man down to his knees, then tie the wire to a big wooden pole. Two men in black clothing appear from the side, each man carrying a long, thin wire in his hands. They push the thin wire through the tops of the young man's ears, and he screams. The three men laugh and yank the wire back on both sides and tie it around the pole.

"This is how Jack wants to keep your head still," one of them tells the young man.

The old man, Jack, thrusts his head back and laughs harder. Jack is a Khmer Rouge! His gun has a long knife attached to the front. He picks the gun up and walks toward the young man. He thrusts the long and shiny knife into the young man's windpipe. Then Jack skins the young man alive as the young man screams and screams. The Khmer Rouge laugh.

"Please, no. Please, no!" she whispers, watching in horror. Her face is as white as a sheet of paper, and she feels sick.

"Now I'll take your heart out," Jack laughs.

"Nooo!" the young man screams.

They continue laughing as Jack skins the young man. He thrusts his knife deeper into the young man's windpipe, then yanks it all the way down to the young man's belly. The young man keeps screaming. Jack puts his gun down and uses his hands to yank the young man's skin to both sides. Then he pulls a human with red, raw flesh attached to his white bones, out of the skin. *The young man's skin peels off from head to toe, like he was a banana.*

She sees no blood on the young man. He is blue all over, and kneels on his skinless knees, staring at her. *He lifts up his skinless hands, as if asking for her help.* Then he falls, face first, to the ground. She feels cold all over. She sees Jack turn toward her.

"Get her!" He points in her direction.

She starts running and runs until she gets home. She runs up the stairs into the house, turning toward her sister, who has a rope tied around her waist. Her caretaker pulls the rope to move her around, because she had been born without legs. Although she has arms, she doesn't use them.

"Bring her in!" she shouts to the caretaker, shaking next to the door. "Bring her in, now!" she shouts again.

"All right!" the caretaker yells before finally untying the sister.

She keeps her eyes down the street, fearful the Khmer Rouge will come before she can get her sister to safety. She runs down the steps, kneels beside her sister, and unties the rope. Her sister is not a child and is heavy, but she picks her sister up and hugs her sister to her chest while running up the steps and into the big house. She runs past her little brother and turns around. He stands next to the door, staring at her with his big brown eyes.

"Come on!" she calls out to him. She is shaking and cold.

He doesn't move. He just stands there looking innocent and confused.

She runs back to him, but with her legless sister in one arm, she can't pick him up. She grabs onto his tiny arm with her free hand and they run. But now she can't run. Her sister is heavy in one arm, and her little brother can't keep up with her. So she walks.

She doesn't know where to go. Wherever she turns, she sees boxes, walls, chairs, and more boxes. They run a few more steps, then crawl under a tall table. She knows when the Khmer Rouge come in, they will see the sisters and brother in front of them. But there are boxes next to the table that hide them from the entrance. She hears them come in, and crawls backward against the wall. *She is caged between her crippled sister and little brother.* Her eyes widen when one of the Khmer Rouge walks toward them. *She has to cover her mouth with her cold hands or she'll scream.* Her little brother stares at the Khmer Rouge with big, innocent eyes. A Khmer Rouge bends over and stares at her. She stares back with frightened eyes. He stares a second longer, then shouts, "Nope!" as he turns away from her.

"No what?" she hears a woman ask. Jack the Khmer Rouge has turned into a woman! The man walks toward another wall and looks behind more boxes.

"Nope, they aren't there or here," he tells the woman.

She feels less frightened.

"Find them! I want them killed," the woman orders.

She can't see the woman. The man walks toward them again, and she starts shaking. Her legless sister never utters a word or even looks frightened. The sister just wears a smug little smile and looks fearless. Her little brother looks innocent and confused. She is shaking and cold.

The Khmer Rouge sits on a box, elbows on his knees, and leans closer to her. He stares at her with his black eyes.

"Will you help us?" she asks.

"Why?"

"Amanda will come back and kill me," she tells him.

"Don't worry about Amanda. She is being transferred to another town." He smiles.

"She'll come back someday. I'll feel safer if we go to another town." Her eyes are opened wide on her pale face. She is cold and shaking.

His hand reaches out slowly for her left breast and grabs it. Then he begins to play with it.

"I can get you to another town if you marry me." His face is inches from hers, and she leans back. "You will marry me," he tells her.

She stares at him, and he stares back. She knows he was one of the men who tortured the young man to death.

She leans toward her little brother until their shoulders touch. But she doesn't want to push him out from under the table, so she leans the other direction. Now her shoulder touches her legless sister's, and she doesn't want to push her sister away. She leans backward until her back touches the wall behind her. She leans forward, but her left breast pushes deeper into his murderous hand. She is sickened by his touch. She is trapped and has nowhere to run. Shaking and cold, she feels sick to her stomach. She can't find her voice. She stares at him and he stares back. Then she blinks for first time. She is very cold, and turns…

* * *

Her eyes open, slowly. The past, present, and future are all awake and united as one at last. *Moy* is finally awake along with her two powerful friends: her inner-self Eng Luong and Luong.

Present

Moy was saved from her attempt to take her own life by American doctors and nurses. This time, she learned the lessons. At the Thai border, she had tried to forget her history and led a life like in a noble fairytale and failed miserably. She faced a future back in Cambodia. Then the memories from the past woke her up and she got out of Sa Khao II and went to Chonburi. In America, she again forgot who she was and almost succeeded in ending everything with a handful of pills.

She may have called herself Luong but she *was* Moy, Keem Lai's daughter. The brave little tiger who feared no one and was owned by no men. Moy was a dragon. She was born in a dragon year, and she would blow fire when she was mad. She had the courage and strength of a tiger and feared no jungles or landmines. She was a little warrior with an iron will. She fought with no weapons except her courage—and that topped all the steel and iron together.

She was also Eng Luong, the wild eagle whose soft heart was filled with love. Moy's memories were not all pretty, the good and bad come paired. Without the lessons from her painful past, she wouldn't have survived in any world. Moy's continued existence on this earth was *because* she had a horrible history. And that history would make her shine in the future.

Moy had fallen flat and hard on her face, but now that she was back up on her feet, she would swing her iron fists!

* * *

Mary and Ed took the family to New Jersey. There, Luong went to see a former roommate from Sa Khao II at the Thai border. Her roommate told Luong that shortly after Eng Luong left, her young man had followed a couple of girls around. Then he got engaged to a girl who lived outside the orphan center.

Later, in 1983, Mary and Ed took the family to New York. Luong went to see another former roommate. This roommate told her, "After you leave, he no sane. He no go to work. He follow every girl who walk past him. Then he ask a girl from outside the center to marry him." She went on to tell Luong that she begged him not to marry the girl, but he didn't listen. She said, "If you marry her, you will have a mess like me."

This roommate was to come to America in 1982, but she married a boy in their block and almost got sent back to Cambodia. Her young husband worked at the IRC office. It took them eleven months, even with everyone's help from the office, to get out. They were very lucky!

"I not know if he marry that girl; we come here a week before his wedding. I think his heart hurt badly and he no care what happen to him," she told Luong in Khmer.

Eng Luong never had any intention of hurting him—far from it. However, she had no choice but to leave Thailand. She hoped his wife would heal his wounded heart and make him happy. She wished him and his wife much happiness and success.

Luong was shocked when the roommate also told her that Pon's family had come to the orphan center looking for Moy.

Of course they came looking for Moy—she had her ma's ring!

* * *

Shortly after Luong returned from New York, she moved out of Mary and Ed's house. There were too many misunderstandings. She went on to live with two more adopted families, one in Littleton, and one in Newton. But she kept in touch with Mary and Ed. Later, Luong said to her caseworker, "I want to live by myself."

She rented a room in a house in Chestnut Hill for three hundred a month. She walked more than an hour each way to and from school, even in rain or snow. She cooked chicken with celery and tomatoes to eat with rice almost every day. Once in a blue moon, she went out to dinner with friends or to see a movie.

Luong worked after school at a supermarket, then at a five-and-dime store. She graduated from Newtown South High School at the age of twenty-three. Some of the teachers and the principal encouraged her to go on to college. She went to the University of Massachusetts in Boston to improve her reading, speaking, and writing skills, working two jobs to pay her way through college. After going to college part-time for nine years, she graduated.

Keem Lai and Wong Lai must have been smiling and crying when they looked down from heaven to watch Moy walk up to the podium to get her diploma.

* * *

One day at work, Luong walked past a superior and the superior said, "You have an ugly face."

She went to HR immediately. There were a couple of mean superiors and managers like that one at work. But there was also a good manager, who said to her, "If you want to do something, set your mind to it and you will get there."

Luong would always remember his encouragement.

* * *

In general, when people are asked where they are from, they reply that they came from the country of X, Y, or Z.

Luong is always tempted to say, "I came from nowhere. I'm a no-land person!"

If the individual asks her, "Was that a cute answer?" she'd reply, "No. I'm from nowhere, but I came from my ma! I have no countries or people who would claim me." Then she would explain that she was not a Chinese citizen because she was born in Cambodia. And to be considered a Cambodian citizen, she had to be the third generation born there.

On July 28, 1988, Luong finally got a land to call her country. She was sworn in as an American citizen at Faneuil Hall in Boston, Massachusetts! For the first time since her grandpa and ma left her, she smiled from deep within her heart and felt proud as she held onto that small American flag in her hand. And she added her ma, Keem Lai's, last name to hers.

In her heart, soul, mind, and body, she is Ung Hong Luong, Eng Luong, *and* Moy. They are one person, and they are me. I am Luong, Eng Luong, and Moy. And I am Luong H. Ung-Lai. Now ask me, "Where are you from?"

The end of the freedom…cage(s)

Luong H. Ung

Newton South High School Graduation
June 8, 1987

Luong H. Ung-Lai

June 1, 1996

Graduation from the University of Massachusetts of Boston

Love From Heaven

Ma, you looked down from heaven

And you saw;

My tears flood the earth
I was scared, hurt,
And abused by others

You came at my call,
You brushed
My tears and fears
Away

Your new hands
Felt like soft, cool, and gentle breezes
On my right cheek and ear

You couldn't hug me
But you kept me warm at night,
In your black winter jacket
Like you were there,
And wrapped your arms around me.

You comforted me
The best you knew how
By letting me see
The beautiful silver moon
Through my sorrow

You saved your ring for me,
Reminding me of your present

A set of embroidered
pillowcases
For me to sleep on
Peacefully,
And holding onto beautiful
Memories.
A mosquito-net-eyebrow
To keep harm away from me,
And a pair of sunglasses
For me to see
A colorful future.

All of that,
It was your way of reminding me
That you still love me very much,
"If I can pull the moon down
for you,
I'll pull it down for you."

I pray to Buddha,
To love and embrace you warmly
And help you rest peacefully, in
Heaven

My ma Keem Lai and my grandpa Wong Lai

Yours forever,
   Moy

April 15, 2014

by
Luong Ung-Lai

June 12, 2012

Author's Note

Please forgive me. I didn't know how to spell my dialect Teochew on first the book, so I spelled it as Chau Chow instead.

Why I told the Americans at the camps that my Father died when I was three years old, that was the story Ma told me, and I stuck to it.

* * *

Who was Wong Lai? I will be brief and to the point. Once, when I was very young, Ma took me to a large jewelry store (all 24-karat gold), in Phnom Penh. She called the owner "big brother," and they had an argument.

"Why you let her call him Grandpa? It not right," he told her.

"It my problem, not your," Ma replied.

Grandpa also took me to visit the same jewelry shop, and he called the owner "brother-in-law." I called my papa "Grandpa" as I grew up. Memories didn't come from A to Z. They came in waves, so I wrote whatever I remembered.

* * *

When my ma and grandpa were alive, they never took advantage of anyone. If they borrowed someone's money, they paid back every penny. If people helped them, even in the smallest way, Ma and Grandpa always gave them a gift or money as a "thank you." Ma and Grandpa weren't rich, but they shared some money with the less fortunate.

I think my ma's spirit knew she picked the wrong people to care for me. I was incapable of doing anything when my ma died. I'm sure Ma's spirit knew when Pon used my gold to buy rice for their family, and when she gambled my gold away. Perhaps it was Ma and Grandpa's way of saying thank you to Pon's family for their help. Still, their spirits, especially Ma's, didn't let her win in any game.

When their daughter used my ma's gold to buy and sell beef in Rock Cow, their rice and cows were stolen. I didn't understand any of it at the time, even after Pon's friend told me what she thought happened. But as I retyped my story and edited it countless times, it hit me. I know not many people believe in spirits, and I'm not telling you what to believe. I just want to share with you what I believe.

"Don't be greedy and take people's things. It no good and sinful," Ma and Grandpa always said.

Here is what I think happened:

My ma and grandpa's spirits weren't happy when Small told me to find my own food. Ma's spirit, especially, didn't want Pon to have my gold. They already had their share. I think Ma's powerful spirit wanted me to know she had worked so hard to buy and save that jewelry for me. And she still chose to share with the needy what she couldn't save for me. That was why the rice and cows were taken from Pon, and people didn't want to buy their beef. Ma's spirit wanted me to have her ring back.

You could say everything that happened was a coincidence, but it seems to be too many coincidences to be coincidental! I strongly believe Ma's spirit helped me get through everything in Cambodia during the Khmer Rouge and then at the Thai border. I will point out why I don't think a few things were just coincidences.

* Shortly after Small told me to find my own food, her husband left her.

* In Rock Cow, I was crying in the store where that young soldier who helped me happened to be.

*When I thought I'd stay in Sa Khao II to marry the boy, and not come to America, suddenly there was Vulture from the Khmer Rouge, coming at me from the opposite direction. He brought back all the horrible memories, and I had to leave. I strongly believe my ma's powerful spirit got Vulture out on the same street with me that day.

If you go back and reread the book again, you will see there were many, many such coincidences. *Things happened at the exact moment of every life-or-death decision I made.* Even when I made a horrible decision, Ma's spirit would show me my mistake, then guide me to a better choice, getting to safety every time!

When I wrote *The Freedom...Cage(s)* over twenty years ago, I didn't think. I just wrote whatever I remembered. At the time, I felt guilty that Ma and Grandpa weren't here in America with me. I was blind to seeing or understanding anything in the books.

My ma's powerful spirit helped me get through everything in Cambodia. Without her, I wouldn't be here today.

I am very grateful for the chance to edit my story again and again—now I have a better understanding.

* * *

Thank you, Buddha, for letting the spirits of my ma, Keem Lai, and my Grandpa, Wong Lai, be my guardian angels, especially my ma.

Thank you, Ma, and thank you, Grandpa, for guiding me through each step of the way, getting me out of Cambodia and Thailand and here to America.

* * *

When my ma was alive, she sacrificed her life for me.

"If anything is to happen, let me be the one to receive them all, but let my child good, good (be well)." Those were the last words she said before drawing her last breath on June 18, 1977.

As a spirit, she gave me a better life and good education. Ma's spirit brought me to America.

* * *

As for all of those people in Cambodia who stole my gold and passed it down to their families, they lied and shamed their children and grandchildren with that stolen jewelry—*my jewelry.*

If Ma and Grandpa were here, they would tell me, "If those people wanted the jewelry, let them take it! If you want the jewelry, then go and buy it. You are safe and graduated from college; that is what is important to us!"

For whatever reasons, those people who got my jewelry either by winning it from Pon's wife in gambling or from selling cows to Pon's daughter, were all chosen. Their children and grandchildren have the honor of a beautiful piece or pieces of legend from Lady Keem Lai and Mr. Wong Lai. My beloved Ma and Grandpa's spirits will guide those people to do the right thing, so I'm sure those people are generous and compassionate to those who are less fortunate. That is why my ma and grandpa's spirits would choose them.

My ma and grandpa had so much jewelry for me, I couldn't wear it all if I had it. Whatever was stolen from me, my ma and grandpa's spirits replaced with something better—*education.* No one can steal my knowledge, or, most of all, Ma and Grandpa's love for me. With that, I am the richest person on earth!

"If I know how to write, I'll write all this in a book so people know what kind of people you are and who I am," I told Pon's wife—and here they are.

The Freedom...Cage(s)

Acknowledgments

Photos, book covers, interior layout, and title created by Luong Ung-Lai

* * *

If my ma and grandpa were here, they would thank those kindhearted International Red Cross doctors and nurses for saving their daughter Moy's life. On behalf of Ma, Papa/Grandpa, and myself, thank you very much.

I'd like to say thank you to all those Vietnamese soldiers who went to Cambodia and fought for my freedom. I pray Buddha blesses them with good health, long lives, and good fortunes. May Buddha love and embrace the soldiers who are already in heaven with him.

I also want to thank the Americans for opening their doors and letting me enter their country. I am proud to be an American citizen and a Bostonian.

May Buddha bless my country's flag—the red, white, and blue star-spangled banner that stands tall under the shining and smiling sun kings forever.

* * *

I'm sure my ma and grandpa's spirits would approve of me dedicating "No Mercy" to the people in Cambodia, especially those who were abused, raped, and tortured to death by the Khmer Rouge. I hope they feel some closure, justice, and healing. May their souls rest peacefully in heaven or live happier lives. And those people who are still alive can pray or thank my ma Keem Lai and my grandpa/papa Wong Lai for it.

Dear readers,

At the moment, I'm unemployed like many of you, but I keep writing. I thank you very much for your support by reading my books. Please look for *Silver Moon, The Pond*, which is coming soon. Thank you again.

* * *

Guess what? I got a part time job for almost a year, and then worked in a full time job but in less than three months, I got very sick… Now I'm back to work on my book again, this time I'm more determined than ever to be a successful writer!

"You fall down and grab two handful of sand up with you," Grandpa had said to me when I escaped home from the children's camp, with a handful of salt and four little fish for our family, and it meant the world to Ma and Grandpa.

With your help by letting your friends and families know about The Freedom…Cage(s) and read them, I'll make all of you proud! I bow to you, thank you.

Your author,

Moy/Eng Luong

Never lose your hope, and hold tight to your dreams—chin up! Go, Boston, go!

Sue Chae Lai/Keem

I think Ma took this picture in Cambodia.

Sue Chae Lai (Keem)

This is my second stepbrother's wedding, the tea ceremony. Ma is standing at the back looking on. Grandpa/Papa and his wife accept the tea from the bride and groom, and the best man is standing next him. And I am standing close to the bride!
This is the only picture of Ma, Grandpa, and me together in Phnom Penh.
Ma paid a hundred thousand ning for this wedding.

1973

This is the only photo I have of Ma and me together.
We took this picture in Phnom Penh during Chinese New Year.
I was nine years old.

Made in the USA
Charleston, SC
20 January 2015